Refugee Crisis:
The Borders of Human Mobility

How should we respond to the worst refugee crisis since the World War II? What are our duties towards refugees, and how should we distribute these duties among those at the receiving end of the refugee flow? What are the relevant political solutions? Are some states more responsible for creating the current refugee situation, and if so, should they also carry a larger burden on solving this situation? Is people smuggling always morally wrong? Are some groups, for example children, owed more than others, and should we thus take active measures to remove them from conflict zones? How are the existing refugee regimes, in Europe, North America, or Australia, challenged by the current crisis? Are some of their measures more justified than others?

Refugee Crisis: The Borders of Human Mobility discusses the various ethical dilemmas and potential political solutions to the ongoing refugee crisis, providing both theoretical and practical reflections on the current crisis, as well as the ways in which this crisis has been handled in public debate. The contributors to the volume include some of the most prominent political theorists and experts on the current refugee situation, as well as some of the upcoming young scholars working on the theme.

The editors are all members of the *Globalizing Minority Rights: Cosmopolitanism, Global Institutions, and Cultural Justice* (GMR) research project hosted by UiT The Arctic University of Norway (NFR 259017).

This book was originally published as a special issue of the *Journal of Global Ethics*.

Melina Duarte is a Post-Doctoral Researcher in Philosophy at UiT working on issues relating to immigration, democratic citizenship, and human rights. Her current focus is on disclosing new ways in which immigration should be handled in times of increasing international mobility and massive forced displacement.

Kasper Lippert-Rasmussen is Professor of Political Science at Aarhus University, Denmark, and Professor II in Philosophy at UiT, and has worked extensively on various issues within political theory, including luck- and relational-egalitarianism, global justice, and methodology of political philosophy.

Serena Parekh is Associate Professor of Philosophy at Northeastern University, Boston, USA, and has worked on areas of social and political philosophy, feminist theory, and continental philosophy. Her current research focuses on global justice, responsibility, and refugees.

Annamari Vitikainen is Associate Professor of Philosophy at UiT working on contemporary political philosophy, especially questions relating to pluralism and diversity. Her recent work focuses on both conceptual and normative issues relating to minority protections in the global arena.

Refugee Crisis:
The Borders of Human Mobility

Edited by
**Melina Duarte, Kasper Lippert-Rasmussen,
Serena Parekh and Annamari Vitikainen**

LONDON AND NEW YORK

First published 2018
by Routledge
2 Park Square, Milton Park, Abingdon, Oxon, OX14 4RN, UK

and by Routledge
711 Third Avenue, New York, NY 10017, USA

Routledge is an imprint of the Taylor & Francis Group, an informa business

Introduction, Chapters 1–10 © 2018 Taylor & Francis
Chapter 11 © 2016 Gottfried Schweiger. Originally published as Open Access

With the exception of Chapter 11, no part of this book may be reprinted or reproduced or utilised in any form or by any electronic, mechanical, or other means, now known or hereafter invented, including photocopying and recording, or in any information storage or retrieval system, without permission in writing from the publishers. For details on the rights for Chapter 11, please see the chapter's Open Access footnote.

Trademark notice: Product or corporate names may be trademarks or registered trademarks, and are used only for identification and explanation without intent to infringe.

British Library Cataloguing in Publication Data
A catalogue record for this book is available from the British Library

ISBN 13: 978-0-8153-8284-3

Typeset in Myriad Pro
by RefineCatch Limited, Bungay, Suffolk

Publisher's Note
The publisher accepts responsibility for any inconsistencies that may have arisen during the conversion of this book from journal articles to book chapters, namely the possible inclusion of journal terminology.

Disclaimer
Every effort has been made to contact copyright holders for their permission to reprint material in this book. The publishers would be grateful to hear from any copyright holder who is not here acknowledged and will undertake to rectify any errors or omissions in future editions of this book.

Contents

Citation Information — vii
Notes on Contributors — ix

Introduction – 'Refugee Crisis: The Borders of Human Mobility' — 1
Melina Duarte, Kasper Lippert-Rasmussen, Serena Parekh and Annamari Vitikainen

1. No safe passage: 'the mapping journey project' — 8
   Diana Tietjens Meyers

2. Global displacement and the topography of theory — 15
   Phillip Cole

3. Misplaced idealism and incoherent realism in the philosophy of the refugee crisis — 24
   Sune Lægaard

4. A fair distribution of refugees in the European Union — 34
   Nils Holtug

5. A spectre in Germany: refugees, a 'welcome culture' and an 'integration politics' — 44
   Nanette Funk

6. Resettling refugees: is private sponsorship a just way forward? — 55
   Patti Tamara Lenard

7. The ethics of people smuggling — 65
   Javier Hidalgo

8. Who owes what to war refugees — 81
   Jennifer Kling

9. What do we owe refugees: *jus ad bellum*, duties to refugees from armed conflict zones and the right to asylum — 101
   Jovana Davidovic

10. Human security and the international refugee crisis — 119
    Aramide Odutayo

CONTENTS

11. The duty to bring children living in conflict zones to a safe haven   134
    Gottfried Schweiger

    Index   153

Citation Information

The chapters in this book were originally published in the *Journal of Global Ethics*, volume 12, issue 3 (December 2016). When citing this material, please use the original page numbering for each article, as follows:

Introduction
Introduction to the thematic issue 'Refugee Crisis: The Borders of Human Mobility'
Melina Duarte, Kasper Lippert-Rasmussen, Serena Parekh and Annamari Vitikainen
Journal of Global Ethics, volume 12, issue 3 (December 2016), pp. 245–251

Chapter 1
No safe passage: 'the mapping journey project'
Diana Tietjens Meyers
Journal of Global Ethics, volume 12, issue 3 (December 2016), pp. 252–259

Chapter 2
Global displacement and the topography of theory
Phillip Cole
Journal of Global Ethics, volume 12, issue 3 (December 2016), pp. 260–268

Chapter 3
Misplaced idealism and incoherent realism in the philosophy of the refugee crisis
Sune Lægaard
Journal of Global Ethics, volume 12, issue 3 (December 2016), pp. 269–278

Chapter 4
A fair distribution of refugees in the European Union
Nils Holtug
Journal of Global Ethics, volume 12, issue 3 (December 2016), pp. 279–288

Chapter 5
A spectre in Germany: refugees, a 'welcome culture' and an 'integration politics'
Nanette Funk
Journal of Global Ethics, volume 12, issue 3 (December 2016), pp. 289–299

Chapter 6
Resettling refugees: is private sponsorship a just way forward?
Patti Tamara Lenard
Journal of Global Ethics, volume 12, issue 3 (December 2016), pp. 300–310

Chapter 7
The ethics of people smuggling
Javier Hidalgo
Journal of Global Ethics, volume 12, issue 3 (December 2016), pp. 311–326

Chapter 8
Who owes what to war refugees
Jennifer Kling
Journal of Global Ethics, volume 12, issue 3 (December 2016), pp. 327–346

Chapter 9
What do we owe refugees: jus ad bellum, *duties to refugees from armed conflict zones and the right to asylum*
Jovana Davidovic
Journal of Global Ethics, volume 12, issue 3 (December 2016), pp. 347–364

Chapter 10
Human security and the international refugee crisis
Aramide Odutayo
Journal of Global Ethics, volume 12, issue 3 (December 2016), pp. 365–379

Chapter 11
The duty to bring children living in conflict zones to a safe haven
Gottfried Schweiger
Journal of Global Ethics, volume 12, issue 3 (December 2016), pp. 380–397

For any permission-related enquiries please visit:
http://www.tandfonline.com/page/help/permissions

Notes on Contributors

Phillip Cole is Senior Lecturer in Politics and International Relations at the University of the West of England, Bristol, UK. He is author of *Philosophies of Exclusion: Liberal Political Theory and Immigration* (2000), co-author of *Debating the Ethics of Immigration: Is There a Right to Exclude?* (with Christopher Heath Wellman, 2011), and co-editor of *Understanding Statelessness* (with Tendayi Bloom and Katherine Tonkiss, 2017).

Jovana Davidovic is Assistant Professor of Philosophy at the University of Iowa, USA, working in the fields of military ethics, philosophy of law, and political philosophy. Her publications include works on humanitarian military interventions, international law, transitional justice, human rights, the changing character of war, and the legal and moral status of combatants. She is interested in the proportionality in war, international criminal law, and conceptual questions regarding human rights.

Melina Duarte is a Post-Doctoral Researcher in Philosophy at UiT working on issues relating to immigration, democratic citizenship, and human rights. Her current focus is on disclosing new ways in which immigration should be handled in times of increasing international mobility and massive forced displacement.

Nanette Funk is Professor Emerita of Philosophy at Brooklyn College, City University of New York, USA, and Visiting Fellow at the Center for European and Mediterranean Studies at New York University, where she co-directs the Workshop on Gender and Transformation in Europe. She is an internationally recognized scholar on gender and post-communism in Europe and her writings have appeared in many journals and collections nationally and internationally.

Javier Hidalgo is Assistant Professor of Leadership Studies at the University of Richmond, VA, USA. He is a political theorist whose teaching and research interests focus on ethics and international affairs, especially the ethical and public policy questions relating to immigration.

Nils Holtug is Professor of Political Philosophy and Director of the Centre for Advanced Migration Studies, University of Copenhagen, Denmark. He is the author of *Persons, Interests, and Justice* (2010); and co-editor of *Nationalism and Multiculturalism in a World of Immigration* (with Kasper Lippert-Rasmussen and Sune Lægaard, 2009), and *Egalitarianism: New Essays on the Nature and Value of Equality* (with Kasper Lippert-Rasmussen, 2006).

Jennifer Kling is Assistant Professor of Philosophy at Siena Heights University, MI, USA. Her work is primarily in social, political, and moral philosophy, with an emphasis on the intersection of ethical and political theories. Currently, her research focuses on the nature and conditions of a state's right of self-defense.

NOTES ON CONTRIBUTORS

Sune Lægaard is Associate Professor of Philosophy in the Department of Communication and Arts at Roskilde University, Denmark. He works on multiculturalism in a range of respects, including discussions of freedom of speech, religion and politics, and issues of immigration. He is also editor of the journal *Res Publica*.

Patti Tamara Lenard is Associate Professor of Ethics in the Graduate School of Public and International Affairs, University of Ottawa, Canada. She is the author of *Trust, Democracy and Multicultural Challenges* (2012). Her current research focuses on the moral questions raised by migration across borders in an era of terrorism, as well as on multiculturalism, trust and social cohesion, and democratic theory, more generally.

Kasper Lippert-Rasmussen is Professor of Political Science at Aarhus University, Denmark, and Professor II in Philosophy at UiT, and has worked extensively on various issues within political theory, including luck- and relational-egalitarianism, global justice, and methodology of political philosophy.

Diana Tietjens Meyers is Professor Emerita of Philosophy at the University of Connecticut, USA. She currently works in four main areas of philosophy – philosophy of action, feminist ethics, aesthetics, and human rights. Her most recent books are V*ictims' Stories and the Advancement of Human Rights* (2016) and *Poverty, Agency, and Human Rights* (2014).

Aramide Odutayo is currently completing an MA in Global Governance at the University of Waterloo, Canada. Her research interests cover topics in the fields of urbanization, international development, international migration, human rights, gender, and social justice. Her work has been published on a variety of forums including *Global Policy Journal*, the *Social Contract*, *E-International Relations*, and *Women and Politics*.

Serena Parekh is Associate Professor of Philosophy at Northeastern University, Boston, USA, and has worked on areas of social and political philosophy, feminist theory, and continental philosophy. Her current research focuses on global justice, responsibility, and refugees.

Gottfried Schweiger works at the Centre for Ethics and Poverty Research of the University of Salzburg, Austria, where he is the Principal Investigator on the project 'Social Justice and Child Poverty'. His books include *A Philosophical Examination of Social Justice and Child Poverty* (with Gunter Graf, 2015), *Ethics and the Endangerment of Children's Bodies* (with Gunter Graf, 2016), and *Ethical Issues in Poverty Alleviation* (co-edited with Helmut Gaisbauer and Clemens Sedmak, 2016).

Annamari Vitikainen is Associate Professor of Philosophy at UiT working on contemporary political philosophy, especially questions relating to pluralism and diversity. Her recent work focuses on both conceptual and normative issues relating to minority protections in the global arena.

Introduction
'Refugee Crisis: The Borders of Human Mobility'

Melina Duarte, Kasper Lippert-Rasmussen, Serena Parekh and Annamari Vitikainen

ABSTRACT
This introduction discusses some of the background assumptions and recent developments of the current refugee crisis. In this issue, the crisis is not viewed as a primarily European, Western or even Syrian, Afghan, or Iraqi crisis, but as a global crisis that raises complex ethical and political challenges for all humanity. The contributions to this thematic issue discuss a variety of questions relating to the rights and duties of different actors involved in the refugee crisis, and assess some of the suggested responses to handling the crisis.

The term 'refugee crisis' has become the phrase of choice in Western media to describe the situation caused by the rising number of displaced persons from the Middle East, Western and South Asia, Africa, and the Western Balkans making their way to Europe and to other Western countries. The crisis is said to have started in 2015 when the tragic incidents in the Mediterranean Sea drew a large amount of attention to the problem (BBC, March 4, 2016). The problem was, according to this perspective, that far too many people were risking their lives fleeing their homes and, in the view of many European citizens and politicians, that far too many people were fleeing to Europe. Sinking rafts and boats in the Mediterranean Sea caused the deaths of thousands of people and the scenario was expected to get worse if preventive measures were not urgently taken (Missing Migrant Project, October 18, 2016). The problem became large enough to be considered a crisis.

While it is difficult to deny that there is a refugee crisis in Europe, the above description of the present situation is misleading or, at least, incomplete for two reasons. First, the mass exodus of people from countries in the Global South is nothing new, but has been ongoing for decades. Second, it is a misunderstanding to think of this simply as a European crisis. Places other than Europe are hosting much larger numbers of refugees: Turkey, for example, is hosting more Syrian refugees than the whole Europe together, and a tiny country like Lebanon has a ratio as high as 1 refugee per 5 inhabitants (Migration Policy Centre, September 2016). According to the Amnesty International (2016b), refugees in Lebanon receive barely US$0,70 cent a day for assistance. The difficulty of accommodating and integrating such large numbers of refugees into countries that have considerably fewer resources than Europe is a feature of the crisis that is often overlooked. Understanding the refugee crisis from a predominantly European or Western perspective is thus excessively restrictive. This Euro- or Western-centrism is unable to account for the many levels upon which the refugee crisis takes place, and for what is at stake in the refugee crisis as a whole.

In this issue, the refugee crisis is not viewed as a primarily European, Western or even a Syrian, Afghan or Iraqi crisis. Here, the current situation is viewed as a global crisis that raises complex ethical and political challenges for all humanity. In this perspective, the current crisis did not begin with the rising number of refugees attempting to reach European or Western soil. Nor did it start with the rising number of Syrians, Afghans, Iraqis crossing the borders of their countries to seek asylum abroad. The global refugee crisis is a decades-long ongoing phenomenon. It must be understood broadly as the forceful displacement of large numbers of human beings from their homes – sometimes due to war, civil war, ethnic or religious persecution by dictatorial regimes like the Syrian state or Islamic State, or simply poverty and destitution – combined with a regime of border controls that creates numerous barriers for their escape.

This last point is crucial. It is not merely that people are fleeing their countries in large numbers, it is also that countries make it increasingly more difficult for them to reach safety or aid, and to be recognized as refugees entitled to aid once they do make it to a safe area. Countries have enhanced control of their borders and reinforced 'border security' through increasing the number of ordinary checkpoints and foot patrols around border areas. Border controls have also been reintroduced in former passport-free travel zones (e.g. the Schengen Area). A number of countries have even recreated a historically condemned form of preventing freedom of movement by building walls and barbed-wire fences (Reuters, April 4, 2016). At the time of writing, at least Hungary, Macedonia, Bulgaria, Greece, Turkey (Walker, September 16, 2016) and Slovenia have built such fences and more European countries are expected to follow in the near future (Tash, March 1, 2016).

This shows that despite acknowledging the human right to seek and enjoy asylum (UDHR, Art. 14), states are taking more and more measures to curtail the flow of refugees into their territories (Parekh 2017). Some measures are clear violations of this human right as well as of the fundamental principles underpinning the 1951 Refugee Convention and 1967 Protocol. For example, the widely accepted principle of non-refoulement has been violated by Turkey which has sent refugees back to Syria (Amnesty International 2016a). Other measures are less obviously violations of international norms but still morally questionable. In the European context, for example, the definition of refugees has been called in to question. An increasingly restrictive notion of what constitutes a refugee has been used by authorities in order to reduce the number of those entitled to assistance. Those who do not fit the restrictive definition are labeled 'illegal immigrants' or 'economic migrants'. Whereas the term 'refugee' denotes a vulnerable individual who is *forced* from his or her home, the term 'migrant' often implies that the individual has *voluntarily* left his or her home. Because their movement is voluntary, migrants do not seem to generate a duty to aid on behalf of receiving states, unlike refugees. The result of this distinction is that while 'genuine' refugees are often allowed to claim asylum, receive aid and have their rights respected, those deemed to be mere 'migrants' can be sent back without any violation of human or refugee rights, since they do not have a right to entry and settle in a foreigner territory. On the contrary, states have been eager to stress that they have the territorial right to exclude them. Yet the conditions that 'genuine' refugees and 'illegal migrants' are fleeing from are often the same and the problem here seems to be more a battle around words to justify different responses (Ruz, August 28, 2015).

At the same time that the concept of 'refugee' is becoming more restrictive, the concepts of 'safe zones' or 'safe countries' are being expanded. States that were once considered unsafe to return migrants or failed asylum seekers to are having their status reevaluated. In such a context, Europe, for example, would not be violating the non-refoulement principle by returning refugees to Turkey (Aaman, March 18, 2016), because before the practice was implemented Turkey was already considered a safe country for refugees (Kingsley, April 1, 2016). The result of this reevaluation is, however, a contestable matter. The Amnesty International (2016a) and the Syrian Observatory for human rights (Kingsley, April 1, 2016) have reported series of abuses from the part of the Turkish authorities that make the reevaluation questionable.

These struggles of creating and maintaining barriers expose the precariousness of human mobility. They show how much the global refugee crisis is pushing universal values of global ethics and global justice to its limits. The refugee crisis has sharpened divisions between 'us' and 'them', 'citizens' and 'foreigners', 'insiders' and 'outsiders'; these divisions often lead to an increase in violence, hatred and hostility between the groups.

Considering this scenario, it appeared of fundamental importance to put the refugee crisis in perspective and to allow for academic discussion of both the theoretical and practical dimensions. In this special issue of the *Journal of Global Ethics*, the first issue of the 'People on the Move' series, the guest-editors selected contributions that were able to enlighten our understanding of the refugee crisis, advance the ongoing debate on the rights and responsibilities of the involved parties, and provide innovative approaches for tackling the situation.

Outline of the volume

The issue is divided into two parts called *Invited Reflections* and *Articles*. In the *Invited reflections*, prominent political theorists and experts of the current refugee situation discuss their views on some of the most pressing challenges, both theoretical and practical, of the current crisis and assess some of the suggested responses for handling this situation.

In theoretical analyses, as well as in public debates, refugees are often viewed as a specific group of people which public opinion, and political institutions are responding to. Refugees are viewed as objects of 'our' actions, and the refugee crisis is interpreted as something 'to be solved'. While there is nothing wrong in aiming to conceptualize the kinds of duties that are owed to refugees, or in trying to find acceptable solutions to the prevailing refugee situation, these debates are often abstracted from the lived realities of refugees and those around them. Refugees are not an abstract group of people, but each has a story to tell of their hopes and aspirations, and of the journey they have embarked upon in order to find safety. Diana Meyers' contribution to this volume, *No Safe Passage: 'The Mapping Journey Project'*, brings forth some of these stories by discussing a recent art installation at the Museum of Modern Art in New York. The stories of the refugees – narrated and illustrated by the refugees themselves – highlight the ways in which these refugees view their journeys to safety, and how their agency is both constructed and constrained by the resistance and hostility of the prevailing political and economic order. The question of refugee agency is also taken up by Phillip Cole in his contribution *Global Displacement and the Topography of Theory*. According to Cole, the exclusion of refugee agency may not only be a problem of social, economic and political practice, but may also extend to the basic structures of ethical and political theory. In order to include refugees as active subjects, Cole argues that refugees must also have a say in the designing of the ethical and political frameworks within which the refugee question is debated rather than being simply included into the pre-existing frameworks of ethical and political theory. Sune Lægaard's contribution, *Misplaced Idealism and Incoherent Realism in the Philosophy of the Refugee Crisis*, further discusses some of the difficulties present in the theoretical and normative debates on the refugee crisis in light of the distinction between ideal and non-ideal theory. By way of analyzing two prominent examples from the debate – Miller's (2016) controversial definition of a refugee and the common argument on the effectiveness of helping neighboring countries of affected zones instead of hosting more asylum seekers in the European states – Lægaard demonstrates how political theorists have often conflated the two stages of ideal and non-ideal theory with the unfortunate results of failing to provide coherent normative principles or practical guidance to the refugee situation at hand.

The three remaining invited contributions move from the issues inherent in theorizing about the refugee situation to a closer analysis of the crisis itself and the proposed models for solving this crisis. Nils Holtug's contribution, *A Fair Distribution of Refugees in the EU*, discusses both the EU countries' obligations to admit refugees from the neighboring countries as well as the morally relevant factors for a fair distributive scheme of refugees within the EU. While Holtug views the current distributive key adopted by the EU to be roughly on the right track, he also points to some weaknesses that must be settled in order for the scheme to be properly morally justified in principle as well as effective in practice. According to him, EU should give substantial support for countries neighboring Syria, relieve these countries by re-settling numerous refugees in the EU, and implement a fair distributive scheme for re-settlements among EU member states. The responses of different countries to the refugee situation within the EU have, of course, been different, and Nanette Funk's contribution, *A Spectre in Germany: Refugees, a 'welcome culture' and an 'integration politics'*, discusses one of these contexts. Analyzing the ways in which the state, civil society, public sphere and refugees themselves have interacted in the integration processes in Germany, Funk advocates a holistic approach to the integration of refugees that builds upon (while critically attending to) the German model. A somewhat different type of policy program, operating for example in Canada since 2013 is discussed by Patti Lenard in her contribution *Resettling Refugees: Is private sponsorship a just way forward?* Lenard provides a normative analysis of both the pros and cons of the public–private partnerships to sponsor refugees, and concludes that, although not perfect, public–private partnerships may provide justifiable supplementary means to offer aid to more refugees in need at little or no extra cost to states' tax revenue.

In the *Articles*, international scholars deal with the various ethical, as well as political, questions relating to the rights and duties of different actors involved in the refugee situation. These actors include, not only refugees and the receiving countries, but also those who are or have been involved in the creating of the current refugee situation, and those involved in preventing or assisting refugees in reaching their destinations.

Javier Hidalgo's paper *The Ethics of People Smuggling* takes on the ethical questions relating to the actions of those who, defying both political and natural border controls, smuggle refugees across borders. As affluent countries are putting a great deal of effort into limiting the number of refugees entering their territories, people smuggling has become a lucrative business for those who have both the knowledge and the means of transferring people across borders with sufficient chances of success. Being both broadly morally condemned and legally prohibited, people smugglers are often viewed as the ultimate evils of the current refugee situation. A careful analysis of the ethical underpinnings of people smuggling may, however, point towards different directions, opening up the possibility of viewing people smuggling as one of the morally permissible ways of assisting refugees.

The two next articles, those of Jennifer Kling's *Who Owes What to War Refugees?* and Jovana Davidovic's *What Do We Owe Refugees: Jus Ad Bellum, Duties to Refugees from Armed Conflict Zones and the Rights to Asylum* discuss the refugee crisis within the Just War tradition. Kling begins from a relatively common assumption among just war theorists that refugees, created by necessary and proportionate wartime actions (such as, for example, legitimate targeting of military bases) are not wronged by these actions, although they are, no doubt, harmed by them. Contrary to this view, Kling argues that refugees, as innocent bystanders, are not only harmed by the necessary and proportionate military actions, but are also wronged by them, and thus owed some form of recompense. Further, Kling argues that the justice based claim for recompense is directed (also) to those actors that have engaged in the necessary and proportionate wartime actions, and that this location of responsibility has some interesting consequences for actual refugee policies across the globe.

Jovana Davidovic's article analyses two different types of duties owed to refugees fleeing from conflict zones, to wit, the duty to remedy past harms and the duty to aid. She points towards certain implications these duties may have for both just war proportionality calculations, as well as for questions of how to discharge these duties in practice. For instance, she argues that the former duty implies that the West in general, and the USA in particular, must assist refugees fleeing war-like conditions in Iraq, for example, by granting them asylum and/or by providing financial assistance to countries and organizations running refugee camps for Iraqi refugees.

Aramide Odutayo's contribution *Human Security and the International Refugee Crisis* provides an interesting overview of some of the punitive policies and practices that that the Western world (especially EU and Australia) have used in their efforts to control the current refugee crisis. These efforts, based on a securitization paradigm that emphasizes national security and strong border controls, have been largely unsuccessful. In contrast to this securitization paradigm, the article discusses some of the benefits and limitations of an alternative framework – that of human security – as providing protections for asylum seekers and refugees in highly non-ideal circumstances.

Gottfried Schweiger's article *The Duty to Bring Children Living in Conflict Zones to Safe Haven* focuses on those most vulnerable within conflict zones, children, and the duties owed to them. Schweiger argues that the special vulnerability and lack of ability of children to exit conflict zones make them a special group of people deserving of special attention. Further, Schweiger argues, these features create a sufficient basis for a duty of the states, and the international community as a whole, to be proactive and bring children, as well as their families, out of conflict zones to safe havens. Acknowledging some of the controversies of the proposal, the paper discusses, and rebuts, some of the common criticisms against the proposal, maintaining that there is a principled duty to bring children out of conflict zones into a safe haven.

Taken as a whole, the articles and contributions in this issue provide a theoretical starting point for a more robust discussion of a global justice approach to the refugee crisis. The articles will no doubt raise as many questions as they answer about the crisis and, hopefully, spark continued debate and discussion about what justice demand that we do in this current crisis and in the future.

Disclosure statement

No potential conflict of interest was reported by the authors.

Funding

This work was supported by Norges Forskningsråd [grant number 259017].

References

Aamann, Preben. 2016. "EU-Turkey Statement, 18 March 2016", European Council, Foreign Affairs & International Relations, Press Release 144/16, March 18. Accessed October, 2016. http://www.consilium.europa.eu/en/press/press-releases/2016/03/18-eu-turkey-statement/

Amnesty International. 2016a. "Turkey: Illegal Mass Returns of Syrian Refugees Expose Fatal Flaws in EU-Turkey Deal. April 1. Accessed October, 2016. https://www.amnesty.org/en/press-releases/2016/04/turkey-illegal-mass-returns-of-syrian-refugees-expose-fatal-flaws-in-eu-turkey-deal/

Amnesty International. 2016b. "Syria's Refugee Crisis in Numbers." February 2. Accessed October, 2016. https://www.amnesty.org/en/latest/news/2016/02/syrias-refugee-crisis-in-numbers/

BBC. 2016. "Migrant Crisis: Migration to Europe Explained in Seven Charts." March 4. Accessed October, 2016. http://www.bbc.com/news/world-europe-34131911

Kingsley, Patrick. 2016. "Turkey is no 'Safe Haven' for Refugees – It Shoots Them at the Border." *The Guardian*, April 1. Accessed October, 2016. https://www.theguardian.com/commentisfree/2016/apr/01/turkey-safe-haven-refugees-shoots-border-illegal-deportations-syrians

Migration Policy Centre. 2016. "The Syrian Refugee Crisis and its Repercussions for the EU". European University Institute, September. Accessed October, 2016. http://syrianrefugees.eu

Miller, David. 2016. *Strangers in Our Midst*. Cambridge: Harvard University Press.

Missing Migrant Project by International Organization for Migration (IOM). 2016. "Mediterranean Update: Migration Flows Europe: Arrivals and Fatalities." October 18. Accessed October, 2016. http://missingmigrants.iom.int

Parekh, Serena. 2017. *Refugees and the Ethics of Forced Displacement*. New York: Routledge.

Reuters. 2016. "How Europe Built Fences to Keep People Out." Edition: United States, April 4. Accessed October, 2016. http://www.reuters.com/article/us-europe-migrants-fences-insight-idUSKCN0X10U7

Ruz, Camila. 2015. "The Battle Over the Words Used to Describe Migrants." *BBC*, August 28. Accessed October, 2016. http://www.bbc.com/news/magazine-34061097

Tash, Barbara. 2016. "This Map Shows How Much the Refugee Crisis is Dividing Europe." *Business Insiders*, March 1. Accessed October, 2016. http://www.businessinsider.com/map-refugees-europe-migrants-2016-2?r=US&IR=T&IR=T

Walker, Alissa. 2016. "5 European Countries Have Built Border Fences to Keep Out Refugees." *Gizmodo*, September 16. Accessed October, 2016. http://gizmodo.com/5-european-countries-have-built-border-fences-to-keep-o-1731065879

No safe passage: 'the mapping journey project'

Diana Tietjens Meyers

ABSTRACT
This essay examines 'The Mapping Journey Project' (2008–2011), an installation artwork by Bouchra Khalili. It consists of eight large video screens and headsets. In each video, a migrant draws a map of her/his journey to and in Europe and narrates her/his route (subtitled in English). In collaboration with Khalili, I argue, these storyteller/draftspersons create a dissident cartography that superimposes their lived geography on the background of legal geography. Thus, 'The Mapping Journey Project' is a work of art that is also a work of advocacy and provocation. Rather than advocating particular policies, however, it advocates in the sense of affirming the dignity of the subjects of the videos and their right to speak the truth of their lives. Moreover, it provokes by elucidating the moral stakes of the current political and economic order and by issuing a pointed demand for humane solutions. So long as vast global disparities of wealth and political power persist, it is no wonder that people who are excluded from the elite privilege of belonging to a prosperous society are burning the borders that protect this unjust regime.

For a philosopher, I am going to address the topic of this special issue in a somewhat unorthodox way. I am not going to critically analyze a concept or defend a practical position. Instead, I am going to discuss a pertinent installation artwork that was on view at the Museum of Modern Art in New York City at the time of writing. I have decided to write about this exhibition for two main reasons. First, my thinking about the refugee crisis – the surge of transnational human movement taking place today – coincides with the artist's understanding of her project. Second, I believe that an esthetic exploration of an issue can be more compelling, and legitimately so, than an abstract argument.

'The Mapping Journey Project' (2008–2011) is the creation of the Moroccan-born, Paris-educated, now Berlin-based artist, Bouchra Khalili. This installation is comprised of eight widely spaced video screens (80″ × 60″) suspended in MOMA's Marron Atrium. The color videos playing on the screens emanate zones of luminosity in the cavernous, dimly lit space. Visitors to the exhibition find a bench with several headsets in front of each video screen. Looking at the screens, they see hands holding marking pens making line drawings on maps. Listening through the headsets, they hear voiceover narratives in European, Asian, and African languages (subtitled in English on the screens) that explain the drawings. The videos are short, running from as little as 3 minutes to as long as 12 minutes. Speaking at an event held at MOMA in conjunction with the exhibition, Khalili stated that she aims to pose a question, spark debate, and give people a means to speak for themselves.[1]

Each video shows a standardized, static representation of geography – a map. The idiosyncratic, kinetic elements of the videos – the motion of drawing and the spoken narration – bring time into the picture. The storyteller/draftspersons are individuals who have traveled in legally impermissible ways. Their simultaneously oral and visual performances depict their travels. As they tell the stories of their journeys, they draw their trajectories on maps. When they are moving steadily from one city to another, their pens glide along the surfaces of the maps. When they find work somewhere or get stuck somewhere, their pens hover above the maps. Represented only by their hands, a bit of forearm or sleeve, and their voices, they are anonymous. Only the space/time coordinates and a few personal details of their journeys are revealed (Figure 1).

Khalili's art practice is important.[2] She does not recruit subjects for her videos using social media or in consultation with NGOs or government agencies serving displaced populations. Her approach is serendipitous and intensely relational. She goes to cities known to be hubs of legally impermissible travel and hangs out:

> The encounter occurs from the moment I accept to get lost in a city. It's a mysterious process, even though it relies on a method.[3]

https://www.moma.org/calendar/exhibitions/1627?locale=en.

The people who interest her approach her. They talk about their experience. She asks a few straightforward, informational questions. She never asks why anyone left home.[4] Mainly she listens. When she thinks an individual is ready to record her or his story, she provides a map and a marking pen, and films the drawing and accompanying testimony in a single take. She does not edit these videos. The subjects speak and draw their piece.

The stories Khalili's subjects tell are short on autobiographical detail. Although one mentions having been a fishermen, most say nothing about their lives before their journeys began. Their resources vary. One leaves home with seven euros. Another's mother gives him 1000 euros to pay a smuggler. The timbres of the recorded voices clue auditors as to whether the storyteller is female or male. We get only indirect, if any, information about their ages. Two mention being apprehended by authorities and being treated as unaccompanied minors – one is sent to a Spanish orphanage, and another is held in an Italian facility for migrants under eighteen years of age. Others sound quite young, but accurate assessment is impossible. All of the stories are told matter-of-factly and unemotionally. The voices are steady. Curator Diana Nawi rightly observes that this installation is neither didactic nor sentimental (Nawi 2015).

In 'The Mapping Journey Project,' individuals' lives are framed as processes of traversing natural terrains and politically demarcated territories. Some people cross mountains or deserts. All but one cross the Mediterranean Sea. We are told and shown on the maps where each person started from, the transit points of her or his journey, and where she or he was at the time the video was made. They are from Algeria, Tunisia, Sudan, Somalia, Morocco, Bangladesh, Afghanistan, and the Israeli-occupied West Bank. They end up in France, Italy, Spain, Turkey, and Israeli-claimed East Jerusalem. Most of them go through or stay in additional countries along the way. They often state how long it took to get from one place to another, whether they walked or used some form of transportation, and how long they stayed in this place or that.

Many mention difficulties they encountered – punishing treks across arid deserts or over forbidding mountains, finding a truck to hide in to get shipped with merchandise to Spain, perilous voyages across the Mediterranean in small boats, people who stole from or lied to them, run-ins with law enforcement agents. Some mention help they received – relatives who provide urgently needed funds, a police chief who detains a boy but soon releases him and gives him a job, the workers in a camp who care for a young woman who survived a boat trip from North Africa to Lampedusa, a commercial vessel that stopped to provide food, water, fuel, and directions to the people packed on a little plastic boat that lost its way on the Mediterranean Sea.

All of the stories make the purpose of the journeys clear. Seven of the eight travelers are seeking work. 'A normal life,' as one says. They remain wherever they find jobs and move whenever they cannot find work. They are employed in agriculture, restaurants, and shops, at a clothing market, as leafletters. Some state that they sent remittances home. There is one romantic story – a Palestinian guy from Ramallah visiting his girlfriend who lives in East Jerusalem.

Every story is geographically complicated but personally sparse. What do the visual depictions add to the stories?

Scale is a telling feature of the imagery. Maps vary in size, and they can be two- or three-dimensional. The ones in Khalili's videos reduce geography to a graphic image on a flat surface. Moreover, they condense large, sometimes vast, areas into the space of a plane that is small enough for a single person to handle and take in at a glance. The maps in the videos represent areas as enormous as the continents of Africa and Europe and the Mediterranean between them, and as small as the cities of Ramallah and Jerusalem and the stretch of land between them.

Regardless of the size of the areas represented on the maps, the hands of the draftspersons look gigantic in comparison. Here it is useful to recall the European Renaissance art practice of scaling the size of the figures in a picture to their relative importance. In this tradition, for instance, the Madonna on her throne is always significantly bigger than the wealthy donors who are portrayed kneeling beside or below her. Following the same logic, these videos showing larger-than-life human hands in relation to compact cartographic representations of tremendous geographical expanses suggest that we must regard the persons whose hands these are as all but infinitely more important than the arbitrary political subdivisions of the planet called nation states.

As I noted earlier, the hands in the videos are marking the maps so as to chart the journeys that the storytellers narrate. So the shapes of the drawings are revealing. Two patterns stand out.

Because the routes are often circuitous, many of the drawings contain perplexing streaks and bulges. For example, one man draws his first attempt to travel from Bangladesh in Asia to Italy in Europe going through India, Russia, and Moldavia where he is stopped and sent home; then he draws his successful second attempt going through Mali and Niger in West Africa and Libya on the North African coast. Such divagations are necessary to dodge border controls, and the shapes of the drawings convey the wariness and desperation of the travelers. The drawings on these maps are reminiscent of maps showing shipping lanes before the Suez and Panama Canals were dug. The only passable routes required circumnavigating whole continents. Although the main obstructions

Khalili's travelers confront are artifacts of political and economic power, as opposed to geological formations, they too are compelled to take roundabout routes.

Because the routes frequently involve trying out possibilities and backtracking, many of the drawings contain jutting or zigzagging lines. A man who has made it to Spain draws a journey that goes from Spain to Italy back to Spain then up to the Netherlands and finally back to Spain. Exploited by an uncle in one place, unable to find work in the next place, retreating to work where his uncle exploited him, successful in obtaining work elsewhere, and finally deceived into returning to his starting point, his drawing is an image of tenacity despite disappointment and futility. The related themes of unavailing effort and dispiriting reversal also appear in the drawings. For example, the thickened tracings of switchbacking lines in one drawing bespeak travel thwarted by expulsion orders – Niger to Algeria and back. The drawings on these maps bear a sobering resemblance to maps of airline flight paths in the hub-and-spoke era, for both the drawings and the flight maps expose systems that prioritize the imperatives of public or private institutions over the interests of travelers.

Plainly the drawings express the subjectivities of the videoed draftspersons – their perseverance notwithstanding their agitation and frustration. In so doing, they attach affective meanings to national sovereignty and border policing with which few museumgoers are likely to have firsthand familiarity. Moreover, in recasting earning a living and gaining legal status as interminable, enervating quests, they endow employment and citizenship with meanings that may resonate with some museumgoers but are apt to be unfamiliar to many others. Grasping these poignant subjective meanings is necessary to understanding 'The Mapping Journey Project,' but it is no less necessary to register that the drawings also express political meanings. Because the maps schematize bounded political entities, the drawings represent Khalili's subjects' engagement with those entities.

One of cartography's charges is to produce graphic representations of the historical outcomes of the politics of geography. In legal terms, this cartographical project reflects the webs of agreements that are articulated in treaties. Maps showing the jigsaw puzzle of nation states depict moments in ongoing histories of bellicosity and diplomacy. Maps showing transnational economic partnerships – before the mid-twentieth century, the coerced alliances of colonial empires; today, the somewhat more reciprocal alliances of the European Union and regional trade pacts – depict moments in ongoing histories of commerce and wealth. During periods when the politics of geography is in flux, accurate mapping requires constant updating. Such is currently the case in the Occupied Palestinian Territory, for new Israeli settlements and checkpoints crop up and right of ways disappear unpredictably.

In contrast to maps of natural topographies and maps of the 'heavens,' the maps in 'The Mapping Journey Project' represent political and economic relationships – groups of contiguous nation states and the EU's single market. As I have mentioned, maps also provide information about shipping lanes and flight paths. Indeed, maps provide information about all sorts of sanctioned itineraries, including trails, roads, railroads, and the like. These maps represent infrastructure and services that comply with government issued safety standards, antitrust laws, and other regulations. Thus, maps of approved transport routes represent intersections between legal authorities, the natural and built environment, and capitalism. It is noteworthy, therefore, that the maps in the videos do not include these approved transport routes. They are beside the point, for each of Khalili's subjects is forging her or his unique itinerary.

Also omitted from the maps in the videos are points of permissible entry and exit at borders. Domestic and international law govern the movement of labor, goods, and capital through these border crossings. However, the demands of economic efficiency often clash with those of national sovereignty and population management because post-industrial capitalist economies depend on low-wage labor that is imported from abroad through clandestine channels if legally sanctioned programs are not available or adequate. With the exception of the video about the Palestinian youth's journey to East Jerusalem to see his girlfriend, 'The Mapping Journey Project' joins issue with this sovereignty-capitalism-migration nexus.[5]

In this connection, a tension between the stories Khalili's subjects tell and the drawings they make deserves attention. The ease and smoothness of their drawing is at odds with the arduous travels they narrate. The storytellers tell of dangerous journeys that test their endurance and consume untold weeks, months, and years under ceaseless threat of discovery, arrest, detention, and deportation. A trip from Bangladesh to Italy, which takes 12.5 hours on a nonstop flight, took one of the storytellers 5 years. Periods of work in interim countries earning enough money for the next leg of the trip interrupt some trajectories. Long waits for smugglers or transportation to be organized or for asylum decisions to be issued hold up others. In contrast, the drawings materialize rapidly. Obviously, the miniaturization of cartography makes this compression of time and distance possible. Still, we viewers need to ask what to make of the aural/visual dissonance Khalili orchestrates.

Most viewers can roughly estimate travel times by public conveyance through official border crossings. Those who perform this little exercise to contextualize their encounter with 'The Mapping Journey Project' may be shocked to find that their estimates diverge so sharply from the astounding spans of time the storytellers attest to. But there may also be convergences between viewers' travel experience and that of Khalili's subjects. Many viewers might remember spending time transfixed on a station concourse in a foreign country while trying to decipher bus or train departure displays in an unknown language or unknown orthography. Similar difficulties surely beset Khalili's subjects traversing the Middle East and Africa on their way to Europe or making their way through Europe. When the drawings depict direct routes from one city to another, the simplicity and speed of the act of drawing may accord with what viewers are likely to consider reasonable, possibly ordinary.

By pitting viewers' expectations about travel against and cuing viewers' awareness of commonalities between their experiences of travel and those of the storyteller/draftspersons, the videos prompt viewers to empathize with and ponder the significance of the delays and ordeals these individuals endure. In other words, the dissonance within the videos presses viewers to think seriously about who these storyteller/draftspersons are and how best to interpret their journeys.

Some of Khalili's subjects claim refugee status and apply for asylum upon arriving in Europe. Colloquial labels that apply to most of them include 'irregular migrant' and 'undocumented migrant' and the highly prejudicial 'illegal alien.' Reaching for neutral language, I have referred to Khalili's subjects as travelers, storytellers, and draftspersons. Of course they are not recreational travelers or business travelers in the usual meaning of those expressions. And I have granted that their travels are not legally permissible. Nor are they authors or artists as those terms are usually understood. Nevertheless, hearing their stories unfold and watching their drawings take shape invite us to problematize conventional language.

Clearly, issues of belonging and citizenship are central to 'The Mapping Journey Project.' So, too, are issues of freedom and agency. Khalili's subjects are not citizens of the 'right' states and lack the skills or wealth to buy their way into destination countries. They are needed in these places, but they are not welcome there. So they exercise their agency to flout laws that interfere with their ability to pursue fundamental human aims – namely, securing work and income sufficient to meet their needs.

Nikki Lohr maintains that Khalili 'does not see these people as migrants, but as members of a political minority, whose journeys are acts of defiance' (Lohr 2014). I take it that the political minority she has in mind is made up of those workers in economies around the world who are not citizens and who do not hold work visas. These workers are doubly disenfranchised. Not only do they lack rights of political participation and labor protection, they and their contributions receive no respect. In my view, then, the isolated, animated zones of illumination scattered in the museum atrium's shadowy space are phantom workers. Politically and socially, they are anonymous and unsung. In many countries today, politicians and citizens vilify and demonize them. Although their political contestation is often solitary and conducted underground, their travels and their labor nonetheless challenge rigid, exclusionary frontiers.

In this regard, the language a subset of Khalili's subjects uses to characterize their endeavors is intriguing. In a talk presented at Iniva at Rivington Place in London, Khalili states that those of her subjects who grew up in North African countries do not speak of immigrating illegally. Rather, they call their travels 'burning.'[6] To prepare for departure, they burn their ID cards and their passports, and when they succeed in getting to Europe, they have 'burned' the border. Through their journeys, they cast off their birth identities, and they symbolically annihilate international borders.

This vernacular might strike some readers as a case of rationalization by euphemism. However, I submit that the metaphor is apt. Consider that right-wing political figures in Britain, France, Germany, Greece, and the US scapegoat so-called economic migrants to stoke nationalist political conflagrations. Likewise it congrues with the 'geography of resistance'[7] that Khalili's subjects are obliged to live. For these individuals, leading a decent human life is incompatible with respect for sovereign borders. In short, burnt borders are the legacy of centuries of global injustice.

In collaboration with Khalili, these storyteller/draftspersons have created a dissident cartography that superimposes their lived geography on the background of legal geography. Thus, 'The Mapping Journey Project' is a work of art that is also a work of advocacy and provocation. The installation does not advocate in the sense of recommending alternative policies. On the contrary, it advocates in the sense of affirming the dignity of the subjects of the videos and their right to speak the truth of their lives. Moreover, it provokes not in the sense of inducing a particular response from viewers, but rather by elucidating the moral stakes of the current political and economic order and by issuing a pointed demand for humane solutions. So long as vast global disparities of wealth and political power persist, as Khalili memorably put it, 'citizenship is like access to the VIP area of a club.'⁸ It is no wonder that people who are excluded from the elite privilege of belonging to a prosperous society are burning the borders that protect this unjust regime.

Notes

1. 'Citizens and Borders: A Conversation with Joseph Carens, Bouchra Khalili, and Samar Yazbek, Moderated by Bernard Haykel.' Museum of Modern Art, New York City, June 24, 2016. A video of the event is available at http://www.moma.org/calendar/events/2121?locale=en.
2. Kaelen Wilson-Goldie provides a helpful discussion of Khalili's interactions with the subjects of 'The Mapping Journey Project' in 'In Focus: Bouchra Khalili.' *Frieze* 2011 (https://frieze.com/article/focus-bouchra-khalili, accessed July 13, 2016).
3. Bouchra Khalili, quoted in Nikki Lohr. 2014. 'The Meaning in Mapping: Bouchra Khalili's Border-Crossing Video Art at the New Museum.' *Observer Culture* (http://observer.com/2014/08/the-meaning-in-mapping-bouchra-khalilis-border-crossing-video-art-at-the-new-museum/, accessed July13, 2016)
4. Part 2 of Bouchra Khalili's presentation at Iniva at Rivington Place, London (https://www.youtube.com/watch?v=nY9jf0S0Hes, accessed July 13, 2016)
5. The video about the Palestinian man's fraught trips to East Jerusalem addresses questions about the geography of occupation and colonization. Because I regard occupation and colonization as indisputably wrong, it seems unnecessary to address this video in a journal devoted to controversies in global ethics. Thus, I will focus on the other seven videos in the remainder of this paper. However, for readers who might be interested, I note that Khalili discusses a more recent cartographic project devoted to the geography of occupation and colonization in a video of a talk she gave at the Sharjah Art Foundation (https://vimeo.com/17756648, accessed July 13, 2016).
6. Part 3 of Bouchra Khalili's presentation at Iniva at Rivington Place, London (https://www.youtube.com/watch?v=EKuiQmCp8rA, accessed July 13, 2016).
7. I borrow this phrase from MOMA's press release for the exhibition.
8. 'Citizens and Borders: A Conversation with Joseph Carens, Bouchra Khalili, and Samar Yazbek, Moderated by Bernard Haykel,' Museum of Modern Art, New York City, June 24, 2016. A video of the event is available at http://www.moma.org/calendar/events/2121?locale=en.

Acknowledgements

Thanks to Lewis Meyers, who visited the exhibition with me and shared his insights about 'The Mapping Journey Project.'

Disclosure statement

No potential conflict of interest was reported by the author.

References

Lohr, Nikki. 2014. "The Meaning in Mapping: Bouchra Khalili's Border-Crossing Video Art at the New Museum." *Observer Culture*, Accessed July 13, 2016. http://observer.com/2014/08/the-meaning-in-mapping-bouchra-khalilis-border-crossing-video-art-at-the-new-museum/

Nawi, Diana. 2015. "Other Maps: On Bouchra Khalili's Cartographies." *Ibrazz*, Accessed July 13, 2016. http://www.ibraaz.org/essays/115#top

Global displacement and the topography of theory

Phillip Cole

ABSTRACT
In this essay, I examine the concept of the refugee within the context of liberal political theory. The argument is that the refugee is displaced both in political practice and political theory – theory has a topology, and inside and an outside, such that even if the refugee as a concept does enter within its boundaries it does so as a marginal figure, constructed as problematic. However, liberal political also has a topography when it comes to the refugee question – it is not just insider theory, but theory constructed within a particular kind of state in a particular location in the world. This means the extent to which liberal political theory can answer the refugee question is limited. The main challenge for theory, I argue, is not to come up with an answer to the refugee question, but to construct a context within which the refugee (broadly defined) is an equal participant in the process of arriving at an answer.

In September 2015, one image dominated the front pages of newspapers across Europe, the picture of a three-year-old Syrian boy, Alan Kurdi, who drowned as his family attempted the crossing from Turkey to Greece, the final leg of their journey from the Syrian city of Kobani, which had suffered repeated attacks by Daesh militants. Now, in one tragic moment, those of us who had been working to change the discourse of suspicion and hostility towards asylum seekers and refugees that dominated political and media discourse throughout Europe saw everything change. There were marches in major cities all with the same slogan, 'Refugees are welcome here'. I took part in one such march in my home city of Cardiff, and as a trustee for the Welsh Refugee Council I witnessed the dramatic effect of that image, as we were overwhelmed with people wanting to offer food, clothes, toys and shelter.

And yet in a few months this mood subsided and the atmosphere of suspicion and resentment returned to European politics. Hostility to refugees cannot be ruled out as one of the factors that led to the decision of the British people to leave the European Union in the June 2016 Referendum. An opportunity for sustained reflection upon the content and basis of the moral obligations and duties towards those fleeing conflict and other dangers was lost. However, as well as an activist, I am also a political theorist, and although there are difficult questions about the relationship between theory and activism and the role theory can play in moments of crisis, one thing we can and must do as theorists is to ensure that we return to the reflective moment and sustain it, to look beyond the rhetoric and the numbers and see if we can offer a coherent ethical vision of what is owed to refugees and why. And even though it is hard to see how theory can make an intervention into the kind of politics we are witnessing, this is a crucial moment to do so, as the sense of crisis in Europe and elsewhere has caused not only organizations like the European Union to find new ways to 'stem the flow', but has also caused some political leaders to question the international legal framework that governs refugees and asylum. That framework may well be reviewed in the coming period, and that review will be led by those who see refugees as a burden and whose main objective is to make it harder for them to reach safety. The contribution political theory can make is to offer an ethical vision which critically engages with that hostility in order to contribute to overcoming it.

However, while theory's task is to challenge political discourse and practice, it too faces fundamental challenges if it is to enable us to articulate that ethical vision. The primary challenge is not so much to arrive at that vision, but to structure a context and process through which it can be reached, and the fact is that political theory itself may be shaped such that it cannot play a positive role in building such a structure. Its *own* structure may be at odds with that project. This may sound odd – surely it is through political theory that we *build* conceptual structures and systems of ideas. But anybody who takes psychology and psychoanalysis seriously is aware that human consciousness does not create ideas in free form, but itself has a structure which constrains what it can create, and that it is only by reflecting back on itself that consciousness can free itself from those constraints and become truly creative. What I want to suggest here is that political theory has a structure which constrains what it can create, and that before it can approach the refugee question and offer an ethical vision in answer to it, it must reflect back upon itself to free itself from those constraints.

At its most basic, the problem is the extent to which liberal political theory accepts and works with certain components of the international refugee framework that should be contested. Of course political theorists are deeply engaged with contesting the definition of who counts as a refugee and why, but one major distinction is between refugees and the internally displaced – in order to count as a refugee one must cross an international border. While the United Nations High Commissioner for Refugees estimates that there are currently 21.3 million refugees globally, that is part of the overall figure of 65.3 million who have been forcibly displaced. For the purposes of this paper, I will use the term 'refugee' to refer to all who have been forcibly displaced, whatever the cause of their displacement and wherever they are displaced to. I will not argue for this as a definition, but in taking this step we set aside many of the presumptions that structure and confine how we can answer the refugee question.

A deeper problem is the extent to which liberal political theory is 'insider' theory, assuming a specific perspective from inside a nation-state, such that the solutions it develops are limited in scope, with the liberal nation-state at the centre and the refugee at the margins. The refugee is the *object* of the refugee question, and as an object must take a particular shape and form to fit within the pre-given structure of the liberal nation-state and the political theory that has that state at its centre. Somehow the refugee must become the active subject of the refugee question, not merely its passive object, by which I mean that not only is the refugee put at the centre of the question, but also plays a full and active role in arriving at its answer.

In approaches to global poverty, there are, broadly speaking, two ways of understanding it, known as the residual view and the structural view. The residual view largely emerges from neo-liberalism and sees the global poor as a leftover from the international economic system – a residue. This residue is not created by the economic system: it is simply unable to absorb it. The solution is to make the economic system more efficient so that it does absorb this leftover element. And so where national economies lie outside of the global economic order, barriers need to be deconstructed so that those economies become incorporated into the international system. Or, where certain sections of a national economy that is incorporated into the international system remain on the outside – for example, publicly owned sectors – then reform has to take place such that they are included. The international system, as it were, moves in and soaks up the poor so that they become part of the global order. The presupposition is, of course, that it is better to be inside the capitalist economic order than outside of it.

The structural approach comes out of the Marxist critique of liberalism and sees the global poor as a product of the international economic order. For the neo-liberal position, the global poor are on the outside of that order but this exclusion has nothing to do with the system. But for the Marxist, they are produced by that system – the order itself produces the economic inside and outside. And so the solution to global poverty cannot be to make the economic order more efficient, because that may have the effect of *increasing* the numbers in extreme poverty. Rather, the solution has to be to radically change the economic order so that it no longer produces an inside and an outside – all are genuinely included in an egalitarian system of production and consumption, a system in which they are free and equal (autonomous) producers and consumers. These two forms of analysis can be applied to many issues, such as the position of women, ethnic minorities and the physically disabled, and not only in relation to the economic system, but also to other kinds of political and social systems. Either these groups lie on the outside because of factors that have nothing to do with the system or because there is a minor inefficiency that can be tweaked, or the system *produces* an inside and an outside such that the order is structured around the exclusion of certain others.

The global displaced can be understood in this way. We can see them as a leftover residue lying outside of the international system of sovereign states, but their exclusion is either nothing to do with that system or is due to some minor inefficiency that can be tweaked. Or we see them as a structural failure, a product of that order, such that finding a solution to displacement means asking radical questions about the international political order itself. This is not so much a dispute between neo-liberals and Marxists, but between reformists and radical critics of the nation-state system. Joseph Carens can, to an extent, be seen as taking the former position, in that he believes his approach to migration and membership is compatible with the nation-state system more or less as it stands. For example, in his discussion of refugees, he explains the obligation nation-states have to refugees in terms of the normative presuppositions of the nation-state system. That system organizes the world so that everybody ought to be assigned to a nation-state. However, in some cases that does not happen because states fail people either deliberately or through incapacity. 'Because the state system assigns people to states, states collectively have a responsibility to help those for whom this assignment is disastrous'

(Carens 2013, 196). The clear implication is that the failure does not arise from the nation-state system itself, but from certain nation-states failing to behave, either deliberately or through incapacity, as we believe nation-states should. The structural view is that refugees are not only forced out of their nation-state, they are forced out of the international nation-state system – and this exclusion embraces the wider sense of 'refugee' I use in this paper. The fundamental problem, then, is not being excluded from a specific nation-state, but being excluded from the nation-state system as such.

But while we have an interesting line of argument here about moral responsibility for the displaced, and whether we should see it a systemic failure or a domestic one, I am not going to pursue this line of argument. My focus in this essay is not how the displaced are produced but how the *idea* of the displaced is produced, not how the political system produces an inside and an outside, but how liberal political *theory* produces an inside and an outside. My main contention is that these two approaches – the residual and the structural – are embodied at the level of political theory itself. What we should notice is that not only are certain groups excluded from economic, political and social systems, but that they are excluded from theoretical systems. Certain groups such as women, the physically disabled, non-white 'ethnic' groups, migrants and the global displaced, have been excluded from liberal political theory. This, of course, is not news – political theorists have been aware of this for decades and many have addressed it. But the point is to notice that we can understand that exclusion either as residual or structural. If residual, all we need to do is tweak our theory a bit to include them, and then carry on more or less as before. If structural, then we have to radically re-think our political theory in order for it to be genuinely exclusive, and that may involve re-thinking everything – we cannot go on as before. My contention in this essay is that this exclusion is structural; the inside and outside is produced by theory itself, and business as usual is not an option.

I first noticed exclusion at the level of political theory many years ago working on my PhD thesis looking at the work of John Rawls in relation to the physically disabled. Rawls explicitly acknowledges that his theory applies to what he describes as the 'normal range'. He says: ' … it is reasonable to assume that everyone has physical needs and physiological capacities within some normal range', and his theory is for 'those who are full and active participants in society, and directly or indirectly associated over the course of a whole life' (Rawls 1978, 70 note 9). His theory therefore explicitly excludes those who are excluded from full and active participation in society. Although he suggests that he may be able to 'attempt to handle these other cases later', it is extraordinary to realize that liberal political theory, as Rawls understands it, is not for everybody, but only for the included. It is also interesting to note that these comments are not taken from his major book, *A Theory of Justice*, but from a paper, and from a footnote in that paper.

And so what we have here is a double exclusion, from practice and from theory, and the exclusion from theory reflects and is based upon the exclusion from practice. Rawls, though, obviously takes the residual view, with the supposition that we can ignore these difficult subjects for now, but once we have worked out the theory for the 'normal' we can bring the 'abnormal' in later – all we need to do is tweak the theory a little to include them and we can go on much as before. The implication has to be, I think, that this is how the problem can be tackled in practice: we can make the practice work better from the point of view of justice for all those included in the practice, and at a later date tweak that practice to include those who have been excluded from it.

However, my view is that this is entirely mistaken and what we have here is a deeply structural challenge. Part of the problem is that when we come to include the excluded, we are attempting to include them within a theory that has been actively structured around their exclusion. This reflects the problem at the level of practice. If our practices have been fundamentally constructed around an idea of what it is to be 'able-bodied', including the physically disabled within them through some 'tweaking' is going to be highly problematic. What is needed is a fundamental re-think of those practices from the ground up which treats all as equal members with no prior distinction between the 'able-bodied' and the 'disabled', and rather than tweaking current practices it may mean starting again from scratch. The same holds for theory. What we realize is that theory has a topology, a shape. Historically, liberal theory has simply excluded the 'other', whether they be the physically disabled or, in our discussion, the global displaced. It has not acknowledged their existence at all and has presented us with a false, particularist, universalism. This means that their presence within theory becomes deeply disruptive and disturbing because, if I am right, it cannot be business as usual only now with the 'outsider' on board. The theory we have ended up with is exposed as deeply flawed and in need of radical critique. Rather than a tweak here and there, we may have to start from scratch.

My proposal is that this is how we should see the concept of the global displaced in liberal political theory. Liberal political theory has notoriously been structured on the assumption that we are dealing with members of a nation-state (and Rawls shows is that, in fact, the focus is much narrower than that, as have feminist theorists and those working on the concept of 'race' and other identity positions). This is an assumption that I have confronted in my work on migration, arguing that the migrant should be an equal figure with the citizen in any ethical discussion of immigration, rather than the interests of the citizen-dominating theory. But equally, international political theory, when it does address the ethics of migration, is equally structured on the assumption that people, even if they are migrants, are members of a nation-state which they have left voluntarily – they have not been *forced* to leave.

This assumption, that the figure of the migrant is one that exercises agency and choice, is fundamental, I think, to how liberal political theory thinks about migration. The migrant does not have to leave their home but chooses to do so, and if they cannot gain access to 'our' particular state, they will be able to choose another one. The displaced person, however, is forced to leave their home and has little or no choice where they go as a result. While we may have addressed the fact that the migrant was not included within liberal political theory, we now have to recognize that the global displaced are not included within *international* political theory, however cosmopolitan we believe that theory to be. And it is crucial to note that this distinction – between the active migrant who has agency and choice and the passive refugee who has neither – around which liberal political theory builds its conception of international migration, simply collapses. Many people who count as migrants rather than refugees move because they are caught up in migratory flows, exercising very little control over where and when they migrate and how, or even why. And many refugees exercise agency and choice over where they go, much to the chagrin of developed-world states. And so one of the crucially important results of opening up the question in this way is that the distinction between the forcibly displaced person and voluntary migrant disappears. Distinctions we thought were clear and which gave us a structure within which to address the question now collapse.

The important point here is that we cannot simply apply the political theory we have to the problem of displacement, because the political theory we have does not acknowledge the existence of the displaced, or rather it can only acknowledge their existence in a particular way. Even if we direct the theory towards displacement as an issue, the theory constructs it as a specific kind of problem, and keeps the displaced at the margins of theory, not allowing them to become the central subject of theory. It has to do this, because if it did allow them to become the central subject of theory, they would expose that theory as fundamentally structurally flawed and incoherent, with all the definitions and distinctions that theory rests upon collapsing around us.

When I wrote my book *Philosophies of Exclusion: Liberal Political Theory and Immigration* (Cole 2000) the major aim of my argument was not, in fact, open borders, but to show that addressing the question of membership has the potential to undermine the entire coherence of liberal political theory. Immigration is not some marginal question which we can add on to theory, but goes to the heart of that theory and exposes it as fundamentally flawed. My conclusion to that book was that liberal theory had a choice, either to embrace open borders or embrace its own incoherence. The question of displacement reveals that the structural flaws go much deeper than I accounted for in *Philosophies of Exclusion*. The problem we face is that liberal political theory has been an 'insider theory', a body of theory that privileges the voice of the insider, the one who possesses statehood, the citizen. That privilege, at the extreme, has meant that this is the only position acknowledged as existing. But even if we recognize the existence of the displaced as a problem for political theory, they are included as a problem for the citizen, a problem that must be solved in the interests of the citizen. Any solution to that problem has to keep the interests of the citizen at the centre, in the same way that the theory has always been structured around the interests of the citizen. The displaced person is the passive object of the refugee question, not its active subject.

Rawls tells us, unwittingly perhaps, that the problem is even worse than this, that the theory has been constructed around the interests of a particular *kind* of citizen, one who is a member of the 'normal range', however, we construct that range. But my contention in this paper is that the problem is even worse than this. Not only has liberal theory been 'insider theory' with a specific *topology*, theorizing from inside a nation-state, it has also had a specific *topography*, theorizing from inside a particular *kind* of nation-state in a particular area of the world. Liberal theory has a *geographical* shape, as a body of theory structuring a viewpoint on migration and membership centred upon the interests not only of those who already have membership of a state, but membership of a particular kind of nation-state in a particular location in the world – liberal democratic states in the Global North. This means that any solution to the problem of displacement that theory produces will be structured around the interests of those specific members. So the relationship we are trying to understand here is not simply between displacement and membership, but between displacement and membership of liberal democratic states in the Global North.

This topography of theory means that any solution to the refugee question constructed within liberal political theory even in its international form cannot be genuinely inclusive and egalitarian, because the negotiation on which that solution is based cannot take place on an equal basis. Indeed, it is likely that any negotiation will still only be between those on the inside, with refugees remaining on the outside, excluded as participants in any negotiation of a solution. There is a core and periphery of theory, with the other – in this case the displaced person – confined to the periphery and the core structured around the interests of the insider, the citizen of a particular kind of nation-state in a particular location.

The challenge we face as theorists is therefore how to break out of this topographic enclosure, but in a way which does not assume there is some neutral theoretical space that we as theorists can occupy so that we can move directly to an answer to the refugee question. Rather, our priority has to be to contribute to the building of a genuinely inclusive theoretical context within which all have equal voices in reaching an egalitarian settlement based on universal principles of justice. In other words, our first task is not to find the right answer to the question, but to find the right way of answering it. This approach is based on the realization that everything has to be up for negotiation – there can be no fixed points, because what we take to be fixed points have been fixed by the old topology/topography of the theory, and it is those fixed points that are the problem. To think that we can arrive at a solution to displacement based around those fixed points is the mistake. We have to start from scratch. And this means that re-thinking is not only the concept of the refugee and their rights, but also the concept of the citizen and their rights – we cannot rethink the meaning of the idea of the refugee without rethinking the meaning of the idea of the citizen, because the inside is defined against the outside and depends upon it. To revise the conception of the outside is to radically threaten the inside. The fact is that it is the rights of the person who is already safe that restrict the rights of those who seek safety. And this, of course, means that the very idea of the liberal nation-state is also thrown into question.

The theoretical basis for discussions of membership and mobility must be challenged. What membership means and the rights that attach to it has to be fought over, rather than taken as our starting point. The fight is not just *for* membership, but also for its meaning. And what we must recognize is that its meaning will be determined not by theorists and policy-makers, but by those who seek it, who act out these ideas in their everyday lives. What is needed is a dialectic between theory and lived experience. This is always how moral and political concepts have been determined – not through abstract thought, but through political and practical struggle, and through ordinary people seeking to improve their lives and the lives of those around them in conditions of oppression. Political theory must become cosmopolitan in the true sense of the word, by providing space for all these voices and experiences, by embracing our common humanity in all its variety and dissolving the boundaries that separate 'us' from 'them'.

The way in which the privileging of the voice of the insider is deeply ingrained within political theory is shown by Seyla Benhabib's use of discourse ethics to establish a human right to membership. Her discourse between the insider and the outsider goes as follows (note that from the beginning she, as the speaker, is the insider):

> If you and I enter into a moral dialogue with one another, and if I am a member of a state of which you are seeking membership and you are not, then I must be able to show you with good grounds, grounds that would be acceptable to each of us equally, why you can never join our association and become one of us. These must be grounds that you would accept if you were in my situation and I were in yours. Our reasons must be reciprocally acceptable; they must apply to us equally. (Benhabib 2004, 138)

In order to be acceptable, such grounds would be to do with qualifications, skills and resources (Benhabib 2004, 139). But note that the crucial aspect of the discourse is that *these must be grounds that you would accept if you were in my situation*. In other words, the outsider must think from the perspective of the insider, and so once more the perspective of the insider is privileged. The sentence should at least read: *These must be grounds that you would accept if you were in my situation and I would accept if I were in yours*. As it stands, there is no reciprocity here. If the grounds for exclusion are to be genuinely 'acceptable to us equally', then they have to be acceptable to the outsider *as outsider*. And equally importantly, they must be contested against grounds for *inclusion* which must carry equal weight in the exchange.

Lori Watson points out:

> The emphasis on reasons we could not reasonably reject as the standard of moral justification requires us to recognize that such reasons have the character they do, in part, because they are reasons we can share – as moral equals. Acknowledging that immigrants stand in a political relationship vis-à-vis the state of intended migration requires acknowledging that the state is obligated to offer justifications that could not be reasonably rejected for its principles. This, however, also requires acknowledging the immigrant as a reason-giver in this context, and as an equal. (2008, 988)

But in order for the migrant or, for the purposes of our discussion, the refugee, to be an equal in this exchange, we must be able to give our reasons from positions of equality, and to make this possible we have to be prepared to think outside of the conventional political frameworks that position the refugee as the 'problem' figure in this relationship. It is not the refugee who is the problem, but the relationship itself, a relationship which privileges the reasons of the 'insider' and renders the 'outsider', in this case the refugee, silent.

The implication of these thoughts is that political theorists, including myself, are not best placed to offer an ethical answer to the refugee question. Instead, we should focus on the prior task of constructing an ethical framework within which the question can be answered. Even then, that ethical framework must be one that recognizes the equality not only of the position of the refugee alongside the other political positions that constitute it, but also the refugee voice in the process of deciding what that ethical framework should look like. And so it may be that the most important right for refugees is not the right to safe passage or to make a new home in a place of sanctuary, but the right to self-representation at all levels of political debate, including political theory itself. To relegate the rights to safe passage and sanctuary as second-order rights may seem paradoxical, but this does point to the fundamental injustice here, the objectification of refugees as passive burdens dependent on the benevolence of states that supposedly champion human rights. Political theory itself must avoid that objectification, and a crucial part of acknowledging the agency of refugees is to acknowledge their participation in answering the refugee question itself, including at the level of theory, that they become its active subject as well as its object.

Disclosure statement

No potential conflict of interest was reported by the author.

References

Benhabib, Seyla. 2004. *The Rights of Others: Aliens, Residents and Citizens*. Cambridge: Cambridge University Press.
Carens, Joseph H. 2013. *The Ethics of Immigration*. Oxford: Oxford University Press.
Cole, Phillip. 2000. *Philosophies of Exclusion: Liberal Political Theory and Immigration*. Edinburgh: Edinburgh University Press.
Rawls, John. 1978. "The Basic Structure as Subject." In *Values and Morals*, edited by A. Goldman, and J. Kim, 47–71. Dordrecht: Reidel.
Watson, Lori. 2008. "Equal Justice: Comment on Michael Blake's Immigration and Political Equality." *San Diego Law Review* 45: 981–988.

Misplaced idealism and incoherent realism in the philosophy of the refugee crisis

Sune Lægaard

ABSTRACT
Many contributions to the philosophical debate about conceptual and normative issues raised by the refugee crisis fail to take properly account of the difference between ideal and nonideal theory. This makes several otherwise interesting and apparently plausible contributions to the philosophy of the refugee crisis problematic. They are problematic in the sense that they mix up ideal and nonideal aspirations and assumptions in an incoherent way undermining the proposed views. Two examples of this problem are discussed. The first example is David Miller's contribution to the conceptual debate about how we should understand refugeehood. The second example is a common argument from the normative debate about how states should discharge their duties to help refugees, namely the claim that states should help in neighboring countries rather than by taking in more asylum seekers. Both are examples of arguments about how we should understand or respond to the refugee crisis, which appear to offer coherent principles for the moral guidance of political actors but which are actually incoherent as principles of practical reasoning for the context they aim to address.

Introduction

The refugee crisis, both in the global sense of the staggering number of refugees in the world at the moment and in the specific sense of, for example, the people fleeing the war in Syria, raises a number of philosophical questions. One set of questions concerns how we should *conceptualize* what is going on. This includes the framing of the entire phenomenon as a 'refugee crisis' and the concept of 'refugee' invoked in doing so. The philosophical question here concerns what we mean by this, why we frame what is going on in these rather than other terms, and what the implications are of doing so. Another set of questions concerns what the appropriate *normative response* to the refugee crisis is: what duties do which actors have to respond to, for example, refugees from Syria, and what is the best way of doing so? While these two questions are analytically distinct, the answers to them are arguably not, since the *labeling* of some people as refugees in ordinary as well as legal parlance implies acceptance of certain *duties* toward these people, minimally the duty of *nonrefoulement* (Lister 2013, 648).

There are genuine disagreements about exactly *in which sense* the people fleeing Syria are refugees, that is, precisely which concept of refugeehood we should use, *exactly which duties* other states have to help them, what the *justifications* for these duties are, and how best to discharge them *in practice*.

While there *are* philosophical questions about the refugee crisis, the practical problem of bridging the gap between the duties of justice and the limited subset of these duties that actual agents, for example states, comply with is not susceptible to philosophical solution. This difference, however, is one that philosophy *can* say something about. I suggest that the difference is not only about a gap between what states ought to do and what they in fact do. I will suggest that the distinction between ideal and nonideal theory (Rawls 1999) also plays a role here, which we should pay attention to when engaging in philosophical discussion of the refugee crisis.

This should come as no surprise, since the crisis clearly is nonideal – otherwise we would not call it a crisis. Nevertheless, I will argue, many contributions to the philosophical debate about both the conceptual and normative issues fail to take proper account of this difference. I will argue that this makes several otherwise interesting and apparently plausible contributions to the philosophy of the refugee crisis problematic. They are problematic in the sense that they mix up ideal and nonideal aspirations and assumptions in an incoherent way undermining the proposed views.

I will present two examples of this problem, one from the conceptual debate about how we should understand refugeehood and another from the normative debate about how states should discharge their duties to help refugees. The first example is David Miller's refugee definition offered in his recent work on the philosophy of migration. The second example is a common argument for why European states should help in neighboring countries rather than by taking in more asylum seekers. Both are examples of arguments about how we should understand or respond to the refugee crisis, which appear to offer coherent principles for the moral guidance of political actors but which are actually incoherent as principles of practical reasoning for the context they aim to address. But these are only intended as illustrations of what I suspect is a more general problem in the philosophy of forced migration.

The refugee crisis as nonideal

The refugee crisis itself is more or less by definition a nonideal problem; although natural disasters can also cause people to flee, a refugee crisis like the one emanating from Syria is obviously an effect of unjust acts on a massive scale perpetrated by both state and non-state actors.

Refugees by definition are people whose states either cannot or will not fulfill their duties to protect the basic human rights of these people, who are therefore forced to flee (Owen 2016, forthcoming). The exact details differ depending on precisely which definition of refugeehood one adopts. On a narrow definition, like that of the 1951 Refugee Convention according to which a refugee is a person subjected to personal persecution who is outside his or her country of origin, the existence of refugees implies that the state in question either itself persecutes or allows other agents to persecute the refugee. On a broader definition of refugeehood, for example a humanitarian one according to which anyone whose basic needs are unmet counts as a refugee (e.g. Shacknove

1985), it implies that the state in question fails in its duties to secure the basic needs of its citizens more generally. Either way, the existence of refugees is nonideal in the Rawlsian sense of being an issue within *partial compliance theory*, since the states in question fail to live up to specific duties (Rawls 1999, 8, 215).

A refugee crisis may encompass additional partial compliance on the behalf of other agents, most obviously other states, depending on whether they live up to their duties to assist refugees. Other states minimally have duties of *nonrefoulement* toward refugees, which in some cases they fail to comply with, for example when Turkish border guards push people fleeing from Syria back across the border. Furthermore, the community of states has collective duties to secure the required assistance to refugees, that is, to secure acknowledged refugees residence in a place where they are secure from persecution (on a narrow definition) or where their basic needs can be met (on a broader definition). Here the well-known problem of the distribution of the responsibility to assist refugees arises (e.g. Miller 2016a). This can engender a condition of collective partial compliance, that is, cases where the duty to assist is not met for some refugees, although it cannot be specified which particular state has failed to live up to its duties, since the duties in question are shared between all states (Owen forthcoming).

The existence of refugees may be nonideal in a further, more theory-driven sense. According to proponents of open borders, the existence of refugees is nonideal in a fundamental sense. Refugees are a product of the partition of the world into states that control the movement across borders – if there were no restrictions on migration, most of the world's refugees would not exist since there would be no borders keeping them in or out. For proponents of open borders, there should not be any border controls at all and therefore the very category of refugees is nonideal. On open borders views, there is really nothing special about the category of refugees. Insofar as refugees are people who have a special status relative to the assumed right of states to control immigration, the need for the category of refugees simply disappears if one rejects this right, as open borders theorists do (Carens 2013, 194; Kukathas 2016; Lister 2013, 653; Oberman 2016).

But in the actual world, where all states hold on to their right to control borders, the category of refugees still picks out a group of people with special needs for a specific kind of assistance and provides a way of granting this assistance acknowledged, at least in principle, by states. The question therefore becomes: how should we understand the category of refugees?

Miller's refugee definition

The category of refugees at stake in debates about whether specific groups of people are refugees is not purely descriptive. What people debate is not whether some people flee (they do), but whether we therefore have duties to help them. To say that someone is a refugee is already to say that states have certain duties toward this person. According to David Miller, states have special duties of care toward refugees encapsulated in the principle of *nonrefoulement* (2016a, 78). Matt Lister similarly initially characterizes a refugee as 'anyone whom a state has a moral duty to admit into itself, despite whatever other immigration policies the state in question may have' (2013, 647). So the question about the definition of refugees is moralized: it concerns how we should delimit the group of people that are owed these duties.

According to the 1951 Refugee Convention, the relevant group only includes people who:

> Owing to a well-founded fear of being persecuted for reasons of race, religion, nationality, membership in a particular social group, or political opinion, is outside the country of his nationality and is unable or, owing to such fear, is unwilling to avail himself of the protection of that country.

But according to Andrew Shacknove's influential criticism, neither persecution nor alienage captures what is essential about refugeehood:

> Persecution is but one manifestation of a broader phenomenon: the absence of state protection of the citizen's basic needs. It is this absence of state protection which constitutes the full and complete negation of society and the basis of refugeehood. The same reasoning which justifies the persecutee's claim to refugeehood justifies the claims of persons deprived of all other basic needs as well. Similarly, alienage is an unnecessary condition for establishing refugee status. It, too, is a subset of a broader category: the physical access of the international community to the unprotected person. The refugee need not necessarily cross an international frontier to gain such access. (Shacknove 1985, 277)

Shacknove therefore argues for a broader humanitarian definition of refugees as 'persons whose basic needs are unprotected by their country of origin, who have no remaining recourse other than to seek international restitution of their needs, and who are so situated that international assistance is possible.'

Miller argues that neither of these positions is correct. He accepts the criticism that the Convention conception is too narrow but argues that the humanitarian conception, on the other hand, is too broad since it fails to explain why refuge is the appropriate response rather than, for example, humanitarian assistance or intervention (2016a, 80). The conceptual room for an intermediate position between the narrow Convention view and the broad humanitarian view becomes evident once we see that there are in fact two distinctions in play in this debate over what is necessary for refugeehood:

(1) Is the necessary threat one of *persecution* or do *human rights violations more generally* count as well?
(2) Can the requisite threat *only* be avoided by migration, or can it *also* be avoided by outside intervention?

Once these two distinctions are combined, we get these possible positions (Miller 2016a, 82):

The position of the Refugee Convention holds that *both* persecution *and* being outside the borders of one's state are *necessary* for refugee status. The humanitarian position, on the other hand, holds that persecution is *not* required for refugee status, but that any form of human rights violation can be sufficient, and that being outside the borders of one's state is also *not* required. Miller's position agrees with the humanitarian view that persecution is *not* required, but agrees with the Convention position that refugee status *does* require being outside the borders of one's state.

According to Miller, people not outside the borders of their state should not count as refugees, to whom states have enforceable duties of justice (cf. Owen forthcoming), although states have other kinds of (unenforceable, humanitarian) duties to them. The proper definition of refugees, according to Miller, therefore is: 'people whose human rights cannot be protected except by moving across a border, whether the reason is state persecution, state incapacity, or prolonged natural disasters' (cf. Gibney 2004, 7; Miller 2016a, 83).

Miller expands on this formulation later:

> refugees are best understood as people whose human rights would be unavoidably threatened if they remain in the place they inhabit, regardless of whether the threat arises from state persecution, state collapse, or natural disaster. The source of the threat does not matter; what matters is whether it could be averted *without* the person moving, for example by creating a safe haven within current state borders for those displaced by civil war or by erecting temporary accommodation for earthquake victims. (Miller 2016a, 167–168)

This seems a sensible proposal for how to define refugees. It tracks what is morally relevant, namely any threat to basic human rights, but retains a focus on what is special about the group of refugees, which explains why states should have duties to grant them asylum (cf. Lister 2013).

The philosophical merits of Miller's proposal notwithstanding, problems arise once we start to think about the actual refugee crisis in the real world, for example the one emanating from the war in Syria. Miller himself notes the problem:

> The problem is that my definition involves a counterfactual element: it asks whether the person in question *could* be adequately protected while remaining in her country of residence. In the case of someone currently staying in an underfunded refugee camp, for example, the answer to this question is very likely to be yes. What is primarily required to secure the human rights of the people staying there is for richer members of the international community to raise the level of support that they provide. But for the people who are actually living in the camp, the relevant question is whether the resources they need to lead decent lives (including opportunities for education and productive work) will *in fact* be provided so long as they remain where they are. They do not want to wait in hope for ten or twenty years. So they have very strong reasons for moving, but since they are already located in places where their basic rights either are or could be secured, they do not qualify as refugees from the perspective of the states they might move to. (Miller 2016a, 168)

In practice, this means that almost all of the people fleeing Syria stop being refugees the moment they move beyond the immediate reach of either the Syrian regime or other actors threatening their human rights within Syria. So the millions of Syrians in the neighboring countries are no longer entitled to claim refugee status in nonneighboring states, according to Miller's definition! Some might think of this as a welcome implication; it means that European states have no duties to accept anyone fleeing from Syria, since these people stopped being refugees once outside their country of origin. So Miller's definition in fact provides a defense of the EU's deal with Turkey, according to which people crossing the Aegean Sea from Turkey to Greece can be sent back without having their asylum applications processed.

But while this implication of Miller's definition might be politically expedient, it strains our conceptual (and moral) intuitions: is it not simply implausible to say that these millions of people fleeing generalized violence as well as persecution are not refugees? Whatever else we disagree about in relation to these debates, surely everyone must agree that the people fleeing Syria are refugees and do not cease to be so on crossing the Syrian border (Blake 2016)?

But the problem with Miller's definition is actually even more fundamental than this immediate implication. As he himself notes, the definition relies on a counterfactual claim. What is important is what *could* happen, not what *actually* happens. This means that, as long as there is a sufficiently close possible world where peoples' human rights are not violated in the place where they currently reside, they are not entitled to claim refugee status elsewhere.

The rationale for this counterfactual element is philosophically sensible: we need an explanation of why states have duties toward refugees to take them in and grant them asylum. If people in need could be helped in other ways, for example by humanitarian assistance in their current place of residence, then asylum is not necessary, and then there is no reason to include them in the group of people to whom states have the duty to offer asylum.

But while theoretically sensible, the counterfactual introduces a nest of both theoretical (philosophical) and practical (political) problems. Theoretically, the problem is to specify how close the possible world in which the people in question do not face human rights violations has to be in order for them not to count as refugees. This is in itself a philosophically hard nut to crack – how can we justify drawing the line in one place rather than another? – and what does it really mean to talk about a 'close possible world' here?

If the question is whether Syrians' basic rights *could be* secured, then the obvious answer is that of course they could – all this would require is that the war is stopped and the regime, as well as any other agents perpetrating human rights violations, ceases doing so. So as long as it is not strictly *impossible* to stop the war, then the people fleeing Syria are not refugees, even if they are *in fact* murdered, bombed, gassed, tortured and oppressed!

This implication of Miller's definition makes plain how unsuited it is as a contribution to a discussion about what real political actors should do in relation to actual refugee crises like the Syrian one. The counterfactual definition of refugees makes questions about whether states have duties to assist refugees dependent on complicated philosophical questions that they as political actors have all kinds of motives for answering in ways that will undermine the aim of helping people in actual need (cf. Gibney 2004, 196; Miller 2016b, 224–225 on the agency problem).

This lack of realism is curious, since Miller himself is a proponent of a 'contextualist' and to some extent 'realistic' form of political philosophy. Contextualism here means that political philosophy formulates principles for specific types of agents in actual contexts (Miller 2013, 43). Realism can mean many different things, and Miller is justifiably critical of the sense according to which politics is seen as inherently conflictual and power driven. However, he supports the need for political philosophy that is realistic in another sense contrasting with utopianism. Realism in this sense requires political philosophy to pay attention to how things actually are in the world, and to adjust any political recommendations in light of this in order to be action guiding (Miller 2016b, 218–219).

Miller's proposal for a refugee definition is supposed to address a practical problem in a real world context, namely how to delimit the group of people states have duties to help. But it is formulated in a way that the relevant actors are unlikely to be able or willing to apply in a way actually serving the aim that the definition was supposed to serve, namely to help refugees. The definition is thus incoherent in a specific way having to do with this combination of realistic aim and philosophical reflections on what ideally should matter.

The immediate vicinity argument

I have argued that the definition of refugeehood proposed by Miller is problematic because it fails to connect to actual refugee crises and the political actors potentially able to help refugees in such cases. I will now move from the conceptual to the normative question. If we bracket the difficulty of defining who count as refugees, there still is the question how states should discharge their duties to help refugees?

One view in this debate is this: European states should channel funds to the areas in the immediate vicinity of Syria where most of the refugees from that conflict are located, that is, Lebanon, Jordan and Turkey, or to 'safe havens' within Syria, for example areas under Kurdish control, rather than spend the resources on managing refugee flows, processing asylum claims and integrating admitted refugees in Europe.

There are several justifications for this (cf. Pogge 1997): one is that the same amount of money will purchase more in countries like Lebanon, Jordan and Turkey than in Europe, because prices and costs of living and integration are higher in Europe. Another justification is that most refugees are located in the immediate neighboring countries – despite perceptions in Europe, the number of refugees making their way to Europe is relatively small in comparison. A third justification is that the refugees actually making their way to Europe are often those least in need of help; they are the most resourceful who would also be the ones most able to make a life for themselves without asylum. Many of the refugees in the neighboring countries, or still caught in Syria, on the other hand, are much more in need of help.

The suggested conclusion based on these justifications is that European states should not take in more refugees, but should rather spend the funds in the immediate vicinity. Call this *the immediate vicinity argument*. The immediate vicinity argument is actually quite strong. The noted three justifications are plausible, both in terms of the empirical and the normative premises they rely on.

There are further justifications for a similar conclusion. A fourth justification is that, if the conflict in Syria should end, it would be easier for refugees to return and help rebuild their country if they remain in the immediate vicinity instead of in Europe. Fifth, if return is not be possible, it would be relatively easier to integrate refugees from Syria in the neighboring countries, given the similarities of language, culture and religion. And finally, even if the conditions for refugees in the immediate vicinity are not good, the prospect of gaining residence in Europe lures refugees on a dangerous journey to Europe during which many of them die and experience various forms of suffering – so the assessment of the conditions in the immediate vicinity should be made against this standard of comparison.

One can be more skeptical about these last couple of justifications, which rest on more questionable empirical assumptions and take policies of European states that might themselves be problematic for granted. In any case, the conclusion can be adequately supported merely on the basis of the first three justifications, so possible failures in the additional arguments do not undermine the claim.

Despite the empirical and normative strength of the immediate vicinity argument, it also runs in to problems when we apply it to actual refugee crises like the Syrian one. The problem is that, even though it is effective and normatively justified to provide assistance in the immediate vicinity, this is not at all a reason to think that the relevant actors will in fact do so. The difference between refugees applying for asylum at the border in Europe and refugees still in the neighboring countries is that there is a strong pressure on European states to deal with the former in accordance with the Refugee Convention, whereas European states can easily avoid donating to the latter. Whereas the granting of asylum to recognized refugees is acknowledged by states as a legal obligation, donation is likely to be seen by the states and their populations as humanitarian aid out of charity and perhaps even as supererogatory. There is therefore no reason – neither in terms of immediately perceived self-interest, nor in terms of perceived normative obligations – to think that states will use the same amount of resources to support refugees in the immediate vicinity as they would use to help refugees applying for asylum on their own territories. For this reason, the proposed shift of resource spending from asylum to donations targeted at refugees in the immediate vicinity, were a state to try to implement it, is likely to result in a net *decrease* in the help provided by the state to refugees.

The problem has a structure reminiscent of the problem with Miller's refugee definition: the immediate vicinity argument is philosophically sound in terms of both its empirical and normative premises and the support they provide for the conclusion. Nevertheless, conditions in the real world to which the argument is supposed to apply make it likely that, were such a policy to be formally adopted by states, the result would not be more effective help to more refugees but less help. So while the argument is an argument about a nonideal situation, it fails to provide a prescription we have reason to think will actually have the desired effect under precisely these nonideal conditions. In effect, the argument claims to be an argument about a nonideal situation, but makes ideal assumptions about the behavior of the relevant agents supposed to act on the reasons provided by the argument. This is a type of incoherence in the argument that undermines it for exactly the purpose it was proposed as a realistic response.

This is not to say that immediate vicinity arguments are completely ruled out. It is only to say that such arguments have to take the context of application into account. An example of a more realistic version of the immediate vicinity argument is offered by Betts and Collier (2015). They propose that displaced Syrians in the neighboring countries should be integrated into specially created economic zones. This would align the economic and security interests of the host states in not being burdened by the presence of the Syrian refugees with the needs of refugees to improve their prospects in the short term. Betts and Collier's zonal proposal is still cast in modal terms – it is said that the Jordanian government *could* modify its restrictions on refugees' right to work to allow the establishment of special economic zones and that Western governments *could* provide incentives for international businesses to establish themselves in these zones. But these counterfactuals are more realistic in the sense that Betts and Collier both present the measures that actors would have to put in place, show that these measures have already been implemented in other contexts, and show that it is in the interest of the relevant actors to do so in the case of the Syrian refugees. Therefore, their version of the immediate vicinity argument avoids the idealizing incoherence.

Conclusion

I have used the ideal/nonideal distinction to draw attention to a specific type of incoherence in the philosophy of the refugee crisis. Rawls's original formulation of this distinction turned on whether one assumes partial or full compliance when arguing about principles of justice (1999). In relation to the philosophy of migration, this has often been formulated slightly differently, namely as the difference between questions about what is morally desirable and questions of agency of actual actors (Gibney 2004, 196; cf. Miller 2016b, 224–225). Here the assumption is that nonideal political philosophy should be action guiding for real actors (Lister 2013, 658, n. 46). Ideal theory comes first in specifying the ideal principles and the morally desirable state of the world to aim for, and nonideal theory then is a second stage where the limitations on the actors that have to put these principles into practice are taken into account (Miller 2016b, 230, n. 2).

While I agree with this general picture of the theoretical division of labor in political philosophy, the two examples of ideal/nonideal incoherence I have sketched show the difficulties of making the transition from ideal to nonideal theory in relation to actual problems like the refugee crisis: in my two examples, the problem is that ideal and nonideal components are present at the *same* stage, for example in the definition of refugees or in the argument for helping in the immediate vicinity, in a way making the proposed definition or policy prescription incoherent. So instead of having ideal theory and nonideal theory at *different* stages, where the first informs the second, my two examples illustrate a *conflation* of the two stages into something that neither works as ideal theory (since it makes claims about a nonideal state of affairs) nor as nonideal theory (since it fails to provide action guidance for actual actors).

I am *not* suggesting that the two stage sequence is mission impossible. I have already noted how Betts and Collier's version of the immediate vicinity argument takes the nature and limits of the relevant agents into account. An alternative version of coherent nonideal theory would be one that considers the conditions making achievement of the morally desirable outcome unfeasible, but then specifies the *dynamic duties* of actually existing agents to change these conditions (cf. Ferracioli 2014, 137) – in other words, to include considerations about how to handle the nonideal limitations such as partial compliance in arguments about the responsibility of actual actors (Owen forthcoming).

Acknowledgements

Thanks to David Owen, Kasper Lippert-Rasmussen, Frej Klem Thomsen, Thomas Søbirk Petersen, Rune Klingenberg Hansen and Jesper Ryberg for comments.

Disclosure statement

No potential conflict of interest was reported by the author.

ORCID

Sune Lægaard http://orcid.org/0000-0002-2554-1132

References

Betts, Alexander, and Paul Collier. 2015. "Help Refugees Help Themselves: Let Displaced Syrians Join the Labor Market." *Foreign Affairs* 94 (6): 84–92.
Blake, Michael. 2016. "Philosophy & the Refugee Crisis: What Are the Hard Questions?" *The Critique*. http://www.thecritique.com/articles/philosophy-the-refugee-crisis-what-are-the-hard-questions/.
Carens, Joseph H. 2013. *The Ethics of Immigration*. Oxford: Oxford University Press.
Ferracioli, Luara. 2014. "The Appeal and Danger of a New Refugee Convention." *Social Theory and Practice* 40 (1): 123–144.
Gibney, Matthew. 2004. *The Ethics and Politics of Asylum*. Cambridge: Cambridge University Press.
Kukathas, Chandran. 2016. "Are Refugees Special?" In *Migration in Political Theory*, edited by Sarah Fine and Lea Ypi, 249–268. Oxford: Oxford University Press.
Lister, Matthew. 2013. "Who Are Refugees?" *Law and Philosophy* 32 (5): 645–671.
Miller, David. 2013. *Justice for Earthlings: Essays in Political Philosophy*. Cambridge: Cambridge University Press.
Miller, David. 2016a. *Strangers in Our Midst*. Cambridge, MA: Harvard University Press.
Miller, David. 2016b. "How 'Realistic' Should Global Political Theory be? Some Reflections on the Debate so Far." *Journal of International Political Theory* 12 (2): 217–233.
Oberman, Kieran. 2016. "Refugees & Economic Migrants: A Morally Spurious Distinction." *The Critique*. http://www.thecritique.com/articles/refugees-economic-migrants-a-morally-spurious-distinction-2/.
Owen, David. 2016. "In Loco Civitatis: On the Normative Basis of the Institution of Refugeehood and Reposnsibilities for Refugees." In *Migration in Political Theory*, edited by Sarah Fine and Lea Ypi, 269–289. Oxford: Oxford University Press.
Owen, David. Forthcoming. "Refugees, Fairness and Taking up the Slack: On Justice and the International Refugee Regime." *Moral Philosophy and Politics*.
Pogge, Thomas. 1997. "Migration and Poverty." In *Citizenship and Exclusion*, edited by Veit Bader, 12–27. Basingstoke: Macmillan.
Rawls, John. 1999. *A Theory of Justice*. Revised ed. Cambridge, MA: Harvard University Press.
Shacknove, Andrew E. 1985. "Who Is a Refugee?" *Ethics* 95 (2): 274–284.

A fair distribution of refugees in the European Union

Nils Holtug

ABSTRACT
In light of the large recent inflow of refugees to the EU and the Commission's efforts to relocate them, I raise the question of what a fair distribution of refugees between EU countries would look like. More specifically, I consider what concerns such a distributive scheme should be sensitive to. First, I put forward some arguments for why states are obligated to admit refugees and outline how I believe the EU should respond to the refugee crisis. This involves, among other things, resettling a proportion of refugees from countries neighbouring Syria in the EU. Second, I consider how the intake into the EU should be distributed between member states, that is, the shares different countries can be expected to admit. I discuss the relevance of a number of different factors that may be claimed to affect such shares, including population size, GDP, number of refugees admitted so far, unemployment rate, country-specific costs and cultural 'closeness'. Third, I consider whether the distributive scheme should be restricted to reflect specific states' responsibility for creating refugees in the first place, levels of racism and xenophobia, and whether other states are required to pick up the slack if some refuse to admit their fair share.

Introduction

According to the UNHCR (2016), we are now facing an unprecedented 65.3 million forcibly displaced persons worldwide, where people are forced to move because of persecution, conflict, generalized violence and human rights violations. This gives rise to large inflows of refugees not least in countries neighbouring conflict zones, but also in the EU. In 2015, a record of 1.3 million migrants applied for asylum in the EU, Norway and Switzerland (Pew Research Center 2016, 4), which was more than a two-fold increase from 2014. Of these, more than half where citizens of Syria (29%), Afghanistan (15%) and Iraq (10%).

Some EU countries have received far more asylum seekers than others. Thus, of the applications for asylum in 2015, Germany (33%), Hungary (13%) and Sweden (12%) received more than half (Pew Research Center 2016, 17). At the other end of the spectrum, Finland, Norway, Denmark, Bulgaria, Spain, Greece and Poland each received 2% or less. To some extent, these differences correspond to differences in population size, but even if we focus instead on numbers of asylum seekers relative to population, there are large differences. For example, while, per 100,000 people, Hungary received 1,770, Sweden 1,600 and Austria 1,000 applications, Italy received only 140, France 110, Greece 100, Ireland 70 and the UK 60 applications (Pew Research Center 2016, 5; cf. IMF 2016, 9–10).

This raises the question of whether the distribution of refugees in the EU is fair and if not, what a fair distribution would look like. This is so not least because asylum seekers and refugees typically impose a cost on destination societies, at least in the short to medium run, and so there is an issue of burden sharing. Indeed, in 2015 the EU Commission proposed a relocation scheme to secure a more balanced distribution and this scheme was later backed in the European Parliament. In the following, I shall consider what a fair principle for the distribution of refugees would look like, that is, how large a share different countries can be expected to take in. More specifically, I shall consider what sort of concerns such a distributive principle should be sensitive to.

Why admit refugees?

Prior to discussing distribution, I briefly consider why European (and other) states are morally required to admit refugees. In part, this is because the question of fairness in distribution relies on there being asylum seekers who have a claim to asylum. But also because the reason why states are required to admit refugees may have an impact on how they should be distributed.

First, there is a humanitarian argument, according to which we have a positive duty of assistance to prevent severe human suffering and/or the violation of basic rights (Carens 2013, 195; Gibney 2004, 233). On a modest version of the humanitarian principle, it may imply that our obligations, with respect to admitting refugees, pertain only to the protection of human rights, where human rights are based on basic needs (Miller 2016, 83). More ambitious versions, on the other hand, may be based on, for example, the utilitarian aim of maximizing total welfare or the (global) egalitarian aim of bringing about global equality.

Not everyone, however, is committed to a (strong) positive duty to prevent human suffering, whether in a modest or more ambitious form. Therefore, let me point also to a second argument, according to which freedom of movement requires that refugees be allowed to cross borders and enter countries in which they may find security (Oberman 2016). Unlike the humanitarian argument, the argument from freedom of movement is based only on a negative duty of states not to interfere with the basic liberty of refugees (more specifically, not to forcibly prevent them from entering the state's territory).[1] And while many will reject the claim that freedom of movement justifies open borders, it is worth pointing out that in the case of refugees, this is a liberty that protects some particularly strong and basic interests, including the interest in escaping persecution, genocide and other forms of violence and abuse.

Dealing with the crisis

Even if there is a general obligation to admit refugees, it does not follow that the EU should admit refugees that have temporarily found refuge in, for example, Turkey, Lebanon and Jordan. Therefore, let me point out why, in the present refugee crisis, I believe that the humanitarian obligation of EU countries is to be fulfilled on the basis of a policy building on the following three elements: (1) substantial (indeed massive) support for the countries neighbouring Syria (or, for that matter, other countries facing huge inflows of refugees that they are unable to handle), (2) relieving these countries further by taking in substantial numbers of refugees in the EU and (3) implementing a fair distributive scheme in the EU such that no country faces an unbearable burden in catering for their share of refugees.

As regards (1), countries neighbouring Syria are hosting very large numbers. Thus, by the end of 2015 Turkey hosted 2.5 million, Lebanon 1.1 million and Jordan 664,100 Syrian refugees (UNHCR 2016). Here, very many live in desperate conditions because of lack of legal rights and lack of assistance. In Jordan and Lebanon, respectively, 69% and 64% live below the UNHCR poverty line (World Bank Group and UNHCR 2015, 8). And refugees are flooding the labour market, are often taken advantage of by employers and are pushing out domestic workers, resulting in serious tensions between national groups. Furthermore, the large number of refugees threatens the already fragile internal stability of not least Jordan and Lebanon (Guzansky and Striem 2013); consider, for example, that Lebanon already houses Hizbollah who are fighting in Syria on the side of Bashar al-Assad. Indeed, sectarian violence is on the rise as is sexual harassment of women, including rape and violence (Samari 2015). Also, incidents of suicide attempts by adolescent Syrians are now reported more frequently (Anderson 2016).

However, aiding neighbouring countries will not suffice. There are at least two reasons for this. First, while the severe problems these countries face are in part due to shortages of funding and the inability to provide opportunities for education and work for refugees, they are also due to, for example, threats to stability, sectarian violence and sexual abuse. These are issues that cannot be fully resolved by increasing aid, they are in part an effect of the sheer volume of the flows. Second, there is an issue of justice in the distribution of refugees. While at the end of 2014, the number of refugees per 1,000 inhabitants in Europe ranged from 0.01 in Latvia, Luxembourg and Slovenia, to 14.8 in Sweden, the number was 232 in Lebanon and 87 in Jordan (IMF 2016, 7–8). More generally, developing countries are hosting 86% of the world's refugees (UNHCR 2016). Arguably, there is no justification for such gross inequality in burden sharing, where the burden, as pointed out above, is not just about economic costs (Carens 2013, 212). Indeed, it is disappointing that the EU, US and a number of other countries recently rejected the UN proposal of resettling 10% of the world's refugees as part of an attempt to deal with the refugee crisis (EurActive 2016).

These considerations also enable me to very briefly address two specific arguments for why aid for neighbouring countries need not be supplemented by a EU intake of refugees, or at least not a significant intake. According to the first argument, for example, Syrians in Turkey, Lebanon and Jordan are not entitled to asylum in Europe because they are now in a safe location where their human rights can be met, and so they no longer qualify as refugees (cf. Miller 2016, 168). According to the second argument, helping refugees in neighbouring countries is more cost-effective than admitting them to Europe, and so it is possible to help more refugees by providing aid (cf. Singer 2015). While neither of these arguments is without merit, I believe that they do not fully take into account the complexity of the refugee crisis in neighbouring countries described above.

There are thus moral reasons to relieve neighbouring countries by admitting more refugees in the EU, but it is quite possible that there are also self-interested reasons. Neighbouring countries are under enormous pressure due to a combination of sheer numbers, costs, political and popular animosity against refugees, and lack of stability.

Their refugee reception systems are in danger of breaking down. And as conditions worsen, many more refugees may try to reach European shores, through increasingly dangerous routes. Therefore, even if we were to consider the refugee crisis only through the lens of European self-interest, the best policy may actually be a combination of massive aid for neighbouring countries and admitting more refugees to prevent a breakdown of refugee reception in countries such as Turkey, Jordan and Lebanon. Indeed, the current response of European states may involve a sort of prisoner's dilemma, where responses at the national level to keep out refugees in a policy of beggar thy neighbour may contribute to a breakdown in refugee reception in the Middle East, but where a coordinated effort to relieve these Middle Eastern countries could have kept the number of asylum seekers in Europe at a lower level.

Of course, much will depend on what sort of arrangements can be struck with transit countries as regards keeping refugees out. But we need to remember that the price of such arrangements can be high in terms of human rights violations, as, for example, European cooperation with Gaddafi in Libya to stop migrants from reaching Europe bears witness to. Likewise, the current EU–Turkey deal to dampen the inflow of refugees is accompanied by Turkey closing their border to Syria, deportations back into Syria, and in some cases even shooting Syrian refugees to prevent them from entering, including women and children (Kingsley 2016).

As regards relieving neighbouring countries by taking in more refugees, ideally this would be done in terms of a resettlement scheme, whereby one could both tackle the problem of smugglers and unsafe routes and simultaneously target the most vulnerable refugees rather than only those who have the economic and personal resources to make it to Europe on their own (cf. Gibney 2004, Ch. 8).

This brings me to the third and last element of the proposed policy, which is also my main topic in the present article, namely implementing a fair distributive scheme in the EU. I shall consider this element in greater detail in the next section, but first I need to make two preliminary remarks. First, there is an issue here of whether such a scheme is compatible with freedom of movement, which as I mentioned may be considered a second argument for why we should admit refugees, besides the humanitarian argument. I shall not go further into this issue here, except by noting that the reasons mentioned for why freedom of movement is particularly important in the case of refugees may not apply when considering the issue of where to settle in the EU. Thus, I side with Blake (2016), Carens (2013, 216), Gibney (2004, 252) and Miller (2016, 86) in thinking that while refugees have a right to protection in a safe country, they are not necessarily entitled to such protection in the country of their choice.

Second, there is an issue of why the distributive question should be considered at the level of the EU rather than at the global level. Here, my answer is that ultimately, a fair distribution will be one that distributes refugees fairly at the global level and that the share that is to be distributed in the EU cannot be settled independently of this. Whether this means that the EU is now taking in too few, too many or an adequate share of refugees, relative to a globally fair distribution, is of course an open question. However, since the issue of the distribution in the EU is an issue that is now being addressed by the Commission and since the question of how to distribute the EU share will in any case have to be answered, this latter question has both practical and theoretical significance.

A fair distributive scheme

As transpires form the above, the distribution of asylum seekers among EU member states is rather unequal, both in absolute numbers and relative to population size. Indeed, both to solve immediate problems of catering for refugees and to secure a more balanced distribution, a temporary emergency relocation scheme was set up in two European Council decisions in September 2015, according to which 160,000 people in need of protection should be relocated from Italy, Greece and Hungary to other member states (European Commission 2015). Nevertheless, not least due to insufficient efforts by member states, it has turned out to be difficult to fully implement the scheme and only a small group has been relocated so far.

A distributive scheme may serve at least two purposes, morally speaking. First, it may be required as a means to secure a fair distribution between different countries. This is the purpose that concerns me here. However, it may also serve a second important purpose, namely to remove at least some of the incentive for member states to provide for refugees increasingly poor conditions, in order to decrease these states' 'pull factor', resulting in a race to the bottom in terms of who can offer the least advantageous level of accommodation.

What would a just distributive scheme look like? Suppose, *ex hypothesi*, that the EU member states were qualitatively identical in every respect, including in terms of size, population, culture, etc. In that case, a perfectly equal distribution would be in order. After all, there would be no reason what so ever why some countries should take on a greater burden than others. But, of course, EU member states are not like that. They differ in many respects, and we may think that some of these are relevant for how large a share they can be expected to take on. In the EU relocation scheme referred to above, a distribution key was proposed according to which shares are to depend on member states' population size, GDP, the average number of past asylum applications and unemployment rates (European Commission 2016). These criteria all seem relevant and what they have in common is that they say something about a state's *capacity to cater for the needs of refugees*, or what Gibney (2004, 241) refers to as its 'integrative ability' (cf. Miller 2016, 86; Schuck 1997, 246). That is why it would not be fair to expect, say, Luxembourg to carry as large a part of the burden as Germany.

Nevertheless, as regards the number of past asylum applications, it should be noted that this criterion reflects more than just a capacity to cater for refugees. Presumably, that capacity is a function not just of how many refugees a country has admitted, but more generally of the size and composition of its immigrant group. It could be argued that the latter would be a more appropriate concern.

Nevertheless, overall, the EU proposal is well in line with what political philosophers have generally argued would be relevant criteria (Carens 2013, 213–215; Gibney 2004, Ch. 8; Miller 2016, 87–88; Owen 2016, 281–282). A further question, however, is whether a distributive scheme should also be sensitive to differences in the specific costs of catering for refugees in different countries. After all, costs seem equally relevant for a state's capacity to cater for refugees. Here, costs will include the economic burden of providing for refugees while their application for asylum is being processed, but also the potential burden of later providing social benefits, educational opportunities, etc. These costs will depend not only how refugees are catered for and the size of social benefits, but also on how easily refugees are integrated on the labour market, which will again depend on a number of factors, including the state of the national economy and the level of minimum wages. The fiscal cost of asylum seekers in percentage of GDP varies considerably in the EU, so that, for example, Sweden is expected to spend 1%, Germany 0.35% and the Czech Republic only 0.02% in 2016 (IMF 2016, 12). Of course, these differences reflect a number of things, including numbers of asylum seekers, the size of GDPs, different assumptions behind estimates in different countries, but also differences in real costs per refugee.

More generally, it is well known that the fiscal impact of non-Western immigration differs between countries, including in Europe. Thus, in the Nordic countries, which are characterized by extensive welfare states, the net fiscal impact of non-Western immigration has been found to be negative, where for a number of other European states the effect is less negative or even positive (Nannestad 2007, 528). To a significant extent, this reflects differences in labour market integration.

So should state shares of refugees be sensitive to differences in the domestic costs of taking care of them? On the one hand, it may be argued if the cost of catering for refugees is high in a certain country because of above average quality of accommodation of asylum seekers, ambitious language and job training programmes, generous social benefits and high minimum wages (making the labour market less accessible for low-skilled refugees), this is a choice made by that country and so something it should be held responsible for in the sense that higher costs do not warrant a reduction in the share of refugees. On the other hand, it may be argued that decent accommodation of asylum seekers, language and job training programmes, etc. are requirements of social justice, and that particular countries should not be 'punished' for satisfying the requirements of social justice by having higher total refugee costs than others.[2]

Here, I believe that the concern for social justice cancels whatever concern we might have had for state responsibility for high costs. If a state is merely conforming to the requirements of justice in its treatment of refugees, its responsibility for doing so cannot be invoked to justify leaving it with higher costs for its share of refugees than other states have. Does this then mean that states that opt for more extensive social rights for refugees are entitled to a lower share? I think this would be the wrong conclusion to draw. If other states have lower costs because they do not fully live up to the requirements of social justice, or if they are unable to provide as extensive social rights because they are poorer, what justice requires is presumably that they increase their social spending on refugees (or try to increase their GDP in so far as, because of relative poverty, they cannot provide adequate conditions for them), rather than that they are allotted more refugees than states that have already implemented the requirements of social justice and/or are richer.

Note also that the EU distribution key discussed above to some extent does accommodate concerns about differences in employability of refugees in different countries, which is important for overall costs, because this key factors in a country's unemployment rate.

A further candidate for a relevant concern, when assessing fair shares, involves a cultural component. For example, it may take into account how easy it would be for particular refugees to adapt to or feel comfortable in a particular society (Carens 2013, 214) or how that society may be impacted by religious and cultural diversity of the relevant kind, for example, in terms of an effective refugee regime (Owen 2016, 282) or social cohesion

(Miller 2016, 88).[3] Now, the cultural component may be more difficult to measure than the other concerns mentioned so far, which may be one reason why it is not part of the EU distribution key (the EU has emphasized the need for objective, measurable criteria). Furthermore, the cultural component may in many cases be more relevant for the question of which refugees should go where than for the question of how large a share a particular country should take. Here, cultural concerns may be part of a wider range of concerns pertaining to which refugees should go where, including concerns about whether a particular refugee has family or networks in a specific country, and where his or her skills may match labour market demands. Finally, when considering the present inflow of refugees in the EU, primarily from countries such as Syria, Afghanistan and Iraq, cultural affinity may not seem a plausible candidate for distinguishing between the distributive shares of European member states.

I have argued that the distributive key adopted by the EU is roughly on the right track, although there are of course many questions that remain to be settled. First, while the EU does adopt weights for each of the concerns it factors in, these may require a more principled analysis. Second, and more generally, I believe that ultimately a distributive scheme would have to be justified on the basis of a more basic principle of justice, such as egalitarianism or prioritarianism (Holtug 2010b), and it may make a difference which such principle we invoke. This, of course, is not to question the relevance of the concerns that form the basis of the EU key, as these will be relevant whatever more specific, even minimally plausible principle we adopt. Third, it is an important aspect of a distributive scheme that it should cater for all refugees with a claim to asylum, and so in the case of the EU for its share of these (but for a different view on this, see Miller 2016, 93).

Restricting the distributive scheme?

In this section, I want to briefly discuss three possible restrictions on, or departures from, the sort of distributive scheme outlined above. It is a very common view among political philosophers working on refugee policy that states have a special responsibility for admitting refugees insofar as they are causally responsible for creating the situation in which they need to flee (Carens 2013, 195; Gibney 2004, 235; Owen 2016, 282; Miller 2016, 90; Souter 2014). For example, certain European states may have special obligations to admit refugees from, for example, Afghanistan, Iraq and Syria, because of their involvement in warfare in these countries. In the present context, what I want to consider is whether states have an obligation to admit specific refugees on the basis of their making them refugees *in addition* to the obligations these states have vis-à-vis the sort of distributive scheme outlined above. The upshot would be that, due to their special obligations, such states would be required to admit more refugees than similarly situated states who did not have special obligations.

However, I have four main worries about restricting the distributive scheme in this manner. First, it may be difficult to transform causal contributions to the creation of refugees into special obligations for specific refugees in a principled manner, not least when conflicts are complex and have many contributing parties, as for example in the present conflict in Syria. Second, there may be causal contributions to the creation of refugees that do not seem to mandate taking in a larger share of refugees than others, for example, when that contribution is an unavoidable side-effect of a just intervention in a humanitarian crisis, say, to prevent genocide. Third, a country may causally contribute to the creation of refugees and yet be rather impoverished, and if so it may not seem fair to expect it to take in more refugees than an otherwise fair distribution would mandate. Finally, special obligations based on causal responsibility may, at least sometimes, seem unfair not only as regards receiving states, but also refugees. Suppose a state, S, is able to admit either of two groups of refugees, A and B, fleeing each their country. Whereas S is engaged in warfare in A's country and therefore a causal contributor to the conditions they are trying to escape, B faces somewhat harsher conditions. Suppose, for example, that the threat to their lives is somewhat greater, they are slightly more frequently exposed to torture and in general the violation of their human rights is a bit more excessive. Suppose finally that S is the only state willing to take in A or B and that it cannot take in both. If causal responsibility is to play a substantial role here, S should admit members of group A. Nevertheless, this may seem to unduly ignore the greater needs of group B.

Another possible restriction on the distributive scheme concerns hostility towards refugees in particular countries, in the form of, for example, racism and xenophobia, and whether taking in (more) refugees will lead to a backlash and even be counterproductive in the long run. Consider, for example, the growth and activities of Jobbik in Hungary and Golden Dawn in Greece. Can xenophobic hostility exempt a country from its distributive share, or at least reduce it? Introducing such a restriction on a distributive scheme may seem problematic as it would reward xenophobic societies and may even create perverse incentives. On the other hand, presumably it would be even more problematic not to take into account the safety of refugees in countries to which they may be relocated. Furthermore, in cases in which relocation would indeed be counterproductive, one may be sacrificing the long-term interests of refugees. Of course, the judgement of when relocation will impose unacceptable conditions on refugees or be counterproductive is often very difficult to make, and certainly this should not be a mechanism that will let countries off the hook of burden-sharing all to easily. Now, there is in any case reason to impose minimum conditions on states they are required to live up to as regards catering for refugees, and such conditions may include protecting refugees from violence and harassment. Furthermore, as Gibney (2004, 245–246) argues, states are morally required to combat racism and xenophobia and in general to promote an atmosphere that is hospitable towards refugees.

Finally, there is an issue of what to do in cases of non-compliance, that is, if some countries refuse to admit what, according to the distributive scheme, is their fair share. For example, in the EU Hungary and Poland have stated they will not partake in the relocation scheme (although, as pointed out above, Hungary was actually one of the countries intended to relocate refugees to other countries). Setting aside the question of what sanctions other countries can legitimately impose on non-compliers, there is a further question of whether other countries are morally required to pick up the slack, that is, to admit more than their fair share. It may seem unfair if states are required to do more than their share, just because other states choose not to do theirs. And, of course, in a sense it is, but I believe that to a significant extent, they are nevertheless required to do so. To bring out the basic intuition driving this judgement, consider the following case. Suppose that on a particular beach, there are 10 lifeguards and 10 children in risk of drowning. Since each lifeguard has equal responsibility, fairness (and efficiency) would seem to require that they each save one child. Suppose, however, that it turns out that nine of the lifeguards are not going to do anything. Surely the last lifeguard should then do more than her fair share, indeed she should save as many of the children as possible, even at some risk to her own safety. Likewise, states are required to pick up the slack when non-compliers refuse to do their fair share, although it may of course be argued that there is a (higher) threshold above which no further help can be required (e.g. because it would be counterproductive in the long run).

Notes

1. For scepticism as regards the case for immigration based on freedom of movement, see Miller (2016, Ch. 3). I critically discuss some of Miller's arguments in Holtug (2011).
2. It may be objected that the requirements of social justice as regards the treatment of refugees in a country would differ significantly depending on whether we assume that our basic principles of justice have global or domestic scope only. In Holtug (forthcoming), however, I argue that not only domestic but also global (luck) egalitarianism implies that we should aim for domestic equality between immigrants and non-immigrants.
3. For a view different from Miller's about of the impact of diversity on social cohesion and its importance for immigration policy, see Holtug (2010a).

Disclosure statement

No potential conflict of interest was reported by the author.

References

Anderson, Sulome. 2016. "Syria's Refugee Children Are Attempting Suicide in Ever Greater Numbers." *Foreign Policy*, June 29.
Blake, Michael. 2016. "Philosophy and the Refugee Crisis: What Are the Hard Questions?" *The Critique*, January 6.
Carens, Joseph. 2013. *The Ethics of Immigration*. Oxford: Oxford University Press.
European Commission. 2015. "Refugee Crisis. Q&A on Emergency Relocation." September 22.
EurActive. 2016. "EU, US Reject UN Plan to Resettle Refugees." EurActive.com, August 4, 2016.
Gibney, Matthew J. 2004. *The Ethics and Politics of Asylum*. Cambridge: Cambridge University Press.
Guzansky, Yoel, and Erez Striem. 2013. "The 'Arab Spring' and Refugees in the Middle East." *INSS Insight*, No. 496.
Holtug, Nils. 2010a. "Immigration and the Politics of Social Cohesion." *Ethnicities* 10 (4): 435–451.
Holtug, Nils. 2010b. *Persons, Interests, and Justice*. Oxford: Oxford University Press.
Holtug, Nils. 2011. "The Ethics of Immigration Policy." *Nordic Journal of Migration Research* 1 (1): 4–12.
Holtug, Nils. Forthcoming. "Luck Egalitarianism and the Rights of Immigrants." *Ratio Juris*.
IMF. 2016. *The Refugee Surge in Europe: Economic Challenges*, IMF Staff Discussion Note, SDN/16/02.
Kingsley, Patrick. 2016. "Turkish Border Guards Kill Eight Syrian Refugees." *Guardian*, June 19.

Miller, David. 2016. *Strangers in Our Midst*. Cambridge, MA: Harvard University Press.
Nannestad, Peter. 2007. "Immigration and Welfare States: A Survey of 15 Years of Research." *European Journal of Political Economy* 23: 512–532.
Oberman, Kieran. 2016. "Immigration as a Human Right." In *Migration in Political Theory*, edited by Sarah Fine and Lea Ypi, 32–56. Oxford: Oxford University Press.
Owen, David. 2016. "On the Normative Basis of the Institution of Refugeehood." In *Migration in Political Theory*, edited by Sarah Fine and Lea Ypi, 269–289. Oxford: Oxford University Press.
Pew Research Center. 2016. *Number of Refugees to Europe Surges to Record 1.3 Million in* 2015. http://www.pewglobal.org/2016/08/02/number-of-refugees-to-europe-surges-to-record-1-3-million-in-2015/.
Samari, Goleen. 2015. "The Response to Syrian Refugee Women's Health Needs in Lebanon, Turkey and Jordan and Recommendations for Improved Practice." *Knowledge & Action*, Humanity in Practice.
Schuck, Peter H. 1997. "Refugee Burden-Sharing: A Modest Proposal." *Yale Journal of International Law* 22: 243–297.
Singer, Peter. 2015. "Escaping the Refugee Crisis", *Project Syndicate*, September 1.
Souter, James. 2014. "Towards a Theory of Asylum as Reparation for Past Injustice." *Political Studies* 62: 326–342.
UNHCR. 2016. *Global Trends in Forced Displacement in* 2015. http://reliefweb.int/report/world/unhcr-global-trends-forced-displacement-2015.
World Bank Group and UNHCR. 2015. *The Welfare of Syrian Refugees. Evidence From Jordan and Lebanon.* http://www.worldbank.org/en/news/feature/2015/12/16/welfare-syrian-refugees-evidence-from-jordan-lebanon.

A spectre in Germany: refugees, a 'welcome culture' and an 'integration politics'

Nanette Funk

ABSTRACT
The German state permitted about one million refugees to enter Germany in 2015–2016, although many were subsequently denied refugee status. Germany adopted an 'integration' and 'welcome' politics, an important, if imperfect, model for a European refugee policy. The integration of refugees required the joint activity of state, of civil society, of the public sphere and of refugees themselves. Civil society initiated a vast amount of essential care work and solidarity with refugees pursued especially, but not only, by women, yet civil society and refugees had no say in refugee policies. German refugee policy and practice raised many normative issues, producing an intense and vigorous national debate about them, in which philosophers and theorists were active. Among the questions debated were whether Germany had accepted 'too many' refugees, the acceptability of the costs of the policy, the risks of harm to the least well off, the purported risks to safety, security and the social order and the purported threats to German culture. I first describe German state policies, practices and civil society efforts and then turn to normative debates. I discuss the limits of the German discourse and suggest how it needs to be expanded.

A spectre is haunting Germany, that of refugees. Everywhere in Berlin people speak of refugees, not sure if they have seen any, or what 'they' look like, given many refugees are kept apart, housed in large institutions. The German state permitted about one million refugees to enter in 2015 alone and Germany adopted an 'integration politics' an important, if imperfect, model for a European refugee policy. But the integration of refugees required the joint activity of state, civil society, the public sphere and refugees themselves. The vast amount of care work and solidarity with refugees initiated by civil society, especially, but not only by women, was essential. A national debate over Chancellor Angela Merkel's policies ensued, in which philosophers were active. I first describe German state policies and civil society efforts, and then turn to the normative issues in the public debate. I note the limits of the German discourse and its significance for a European refugee policy.

Asylum seekers come to Germany

In 2015–2016 Germany embarked on a 'Welcome Politics' ('Willkommenspolitik') of care for refugees, and an 'Integration Politics', with Chancellor Merkel's famous statement on 5 September 2015 'Wir schaffen das' ('We can do it'). For about one month Germany opened its border to refugees who had struggled to get to Germany, and permitted them to apply for refugee status, overriding the EU Dublin III Agreement requiring refugees to apply for asylum from within the first EU country they entered (Regulation (EU) No 604/2013 of the European Parliament and of the Council 2013).

The estimated number of refugees arriving in 2015 is somewhat misleading, since some left for Scandinavian countries, leaving about 800,000, about 1% of the German population. The largest group came from Syria (30%), of which 25% were Kurds, followed by Iraq, Afghanistan, Iran and Eritrea, in that order, along with many from North Africa, especially Morocco and Tunisia. Some also came from Pakistan. Twenty-five percent came from the Balkans, especially Albania, Serbia, Kosovo, Bosnia – Herzegovina and Macedonia, and were rejected as economic migrants coming from 'safe' countries (Bamf 2015, 17, 21).

To prevent refugees from entering the EU through Greece, the EU made a morally problematic 'deal' with an increasingly repressive President Erdogan of Turkey. Erdogan would monitor Turkey's coastline and admit refugees Greece rejected for asylum, in return for six billion euros for care of refugees and consideration of visa free travel to the EU for Turks. The EU would accept one refugee already in Turkish refugee camps for each refugee Turkey took from Greece. As a consequence, many fewer refugees entered Germany in the first seven months of 2016, and even fewer are expected thereafter, although much of this deal is not being implemented.

The state

German refugee policy is admirable in many ways in its efforts to fulfill its moral duties to refugees. It is legally based on Paragraph 16a of the German Basic Law, equivalent to a constitution, the Asylum Law and the Integration Law, passed 7 July 2016. Refugees are granted either asylum or protected refugee status for three years, or 'subsidiary protection' for one year. If deemed to come from a 'safe country' they are summarily rejected and scheduled for deportation, with a deportation ban possible for one year if deportation would endanger their life, because of their health or conditions in their home country. During this time they are 'tolerated' ('geduldete'). Extensions are possible in all categories and are often granted and appeals are possible. Asylum or protected refugee status requires a 'well-founded fear of persecution in his [sic] country of origin' 'on account of his [sic] race, religion, nationality, political opinion or membership of a particular social group' [Paragraph 3]. 'Subsidiary protection' (Paragraph 4 (1)) is for those for whom there are 'substantial grounds for believing that he [sic] would face a real risk of suffering serious harm in his country of origin', including from 'international or internal armed conflict' (Asylgesetz 2015). De facto this excludes the roughly one-third of refugees coming from North Africa (Tunisia, Morocco and Algeria), and the Balkans. Refugee status determines whether and when one can bring one's family (those with subsidiary protection have to wait two years) and access to benefits, whereby those granted a recognized refugee status have priority for job training and language courses.

Until their asylum status is decided, refugees often live in large-scale state-funded housing run by private organizations, in both large cities and small towns. In large cities, they often live with more than 1000 people, for over a year, in huge empty airports and hangars, sports centers, former city and state buildings, containers, and school gyms. Their quarters are cramped, with little privacy, and they live amidst political, religious, cultural and gender tensions. Conditions varied tremendously, but in the best of cases it was dreary. Distinctions in refugee status caused tensions with those from 'safe' countries resentful of Syrians and Iraqis with favorable refugee status. Refugees are later to be distributed proportionately throughout Germany, with the threat that if they do not remain where placed, their benefits will be reduced.

But laws and policies and the manner in which they were applied changed continually. Insufficient staffing led to huge backlogs in processing asylum applications in 2015, so that only half the refugees who entered could file for refugee status in 2015. In that year virtually all Syrians whose cases were decided were accepted as 'protected refugees' and virtually none received the lesser subsidiary protection, but in the first seven months of 2016 about 20% of Syrians received that status (Bamf 2015, 2016). In 2016, only 60% of all refugee cases decided were granted some kind of protected refugee status (Bamf 2016). Political pressure to settle asylum cases in 2016 led to many more, often hasty, decisions. Germany also sent back over 16,000 refugees to their home countries in 2016, proportionately more than in 2015, one quarter Afghanis, others Syrians and Iraqis. Yet more are sent back to Austria at the border (Bielicki 2016; "Deutschland Schickt Viele," August 10, 2016).

Nevertheless, Germany's refugee policy is an important model, justifiable not only by a duty to permit refugees entry into Germany, but also by a positive duty to provide the necessary conditions enabling refugees to eventually live with dignity as full and equal members of the society. The policy includes state provision of minimum conditions – housing, medical care and minimum living expenses (about 390 Euros or necessary consumer goods) roughly the equivalent of German welfare. Secondly, it includes job training and language courses paid by the state, to provide social and labor market integration – an 'Integration Policy'. Language courses include not only teaching German, including job-relevant language, but also legal and social norms, including those regarding gender.

These courses are an offer, but conjoined with a threat. Those granted refugee status are *required* to take these courses and if they do not, or if they fail or drop out, their benefits will be reduced. If they take the courses they can get permanent residency after five years. Those officially awaiting deportation ('tolerated') have an incentive to take such courses. While in such courses they can remain in Germany, and if they pass, can remain another six months to find a job; if they get a job they can stay another two years (Deutscher Bundestag 2016). The process is complicated, confusing, fraught with bureaucracy and many pitfalls, not the least of which is refugees' difficulty in learning about their opportunities, learning German and qualifying as skilled workers.

The state was unprepared, although it had good reason to expect many refugees. To its credit, in response to criticisms (e.g. that language courses were inadequate – too short and not enough of them – the state modified and expanded language and job training courses). An Integration Law passed in summer 2016 permitted all living in collective housing to take workfare jobs (about 80 cents/hour), and created 100,000 such jobs; for the next three years, in hiring a refugee for a regular job prospective employers no longer had to show that no German worker was qualified, a bureaucratic hurdle employers resented (Deutscher Bundestag 2016).

The trick will still be providing enough courses and getting businesses to cooperate by hiring and training refugees. Angela Merkel uses moral persuasion, but has no legal authority to require businesses to do so. The cost for all programs and needs of refugees, including housing, is substantial, perhaps 20 billion euros in a year. The goal of German refugee policy and practice is two pronged – to integrate those permitted to remain, thereby avoiding the creation of parallel societies and providing a needed labor pool, but also to reduce the number of refugees who enter or can remain in Germany.

German civil society

State policy to absorb the many refugees could not have been implemented without civil society. In acts of solidarity, vast numbers of people volunteered, jumping in to fill enormous gaps in state efforts and to reduce refugees' pain, isolation and confusion. Civil society volunteers carried out the state's 'welcome culture' ('Willkommenskultur') given that the state had lacked adequate administrative organization, and had allocated insufficient resources. Civil society's efforts were vast, polyphonic and everywhere – in small towns and large cities, urban and suburban, in eastern and western Germany, by Christian and Muslim, students and professors, old and young, retired and working people, overwhelmingly, but not only, by women. They provided a public presence to counter other Germans' growing anti-refugee attitudes, and the growth of the anti-immigrant Alternative for Deutschland (AfD) party, which in some German states has almost 15%, or more, of voters.

Volunteers provided refugees crucial assistance with everything from A to Z. They made refugees feel accepted and safe, provided personal contacts with friendly Germans, not only with overwhelmed, sometimes unfriendly bureaucrats. They helped with bureaucratic hurdles, mysterious forms, and legal appeals involved in getting refugee status. They accompanied refugees to important immigration interviews and translated for them. Volunteers were creative, for example, they used crowdfunding to pay refugees' rents, looked for housing for refugees, and invited refugees to live in their homes and communes. Others helped refugees get medical care, created mother–child groups, formed quilting circles and women's groups, provided contacts to midwives and accompanied pregnant women to medical appointments. They organized social activities, including joint meals and cooking opportunities especially important to women refugees and joint musical opportunities, cultural events, festivals and outings with neighborhood residents for men and women, and sports clubs activities for men, all fostering social integration. Yet others taught German and helped with homework. Some volunteers, often thereby overwhelmed, adopted a particular family for over a year, serving as their all-purpose support.

Some young German Muslims created hip videos to dispel stereotypes about Muslims. Even after a year this supportive atmosphere is strong, if not predominant, and refugees have confirmed volunteers' centrality in making them feel welcome (IAB 2016). Though crucial to the success of the refugee policy and often more informed about refugees' problems than administrators, civil society volunteers generally did one-on-one care work, but had no say in defining policies.

However admirable civil society activity was, there were also normative problems. The state and civil society often acted *for* refugees, instead of empowering them, where possible, to be agents on their own behalf. The latter is both a value in itself and of instrumental value as well because refugees were aware of problems that others, including volunteers working closely with them, often were not, for example, Salafists managing to enter refugee housing to recruit refugees, frightening them (Neshtov 2016). Refugees lived in large scale, sometimes prison-like housing, sometimes for over a year. They were unable to cook for themselves, and lacked residence councils that would have given them some say in the conditions in which they lived. The resulting institutionalization discouraged their agency. It is also frustrating for people who did so much on their own behalf to get to Germany. Mechanisms for refugee self-representation in the public sphere, for example, a right to speak in community discussions on refugee matters affecting them, were rare, with some exceptions existing in Bavaria.

Some refugees and former refugees did manage to act on their own behalf in the public sphere, for example, a Syrian former teacher created a sightseeing tour from the perspective of refugees; men and women wrote and performed lively poetry and rap music about their experiences, criticizing 'integration' as a one way street that required efforts on their part, but none by non-Muslim Germans to reject stereotypes about Muslims. An organization of earlier women refugees investigated conditions for recent women refugees and created public events to raise awareness about women refugees and counter stereotypes; they brought together other active women's organizations.

The public sphere: a philosophical intervention

In spite of a 'Welcome Culture' there is also significant hostility to refugees and widespread criticism of Germany's refugee policy. The issues raised by the pursuit of any refugee policy is a subject for serious applied ethics, and such a debate occurred, mostly about criticisms dominant in the public sphere. It is important for philosophers to take part in these debates, as many did in Germany, both in a widely available popular philosophy magazine for non-philosophers *Philosophie Magazin* ("Was tun?," 2016; "Wo Endet Meine Verantwortung" ["Where does my responsibility end"] 2016), in online blogs, newspapers and in writings for more professional audiences.

Konrad Ott (2016) criticized defenders of Merkel's refugee policy as pure deontologists, committed to aiding refugees purely as an end in itself – an 'ethics of conviction' (Gesinnungsethik') – regardless of consequences. He argued, in contrast, that a consequentialist ethics, 'an ethics of responsibility', showed Merkel's policies to be morally unjustifiable. Yet many of those defenders actually took into account consequences, as any responsible deontologist would. Analytic philosophers, in the volume, "*Welche und wie viele Flüchtinge sollen wir aufnehmen?*" *Philosophische Essays* ["Which and how many refugees should we take?" Philosophical Essays.] (Grundmann and Stephan 2016), supported by the German Society for Analytic Philosophy, argued that a defense of Merkel's policies did not ignore consequences. Brezger (2016) accepted that there were limits, but on no plausible criteria had they been reached, for example, serious social disorder (Brezger, Hoesch), inability to care for and accept refugees in the future (Frick 2016, 43), harms to one's own citizens' social well-being and security (Hoesch). Ott had simply created a strawman.

One issue is *how many* refugees a country has a duty to accept. As was widely reported in the media, the governor of Bavaria claimed that there was an 'upper limit', of 200,000 (Reuters 2016), Safranski (Helg 2015) asserted there were 'too many' refugees, and Sloterdijk (2016) that Germany was being 'overrun'. A major normative debate ensued in which many others challenged these claims.

A second critique of accepting Muslim refugees is that Muslims *threaten German cultural identity* (Ott 2016, 43), a moral ground given to limit refugees. As is often the case, gender norms, women's freedom and the wearing of the burka, became the symbol of this danger, though hardly any Muslim women in Germany wear burkas. This reflected widespread public fears, anxiety and insecurity. Cultural change was also presumed to be only a threat, never an enrichment.

Some objected that Germany's 'Leitculture', its 'dominant culture', would be destroyed. But 'Leitculture' is a problematic, terminally vague category. Is there a 'Leitculture', and what is it? Is there any agreement about it? Is it what has always existed in Germany, and is there such a creature? Is it a shared religion, as its advocates suggest? Is it Christianity? Judeo-Christianity? But Muslims have been in Germany at least since the 1970s. Or is it a political commitment to democracy and religious tolerance? If so, acceptance of Muslims would only confirm that 'Leitculture'.

Threats to safety and social peace, including from anti-refugee hostility and violence, is a third justification, many, including Ott (2016, 97–99, 129), gave to limit refugees. Gesang (2016), Wendt (2016, 55) and Twele (2016) also took into account *anti-refugee* violence but, unlike Ott, argued for the need to try to aid refugees near their own cultures. Ott did not cite evidence or provide criteria for an unacceptable level of disorder. Wendt (2016), Brezger (2016) and Imhoff (2016) responded to this omission.

Again, threats to women's safety and freedom are cited, for example, the massive group sexual attacks in Germany against many, many women on New Year's Eve 2015. Though women's safety is certainly very important, other than on that one night, no other such group attacks were reported. It needs to be analyzed who was purported to be involved, and what can be done to avoid such occurrences. Four violent acts by refugees in summer 2016, three of which were definitely not terrorist acts, nevertheless fueled fears of violence and terrorism.

Another major argument concerns the *costs* of refugee programs and its consequences. Ott argued that the costs would harm citizens, especially the least well off, by leading to increased taxes, a higher retirement age, and reduced state benefits (Ott 2016, 99–101). He did not, however, cite evidence, nor consider policies to counter such risks, which Gosepath (2016a), Gesang (2016), Hoesch (2016) and Twele (2016) offered.

Finally, there is the question of *individual* duty and not only the state's duty to aid refugees. Gosepath (2016a, 2016b) argued that under such emergency conditions individuals also have a duty, as long as it does not impose undue burdens. Such a claim is, in part, compatible with any policy.

Since these debates raise issues likely to lie behind other EU countries' refusals to accept refugees, or other European countries' refugee policies, it is instructive to consider some of these arguments further.

1. Whether 'too many' refugees are accepted begs for criteria of what are 'too many'. As Hoesch (2016) and Brezger (2016) persuasively argue, there is no *absolute* limit. Ideally each country should take only its fair share, but in non-ideal conditions there can be a

moral duty to do more, as was recognized in 2015–2016. Hoesch argued that, because refugees' lives were endangered in their home country, they morally cannot be returned there. When refugees present themselves at a country's borders and there are no neighboring states that have not already taken their fair share, who would also accept refugees, as was the situation in Germany in 2015–2016, then that country becomes the refugees' last chance to be saved, creating a duty to accept more than one's fair share (Hoesch 2016, 29). To accept those refugees was therefore not morally to accept 'too many'.

This argument requires criteria for a country's fair share of refugees, which Hoesch and Brezger offered. Hoesch proposed a complex criterion including: a country's capacities, indebtedness, land, population, GDP, political climate and the public will to accept refugees. He further argued that a country's fair share rests not only on a duty to aid, but also on duties of territorial justice, that is, that it is only luck that others were not born in this territory, as well as compensatory duties due to harm one's country had caused to those countries from which refugees were fleeing (Hoesch 2016, 16–22). How to weigh these factors and apply them would require further argument.

Likewise, moral and political discussion is necessary on how to render effective EU wide refugee policies predicated on a just distribution of refugees (Katzer 2016). Questions need to be addressed such as: whether to use *threats*, such as partially withholding EU transfers to those EU countries that do not implement such policies, or to use *offers*, either the offer of an opportunity to opt out of accepting refugees by contributing proportionately to those EU countries that do, or an EU offer to fund aid to refugees in countries that accept them. Gosepath (2016a, 2016b) and Twele (2016, 39) propose the latter, based on a proportionate tax that all EU states would pay for this purpose.

Further public discourse is also necessary on the EU need not only to provide greater developmental aid to alleviate the conditions that lead people to become refugees, but also on the need of the EU to cease producing those conditions through economic, trade, political, environmental and military policies toward those countries from which refugees flee.

2. The second objection is to the risks to internal peace, from both refugees (Ott 2016, 99) and one's own citizens, for example, hostile Germans who attack refugees and refugee homes (Ott 2016, 93). Such anger can come from the least well off, fearful of losing jobs to refugees. Philosophers, however, need to argue, as did Wendt (2016, 51–54) and Imhoff (2016, 114), that although 'internal peace' and security are important moral goods, that security has to be 'drastically reduced', with 'pervasive instability and insecurity' (Wendt 2016, 52–54) before it justifies rejecting refugee policies. Wendt showed that, looking at police crime statistics for 2015, including from both violent attacks on refugees and refugee homes, as well as refugee crimes, that in Germany insecurity did not rise to that level (2016, 52–53).

Because economic insecurity leads to exaggerated fears, Gesang (2016) argued that policies to decrease unemployment are necessary to reduce violence. I would add that other means also need to be first adopted to reduce violence, including: further support and social integration of refugees, including education of Germans to dispel stereotypes about Muslims, Islam and Muslims in Germany; a non-sensationalist media; state policies that do not unwarrantedly provoke general anxiety, and greater police protection for refugees, before it is morally permissible to consider dangers to refugees as a grounds to limit their entry (Gesang 2016, 93; Wendt 2016, 52). It is questionable whether violence against refugees who have a legal right to remain, is a *morally* relevant ground for restricting entry of more refugees, rather than a prudential consideration. Attacks on abortion providers in the US are not moral grounds for restricting providers, but for restricting their attackers.

Gesang (2016, 93) and Twele (2016) echoed by others argued that such fears were a reason to accept refugees gradually, aiding them in their own countries or nearby, in similar cultures (Gesang 2016, 93). But this ignores that those countries have already accepted many more than their fair share of refugees.

3. The final set of arguments concerns the economic impact and high costs of the integration policy, and increased and purported endless welfare costs, about which many made pronouncements. Ott claimed that the policy was unfair to the least well off since the state would reduce state benefits, and raise taxes and retirement age to pay the high costs. Many claimed that the integration policy and job training will fail anyway, with many, many refugees remaining unemployable, increasing welfare costs. At best, refugees, it was argued, will only be employable in the least well-paying jobs (Ott 2016, 101). The least well off would thereby lose jobs and suffer lowered wages due to competition from such refugees (Ott 2016, 99–101).

In response, as Gesang (2016), and Twele (2016, 42–43) argued, if this were to indeed become likely, justice would require the state to instead increase revenues through a fair, progressive solidarity tax, or a wealth tax (Twele 2016, 38), thereby protecting the least well off. Germany had instituted such a solidarity tax on behalf of the GDR after German unification. Gosepath's arguments that citizens had a duty to accept some burdens to save refugees justify such non-onerous taxes. He and others proposed EU and worldwide solidarity taxes, possibly to aid all those in poverty. Another possibility, however, is that the EU end its austerity policies thereby enabling job creation in member states, reducing one ground for hostility to accepting refugees and reducing risks to the least well off.

Arguments based on costs turn on the likely costs for refugees (Gesang 2016, 89). But the International Monetary Fund (IMF) projected in 2016 Germany would spend only 0.35% of the GDP (11 billion euros). Even if it is in fact double or more each year, as may be the case, it is still under 1% of total GDP and would not require reducing social benefits in 2016 given that Germany even had a budget surplus.

Cost assessments alone are also misleading, since state programs for refugees are also Keynesian programs, pump-primers that create jobs, thereby increasing tax revenues. The IMF projects 0.5–1.1% additional growth in Germany due to refugee spending. Jobs are created, including low-paying jobs, in service, food preparation and delivery for those in large-scale refugee housing, in construction of new refugee housing and schools, and in additional retail jobs from refugee consumption.

Increased revenue from taxes refugees and their future employees pay offset costs. Future refugee employment projections also cannot be based on the low percent of refugees presently employable, since some will improve their language and work skills, especially young persons, if integration courses are adequately funded. Though economists grant that short-term costs and, perhaps middle range as well, will outweigh increased revenue, projections cannot be made for the long run.

Objections that Germany could reduce its costs by eliminating its integration policy, with expensive job and language training courses, are unpersuasive. It is reasonable to expect that such courses reduce long-term welfare costs by increasing employability, thereby reducing illegal employment at less than minimum wages and crime, and increase state revenue through refugees paying more taxes.

The need for a holistic approach

The danger is that in any given European country, discussion of refugees and refugee policy will focus overwhelmingly on criticisms about its domestic impact, neglecting both refugee concerns and the conditions in the countries from which refugees originate, as well as those of European and non-European countries through which refugees stream, and Europe's role in the creation of all those conditions. This is exactly what happened in Germany.

A holistic view of refugee issues is needed, one informed about the broader context and how it impacts on domestic concerns. Such considerations might well stretch upward conceptions of an 'upper-limit', revise conceptions of what counts as a 'safe' country, lead to greater discussion of the duty to accept economic refugees (Gesang 2016, 86; Hoesch 2016), stimulate increased EU development aid and change in military, political, economic and trade policies toward countries from which refugees come. It could also influence discussions about the Dublin III agreement, which imposed especially unfair costs, both social and financial, on EU border states, particularly Greece. It might even revive discussion of the austerity policies and debt burden imposed on Greece, a dead issue in Germany, in spite of Germany's role in that policy. Greece thereby became less able to handle already unfair refugee costs, left refugees in Greece in terrible conditions, created a strong risk of fascism and increased the number of unemployed Greeks who are, in effect, potentially in flight to Germany.

Further moral debate is needed about the EU agreement with Turkey about refugees. An argument suggesting that the agreement was with Turkey, not Erdogan (Gosepath 2016b) makes a spurious distinction; given Erdogan's increasing autocratic powers, it is even less plausible. Reports available since at least May 2016 established the inability of some refugees in Turkey to support themselves, or even file for asylum.

Germany, which accepted by far the greatest number of refugees in the EU in 2015–2016, introduced an admirable, if imperfect policy, predicated on providing subsistence, state-funded job training, language education and social integration. This policy deserves consideration as a model for a needed EU wide state refugee policy, one not based primarily on policing borders. Developments in Germany show the need for state and civil society participation and a public discourse broadened beyond debate about criticisms of refugee policy, both to achieve a just refugee policy, and to reduce the number of refugees seeking aid. Philosophers have an important role to play in such debates and need to engage actively in such discourse everywhere, as they did in Germany.

Acknowledgements

I want to thank Andrew Wengraf, Chloe Smolarski, Barbara Dietz, and Marina Grasse, who were each of help in a very different way.

Disclosure statement

No potential conflict of interest was reported by the author.

References

Asylgesetz. 2015. Accessed August 18, 2016. http://www.asylgesetz.de/§/.
Bamf (Bundesamt für Migration und Flüchtlinge). 2015. *Das Bundesamt im Zahlen. 2015*. Accessed August 25, 2016. http://www.bamf.de:SharedDocs:Anlagen:DE:Publikationen:Broschueren:bundesamt-in-zahlen-2015-asyl.html.
Bamf (Bundesamt für Migration und Flüchtlinge). 2016. *Asylgeschäftsstatistik. Asylgeschäftsstatistik für den Monat*, Juli, 2. Accessed August 22. http://www.bamf.de/SharedDocs/Anlagen/DE/Downloads/Infothek/Statistik/Asyl/201607-statistik-anlage-asyl-geschaeftsbericht.pdf?__blob=publicationFile.
Bielicki, Jan. 2016. "Was geschieht mit Abgewiesenen an der Grenze?." *Süddeutsche Zeitung*, August 13–14.
Brezger, Jan. 2016. "So viele wie nötig und möglich! Die Pflicht zur Aufnahme von Flüchtlingen und die Spielräume politischer Machbarkeit." In *"Welche und wie viele Flüchtlinge sollen wir aufnehmen?" Philosophische Essays*, edited by Thomas Grundmann and Achim Stephan, 57–69. Stuttgart: Reclam.
Deutscher Bundestag. 2016. *Gesetzentwurf der Bundesregierung. Entwurf eines Integrationsgesetzes*. 20.06 Wahlperiode. Accessed August 15. http://dip21.bundestag.de:dip21:btd:18:088:1808829.pdf.
"Deutschland Schickt Viele Flüchtlinge Zurück." 2016. *Süddeutsche Zeitung*, August 10, 1.
Frick, Marie-Luisa. 2016. "Wenn das Recht an Verbindlichkeit Verliert und die Zonen der Unordnung Wachsen, rettet uns keine kosmopolitsche Moral." In *"Welche und wie viele Flüchtlinge sollen wir aufnehmen?" Philosophische Essays*, edited by Thomas Grundmann and Achim Stephan, 70–83. Stuttgart: Reclam.
Gesang, Bernard. 2016. "Sind Obergrenzen für Asylbewerber Moralisch zu Rechtfertigen und wo Liegen sie? Auf dem Weg zum Integrierten Asylberechtigten." In *"Welche und wie viele Flüchtlinge sollen wir aufnehmen?" Philosophische Essays*, edited by Thomas Grundmann and Achim Stephan, 84–97. Stuttgart: Reclam.
Gosepath, Stephan. 2016a. "Es Gibt Eine Globale Hilfspflicht." *Philosophie Magazin* 4: 55–57.
Gosepath, Stephan. 2016b. "Die Lage in türkischen Flüchtlingscamps muss verbessert werden." Stephan Gosepath in discussion with Petra Ensminger. Deutschlandfunk. April 24. Accessed August 1. http://www.deutschlandfunk.de/philosoph-stefan-gosepath-die-lage-in-tuerkischen.694.de.html?dram:article_id=352247.
Grundmann, Thomas, and Achim Stephan, eds. 2016. *"Welche und wie viele Flüchtlinge sollen wir aufnehmen?" Philosophische Essays*. Stuttgart: Reclam.
Helg, Martin. 2015. "Die Deutschen sind in der Pubertät." Interview with Rüdiger Safranski, *Neue Zürcher Zeitung am Sonntag*, November 8. http://www.nzz.ch/nzzas/nzz-am-sonntag/ruediger-safranski-interview-die-deutschen-sind-in-der-pubertaet-ld.2940.

Hoesch, Matthias. 2016. "Allgemeine Hilfspflicht, Territoriale Gerechtigkeit und Wiedergutmachung: Drei Kriterien für Eine Faire Verteilung von Flüchtlingen – und Wann sie Irrelevant Werden." In *"Welche und wie viele Flüchtlinge sollen wir aufnehmen?" Philosophische Essays*, edited by Thomas Grundmann and Achim Stephan, 15–29. Stuttgart: Reclam.

IAB (Institut für Arbeitsmarkt-und Berufsforschung). 2016. Forschungsbericht 9/2016. *Geflüchtete Menschen in Deutschland – eine qualitative Befragung*. Accessed October 19. http://www.iab.de/185/section.aspx/Publikation/k160715301.

Imhoff, Simeon. 2016. "Über Hilfe und Aufname: Zwei Pflichten und Ihre Grenzen." In *"Welche und wie viele Flüchtlinge sollen wir aufnehmen?" Philosophische Essays*, edited by Thomas Grundmann and Achim Stephan, 110–119. Stuttgart: Reclam.

Katzer, Matthias. 2016. "Die Goldene Regel und Unser Umgang mit Flüchtlingen: Ein Dialog." In *"Welche und wie viele Flüchtlinge sollen wir aufnehmen?" Philosophische Essays*, edited by Thomas Grundmann and Achim Stephan, 98–109. Stuttgart: Reclam.

Neshtov, Tim. 2016. "Ganz Leise." *Süddeutsche Zeitung*, August 19, 3.

Ott, Konrad. 2016. *Zuwanderung und Moral*. Stuttgart: Reclam.

Regulation (EU) No 604/2013 of European Parliament and of the Council of June 26, 2013. 2013 Official Journal of the European Union. http://www.refworld.org/docid/51d298f04.html.

Reuters. 2016. "Seehofer fordert Obergrenze von 200.000 Flüchtlingen pro Jahr." *Inlandsnachrichten*. January 3. Accessed August 12. http://de.reuters.com/article/deutschland-fl-chtlinge-seehofer-idDEKBN0UH08620160103.

Sloterdijk, Peter. 2016. *Cicero. Magazin für politische Kultur*. 2, 14–23,"Das kann nicht gut gehen. Peter Sloterdijk über Angela Merkel, die Flüchtlinge und das Regiment der Furcht." Questions by Alexander Kissler and Christoph Schwennicke. Accessed September 20. https://issuu.com/andreasboeder/docs/caesar0216.

Twele, Marcel. 2016. "Von Menschenrechten und Hilfspflichten." In *"Welche und wie viele Flüchtlinge sollen wir aufnehmen?" Philosophische Essays*, edited by Thomas Grundmann and Achim Stephan, 30–44. Stuttgart: Reclam.

"Was tun?" 2016. *Philosophie Magazin*. 2, 40–65. Accessed September 10. http://issuu.com/philomagde/docs/pmdetab26leseprobe/3?e=3894071/32522327.

"Wo endet meine Verantwortung? ["Where does my responsibility end?"] Dossier." 2016. *Philosophie Magazin*, 4, 44–67.

Wendt, Fabian. 2016. "Gerechtigkeit ist Nicht Alles: Über Immigration und Sozialen Frieden." In *"Welche und wie viele Flüchtlinge sollen wir aufnehmen?" Philosophische Essays*, edited by Thomas Grundmann and Achim Stephan, 70–83. Stuttgart: Reclam.

Resettling refugees: is private sponsorship a just way forward?

Patti Tamara Lenard

ABSTRACT
According to the United Nations High Commissioner for Refugees, there are over 20 million refugees worldwide, less than 1% of whom are referred for resettlement to third countries permanently. One obstacle to resettlement stems from the alleged lack of resources in settlement countries. A possible way forward is a refugee selection and admission regime that shares costs between governments and private citizens, to permit states to admit greater numbers of refugees where their citizens are willing and able to contribute their own, private, resources to the resettlement project. Taking Canada's private sponsorship scheme as a model, I argue that there are pros and cons to public–private cooperation in refugee resettlement. On the one hand, they permit the resettlement of greater numbers of refugees and they permit private citizens committed to aiding refugees to do so in concrete ways. On the other hand, they require oversight to protect refugees who are, otherwise, fully dependent on their sponsorship groups and there are cultural differences that make the offering of support challenging. In particular, while sponsorship groups ought to aim at securing the independence and autonomy of newcomers, they can sometimes behave in culturally inappropriate and paternalistic ways, which generate resentments between refugees and their sponsoring groups.

According to the United Nations High Commissioner for Refugees (UNHCR), there are over 20 million refugees worldwide, less than 1% of whom are referred for resettlement to third countries on a permanent basis.[1] The vast majority of refugees languish in camps, waiting for the violence and persecution that propelled their flight to abate, so that they can return home safely. Others are offered temporary asylum in third countries, on the expectation that they will be repatriated as soon as their home countries are stable enough to provide minimum protection for their basic human rights. Only those who are most vulnerable in their countries of refuge – because they are ill, or children, or women-without-adequate-protection or LGBTQ – are recommended for resettlement, and not all of these individuals are ultimately able to resettle abroad. There are, as political theorists of migration note, multiple obstacles that stand in the way of offering permanent refuge to those most in need,[2] and one among these obstacles is the alleged lack of resources in settlement countries. Governments in many resettlement countries claim that they simply are not able to afford the costs of resettling the number of refugees in need;

they are deficit-ridden and so cash-strapped, and argue (not unreasonably) that they must focus their limited resources on the needs of their citizens rather than on the needs of those who are abroad. And yet, many citizens of potential resettlement states decry their governments' unwillingness to dedicate more resources to those in desperate circumstances.

There is a possible path through this impasse – a refugee selection and admission regime that explicitly shares costs between governments and private citizens, to permit states to admit greater numbers of refugees where their citizens are willing and able to contribute their own, private, resources to the resettlement project. The Blended-Visa Office Referred programme, operating in Canada since 2013,[3] is one such programme, and it is the intention of this short discussion piece to evaluate its structure and practice from a normative perspective. Canada is not alone in operating programmes that permit public–private cooperation in the sponsorship of refugees, but its programme is the longest-running and most successful in the world.[4] As a result, although I intend this piece to consider the normative benefits and challenges of these programmes *in general*, it will necessarily draw significantly on the Canadian experience.

I conclude tentatively that the private–public cooperation – though not without its challenges, both practical and normative – does appear to be a strategy that, more broadly adopted, could offer aid to more refugees in need, at little or no extra cost to settling states. In this piece, I begin with a brief outline of how Canada has proceeded, since 1976, when it formally gave citizens the ability to 'sponsor' refugees in need for resettlement, that is, to take on the responsibility, both financial and emotional, of supporting specific refugees resettling to Canada. I will then – taking the broad framework of this programme as a model – offer a normative examination of these programmes.

As I see it, the goods provided these programmes are these: they permit the resettlement of greater numbers of refugees, in a cost-effective way, and they permit private citizens committed to aiding refugees to do so in concrete ways. On the other hand, the challenges posed by these programmes are significant: they must genuinely be and remain partnerships, so that they add to a state's overall commitment to refugees; they require oversight to protect refugees who are, otherwise, at the mercy of private sponsorship groups in a range of ways; and there are cultural differences that make the offering of support challenging in unexpected ways. In particular, while sponsorship groups ought to aim at securing the independence and autonomy of newcomers, they can sometimes behave in culturally inappropriate and paternalistic ways, which can generate resentments and distrust between refugees and their sponsoring groups.

Private sponsorship of refugees in Canada and globally[5]

Many democratic states include quotas for refugee admissions as part of their overall immigration policy. These refugees are admitted and, typically, are supported by the state until they are able to be self-sufficient. These 'government-assisted' refugees have access to a range of services – many funded by the government – which offer support in finding accommodation, health care, language instruction, employment, and so on. The term 'sponsored' has been adopted for refugees who are admitted under schemes that permit private citizens more direct involvement in their support. These 'privately sponsored' refugees are identified by citizens in the host state, who then submit an application outlining the support (financial and emotional) that their sponsoring group is able to provide. These applications are submitted to the central government, which adjudicates the cases. So, to summarize, what distinguishes privately sponsored refugees from government-assisted refugees are that the former are (often) identified by citizens, who commit to some form of financial and emotional support.

Canada is not the only country in the world to permit the private sponsorship of refugees, but it is the country with the longest running and most successful programme. Several countries have experimented with short-term private sponsorship schemes in response to the Syrian crisis (Germany, Argentina, Ireland, and Switzerland); Australia launched a private sponsorship programme in 2013; and in New Zealand, 300 individuals per year may be sponsored privately via the 'Refugee Family Support Category'.[6]

Since the 1960s, Canada has admitted significant numbers of refugees ('government-assisted refugees') as part of its humanitarian mission, and has since then consistently responded to urgent crises by augmenting the number it admits in any given year. While the practice of private sponsorship had been operating in an ad hoc way in Canada for many years prior, and in response to specific crises, the 1976 Immigration Act formalized the Private Sponsorship of Refugees Program (PSRP). This Act put in place a set of regulations to permit private citizens, in groups of five, or in association with so-called 'sponsorship agreement holders' (these are pre-vetted community organizations that signed formal memoranda with the government approving their right to sponsor refugees) to identify refugees in need, for whom they would be willing to take full financial and emotional responsibility for the period of a year. Such groups agree to raise approximately the equivalent of what social assistance would pay for one year and agree to take responsibility for the settlement and integration of newcomers,[7] including finding appropriate accommodation, health care, language lessons, foreign credential recognition, and support in understanding the labour market. This programme 'allows private actors – individuals and organizations – to make choices that will directly contribute to the protection of persons suffering from human rights violations ... private actors fulfill certain international obligations traditionally regarded as a duty and a prerogative of states'.[8] Privately sponsored refugees – as is the case with all refugees who are selected for resettlement in Canada – *arrive* as permanent residents of Canada. In other words, the asylum offered to these individuals is *permanent*. What marks the Canadian programme as distinct, then, is not only that it is the longest running programme, but also it (1) is open to all nationalities; (2) does not require a family or any other form of personal connection between sponsoring group and refugee;[9] (3) is *additional* to whatever government quotas exist for refugee admissions each year;[10] and (4) permits any willing citizen to participate in the scheme.[11]

Although elements of the programme have come under scrutiny,[12] by all accounts the programme is extraordinarily successful: since its inception, private Canadian citizens have supported the arrival and integration of approximately 200,000 refugees (just under half the number that Canada as a whole has resettled in that same time period), and evidence suggests that privately sponsored refugees are more successful along standard measures of integration than are refugees admitted by the government.[13] Their average annual income is higher than government-assisted refugees and they are thus more likely to be economically self-sustaining.[14] On average, they report high levels of satisfaction with their transitional experiences and often remain life-long friends with their sponsorship group.[15]

In 2013, the government amended its private sponsorship legislation to add a new programme, called the Blended-Visa Office Referred (BVOR) programme. This programme also permits Canadian citizens, in various formations, to support refugees in need, but in the form of a more explicit public–private partnership between specific citizens and the Canadian government.[16] Whereas the original PSRP invited Canadian citizens to identify individuals abroad, in need, and to raise the full cost of their first year in Canada, the BVOR programme offers to share the financial costs with private groups (i.e. the government and the sponsorship group split the financial costs more or less evenly). What distinguishes this programme is that the government pre-identifies refugees in need, in consultation with the UNHCR (which recommends refugees for resettlement), and clears them for travel. Canadian citizens who have themselves been pre-cleared for sponsorship are then provided with the 'BVOR list', which identifies refugees by some basic demographic information, including age, country of origin, family structure, sex (and sexuality where it is relevant), and specific medical (including mental health) needs. Sponsorship groups then ask for a 'match' with an individual or family, and a 'matching centre' is responsible for making appropriate matches. Whereas Canadians who participate in the PSRP select refugees on their own and take on the full cost of one year of settlement, Canadians who participate in the BVOR select among refugees pre-vetted by the government of Canada in collaboration with the UNHCR, and while they take on the full *emotional* costs of settlement for the year, Canadians and the government split the financial costs of settlement.

The introduction of the BVOR programme was met with scepticism – it was understood by its opponents as a cost-saving mechanism, that is, as an attempt by the government to offload the cost of Canada's humanitarian obligations to private citizens.[17] In particular, it was criticized as failing to respect the principle of 'additionality' that was said to be at the heart of the original private sponsorship programme, which had been constructed to permit Canadian citizens to *add* to Canada's humanitarian efforts by increasing the total number of refugees admitted to Canada.[18] This criticism has not fully abated, but no one can deny that it has proven to be a wildly successful way in which Canadian citizens have been able to respond quickly to the Syrian refugee crisis; indeed, the most frequent criticism launched at the programme, and the PSRP generally, has been that processing of refugees has simply been too slow to keep up with Canadian 'demand' for refugees. Minister of Immigration, Refugees, and Citizenship recently (proudly) proclaimed his unique status as the only Minister of Immigration in the world who is being criticized for admitting too few refugees and too slowly: 'I probably have a problem that no other Immigration Minister has. I can't produce refugees quickly enough to satisfy the incredible demand of all these generous Canadians who want to bring them in. That's a good problem to have'.[19]

There are many parochial details here, about the operation of the programme, and its successes and failures. But what I want to highlight here is the private–public partnership in refugee support that is at the heart of the BVOR and PSRP, to examine the merits and demerits of this way of proceeding in the face of unmet need for resettlement.

Public–private partnerships to sponsor refugees: The Pros

In examining public–private partnerships to support refugees, there are three parties that stand to gain: a host state's government, refugees (both globally and from the perspective of those who are admitted), and private citizens of a state. Let me outline in brief the benefits for each of these parties.

The benefits for welcoming states are clear. In the setting of immigration policy broadly understood, states face multiple pressures, to deploy immigration to support economic growth, to prioritize family reunification, and to admit refugees, among others. The pressures to admit refugees stem from the global community – in the case of refugees, instantiated in the UNHCR – and also from the welcoming state's own sense of itself as a humanitarian actor on the global state. There is of course much analysis that evaluates the *costs* of admitting refugees, and on the basis of this analysis there is much dispute about whether the costs are long- or short-term, and how these costs should influence a state's willingness to admit refugees. The benefit of public–private mechanisms for admitting refugees is clearly a defraying of the cost of refugee resettlement, in at least two ways. One way is the sharing of the financial burden – in the Canadian case, the financial burden of BVOR admissions are shared equally between the government and the private sponsorship group, and the financial burdens of privately sponsored refugees are borne entirely by private citizens. Now, as I indicated, in Canada and elsewhere one debate is whether private sponsorships, and public–private partnerships, to admit refugees, are *additional* to or *in place of* government-assisted refugee quotas. The extent of financial benefit to the government may therefore appear to rest solely on whether it is off-loading the costs of refugee resettlement to private citizens.

But, that is not the whole story. As I said earlier, there is considerable evidence in Canada to suggest that privately sponsored refugees are among the most productive of refugees. This economic benefit is attributed to the emotional and cultural support offered by private sponsorship groups, which is understood to be a key element of effective integration of newcomers into Canadian society. The emotional and cultural support are costs are absorbed in almost entirely by the sponsorship group, but translate into economic benefits for the welcoming society as a whole. All (permanent) newcomers to Canada are offered access to a wide-range of government-supported services, ranging from language classes, to job readiness support, and so on; the financial costs of these services are borne by the state, but the connection of newcomers to these services is borne by the sponsors. On the list of jobs taken by private sponsors is to connect newcomers to these services, as quickly as possible on arrival, and more importantly to offer emotional support to individuals who are often overwhelmed by arriving to, and making their way in, an entirely new cultural environment, without the supports of friends and family.

Correspondingly, the benefits to refugees comes in two forms. One form is that, so long as the principle of additionality is respected, the result of cost-sharing mechanisms for refugee admission and integration is the entry of greater numbers of refugees than in alternative scenarios. The second is in the form of the emotional support offered by private sponsorship groups, which provides an irreplaceable resource for individuals who have been forced from their homes by violence and persecution, and who are thereby in the position of having to start their lives again. Members of sponsorship groups are the often the *essential* connection to Canadian society for newcomers, who rely on their sponsors to counter the loneliness and isolation that accompanies the refugee experience.[20]

There are also benefits to citizens as well, in multiple forms. One clear benefit is this one: individual citizens who are appalled by refugee crises, in general or in specific cases, are given a way to act in the face of them. They are permitted to gather resources to offer permanent homes to those in desperate need; they have a concrete way in which to act to make an important (however small) contribution to relieving suffering. In a global environment in which only small numbers of individuals feel compelled to act in the face of significant global inequalities and suffering, individuals who believe they have a duty to aid those in need (regardless of borders) can participate in private sponsorship schemes as a way to carry it out. And in domestic environments where citizens are not always persuaded of the importance of prioritizing global justice over social justice,[21] those who wish to act in defense of global justice can do so, by mobilizing their own resources. A second benefit stems from the personal connections that citizens make with newcomers. As stories of the relations among refugees and the Canadian citizens who have worked so hard to give them a new a home are told, among the frequently heard stories are about how Canadians have been touched by the strength and openness of refugees who have arrived, and how satisfying it is not simply to 'donate to a good cause' but to be able to develop life-long relations with a 'new family'.[22]

I suspect there is a third and as of yet unquantifiable benefit as well. In September 2015, many around the world were struck by the image of Alan Kurdi's lifeless body lying still on a beach having drowned in an attempt to reach safety in Europe. Canadians were especially struck, by the knowledge that there was a 'Canadian connection' to Kurdi – it was initially (though falsely) reported that his family had been denied status in Canada, but it is nevertheless true that members of his extended family were living in Canada, having been granted refuge some time earlier.[23] This story (and the more general reports of the horrors taking place in the Mediterranean Sea) galvanized people around the world to offer their support to these desperate individuals. Videos circulated of cities cheering as refugees arrived; private citizens banded together to mobilize to offer housing to refugees,[24] and so on. Popular opinion around democratic states moved dramatically in favour of admitting more and more refugees, and persisted until several months later when reports of men of Middle Eastern descent acting collectively to harass women on New Year's Eve emerged in Cologne. From then, and combined with anxieties that the refugee route was in fact being exploited by members of Daesh to gain entry to European states, public opinion began to turn away from extending generosity towards a scepticism of these (allegedly) potentially dangerous newcomers. Yet, in many ways, Canada proved robust against this shift away from support of, to skepticism of, refugees.

One possible explanation for this robustness, in my view, is the strength and depth of the private sponsorship regime in Canada. Canada is well-equipped in general to resettle newcomers, and takes pride in the ability of its extensive settlement services to integrate large numbers of newcomers from all over the world. But the presence and operation of these settlement services is insufficient to explain why Canadians refused to turn against refugees: rather, the involvement of so many Canadians in the private sponsorship of refugees is an essential part of the explanation. The numbers of individuals resettled to Canada by private sponsorship groups in response to the Syrian crisis are not yet clear, but they may be as high as 18,000 refugees (and the number continues to rise). A sponsorship group is at minimum five people, and is usually much larger than that. These individuals typically reach out to many more people to fundraise, to donate goods (including furniture and clothing) and to provide essential services to refugees on their arrival. Sponsors reach out to the extensive network of settlement services in order to create the conditions under which 'their' refugees can be successful in Canada. They get angry and frustrated with the government when 'their' refugees face bureaucratic hurdles in exiting their state and boarding a flight to Canada (a newspaper referred to them as an 'angry mob of do-gooders'[25]); they call on their government to expedite the entry of refugees to Canada, and to admit more refugees and faster, so that they can get on with the work of resettling those in need. These citizens become advocates for 'their' refugees – indeed often for refugees in general – as they attempt to gain a foothold in their new home.[26] Ultimately, in my view, *too many* Canadians were personally involved in the admission and settlement of refugees to permit the emergence of an anti-refugee perspective to gain significant traction.[27]

Public–private partnerships to sponsor refugees: The Cons

Yet, these private–public partnerships are not without genuine and normatively troubling challenges. One significant challenge to public–private partnerships to sponsor refugees stems from the worry as I indicated above – expressed, for example, in the Canadian case – that public–private schemes are treated by the government as 'cost-saving' strategies rather than 'cost-sharing' strategies, that is, that the government may be failing to respect the 'additionality' dimension of the private sponsorship scheme.[28] According to this view, the primary responsibility for admitting and settling refugees lies with the state, and not with private individuals. Private sponsors are (sometimes) motivated by a desire to increase the *total* number of refugee admissions, but governments facing budget deficits may desire to rely on private sponsors to simply meet refugee quotas that it has already set. Private sponsors want to know that they are not simply doing what they believe is the government's job, in other words. I think the pressure on governments to be open and transparent about who is absorbing the cost of which refugees and how many is significant (the tendency of the Canadian government to refer to BVOR admissions in the 'government-assisted' column has historically exacerbated this worry among Canadians). Private–public sponsorship programmes will ultimately fail if they are not perceived to be genuine partnerships, in other words.

A second challenge has to do with the imperfect oversight of private sponsorship groups as they welcome and work with newcomers. As part of their application, sponsoring groups must 'prove' their willingness and ability to do the settlement work required of them; sponsoring groups are required to commit to specifically delineated settlement tasks, and to indicate how they plan to approach a range of others (e.g. to indicate how they intended to identify culturally appropriate counselling and which organizations they will approach to offer job training skills). The objective is to ensure that sponsoring groups are given at least some direction with respect to the job they agree to undertake by acting as private sponsors. This in-advance work offers an opportunity for the government to specify what they expect of private sponsors, and it gives private sponsors clear direction with respect to their tasks. Although the preparatory work appears to have been helpful for both private sponsors and the refugees they aim to support, there remains no *post-arrival* check-in, or evaluation, of the jobs done by private sponsors, and refugees therefore remain vulnerable to the efforts that these sponsors are willing and able to expend. One newcomer observed, for example, that for 'most things, the sponsor didn't help much. Our sponsor used to tell us that his role was only to bring us here, and once we are here, we are responsible for ourselves'.[29] Of course refugees, as with all newcomers, can access settlement services of all kinds – with or without the intervention of their sponsors – but the fact remains that newcomers with private sponsors will rely on them to act as their conduit to what is available to them in the welcoming state.[30] This vulnerability is exacerbated by the profound gratitude that refugees have for their sponsors, recognizing them as individuals who are essentially responsible for giving them an opportunity to live in safety and freedom.

A third challenge is related to the one indicated just above, and has to do with the 'cultural' challenges associated with interactions among people with different cultural norms and expectations for interactions, and the connected fact that trust relations are often facilitated by shared cultural norms (and made more challenging in their absence).[31] There are multiple dimensions to this which I can only gesture at here. One challenge stems from the tension between private sponsoring groups who are charged with navigating the employment market on behalf of their newcomers and the cultural norms and preferences that newcomers have with respect to employment. For example, private sponsors may expect women from religiously conservative cultures to find employment; women from these cultures may resist this, having lived in environments where it is conventional to depend on men to provide for them. Or, newcomers may arrive with a sense of what kind of job they find respectable, and private sponsorship groups may pressure newcomers to take 'any' job, just as a way to break in to the labour market. This is exacerbated in cases where newcomers are high-skilled, and resist taking menial jobs which they perceive as beneath them. Or, newcomers may fail to understand that sponsoring groups are genuinely doing their best, and resent that the conditions of their lives are not better than they are. One friend reported frustration to me that the head of the household she has worked to sponsor continued to believe that he was overpaying for an apartment she had worked hard to secure on his family's behalf.

A final challenge stems from the way in which newcomers are expected to respond to the advice and information offered by sponsoring groups. The specific objective of sponsoring groups is to support newcomers as they integrate, that is, to support newcomers in their journey towards independence. This requires that sponsoring groups take seriously the role of providing information about paths forward in the welcoming society, but it also requires taking seriously the cues provided by the newcomers with respect to their own objectives and ways of meeting them. Sponsoring groups may also mistakenly believe that newcomers should be grateful to them for the work they have done, and interpret newcomers as ungrateful or irrational if they choose to discard advice or information offered to them. Pressures that signal to newcomers that they are required to take advice or goods offered by their sponsoring groups reflect a kind of 'we-know-best' paternalism, which serves to undermine rather than support the development of autonomy and independence among newcomers.

Conclusion

The purpose of this short discussion is to highlight one possible path forward in the global project of resettling refugees. I began by pointing to the small number of refugees that are ultimately resettled in third countries, to begin their lives anew. In the absence of a collective will to work harder as a global community to respond to the waves of refugees escaping violence and persecution, expanding the use of public–private partnerships to sponsor refugees in democratic states may offer another path forward.[32] As I described, these partnerships permit private citizens to work in conjunction with governments to raise the funds, and provide the emotional resources necessary, to permit the resettlement of more refugees in need. They are not perfect – they rely on the existence of trust relations between governments and private citizens, and in part because of inadequate oversight they render newcomers vulnerable to their sponsors as I have outlined. But, in Canada they have largely been an effective and rewarding way for those who are moved by the plight of refugees to work to support them in tangible and meaningful ways.

Notes

1. United Nations High Commission on Refugees, 'Resettlement', http://www.unhcr.org/resettlement.html.
2. Matthew Gibney, "A thousand little Guantanamos: Western states and measures to prevent the arrival of refugees," in *Migration, Displacement, Asylum: The Oxford Amnesty Lectures 2004*, ed. K. Tunstall (Oxford: Oxford University Press, 2006).
3. Citizenship and Immigration Canada, "Blended-Visa Officer Referred Program – Sponsoring Refugees", http://www.cic.gc.ca/english/refugees/sponsor/vor.asp.
4. Lest I be accused of jingoistic pride, let me specify that by 'most successful' I mean in terms of number of refugees admitted as part of these schemes.
5. For a more extensive history of the programme, see Barbara Treviranus and Michael Casasola, "Canada's private sponsorship of refugees program: A practitioners perspective of its past and future," *Journal of International Migration and Integration/Revue de l'integration et de la migration internationale* 4, no. 2 (2003).
6. For summaries of these schemes, see Judith Kumin, *Welcoming Engagement: How Private Sponsorship Can Strengthen Refugee Resettlement in the European Union* (Brussels: Migration Policy Institute Europe, 2015). pp. 5 and 30–34.
7. In Canada, it is conventional to keep private the category of immigrant admission – that is, to refer to newly arrived refugees, and all other immigrants, simply as newcomers. I will maintain that convention here, and should be understood to be referring to refugees unless I specify otherwise.
8. Ekaterina Yahyaoui Krivenko, "Hospitality and Sovereignty: What Can We Learn From the Canadian Private Sponsorship of Refugees Program?," *International Journal of Refugee Law* 24, no. 3 (2012): p. 594.
9. Although, in the past, it has been deployed primarily by families and friends. This makes sense, since resettled refugees are the most likely to be able to name specific others in need of resettlement.
10. There are caps to the number of privately sponsored refugees who can be admitted – they hover around 6–7000 per year. Private sponsoring groups in Canada have however been pressuring the government to lift caps, noting that if private citizens wish to donate their resources towards humanitarian activity in this way, they should not be restricted from doing so. While I generally agree with this view, the costs to the government – in processing applications and doing security and medical checks on potential newcomers – are not zero, as some advocates appear to suggest.
11. Applying citizens are subject to a range of background checks in advance of having their application approved.
12. Central among the criticisms is that the processing time of private applications to sponsor is very slow. Reports vary about the length of time that it takes Canadian visa officers to process applications, but they have been as long as four years. See, for example, Yahyaoui Krivenko,

"Hospitality and Sovereignty: What Can We Learn From the Canadian Private Sponsorship of Refugees Program?."
13. For example, see Morton Beiser, "Sponsorship and resettlement success," *Journal of International Migration and Integration / Revue de l'integration et de la migration internationale* 4, no. 2 (2003).
14. Steve Meurrens, *The Private Sponsorship of Refugees Program after Alan Kurdi*, Policy Options (Ottawa: Institute for Research on Public Policy, 2015). pp. 3–4.
15. For example, see Tom Carter et al., "The Resettlement Experiences of Privately Sponsored Refugees: Phase Two Report Preapred for Manitoba Labour and Immigration," (Winnipeg: University of Winnipeg, 2008).
16. This is an important clarification. In some sense, refugee resettlement is always a public-private partnership in Canada, since private organizations do much of the resettlement work, often with funding from the government. In some cases – in particular, in the US context, this partnership is sometimes misleadingly referred to as 'sponsorship'.
17. Canadian Council of Refugees, "Important Changes in Canada's Private Sponsorship of Refugees Program", January 2013, http://ccrweb.ca/en/changes-private-sponsorship-refugees.
18. *Ibid.*
19. John McCallum, "Speaking Notes for John McCallum, Minister of Immigration, Refugees, and Citizenship at a luncheon hosted by the Canadian Club of Ottawa", June 14, 2016, http://news.gc.ca/web/article-en.do?nid=1086189.
20. This reliance is documented beautifully in Carter et al., "The Resettlement Experiences of Privately Sponsored Refugees: Phase Two Report Preapred for Manitoba Labour and Immigration".
21. David Miller, "Social Justice versus Global Justice," in *Social Justice in a Global Age*, ed. Olaf Gramme and Patrick Diammond (Cambridge, MA: Polity Press, 2009).
22. Jodi Kantor and Catrin Einhorn, "Refugees Encounter a Foreign Word: Welcome" *New York Times*, July 1 2016.
23. National Post Staff, "Canada says it never denied a refugee application for Alan Kurdi and his family," *National Post*, September 3 2015.
24. Jessica Elgot, "'Airbnb for refugees' group overwhelmed by offers of help," *The Guardian*, September 1 2015.
25. Catherine Porter, "How to deal with an angry mob of do-gooders," *Toronto Star*, March 31 2016.
26. Thomas Denton, "Unintended Consequences of Canada"'s Private Sponsorship of Refugees Program," in *International Metropolis Conference* (Tampere Finland 2013).
27. That is, the Canadian public was of course not unified with respect to what responsibilities it should take in relation to refugees; rather, the voice of those who were in favour of doing more and better for them was prominent in Canadian public discourse over many, many months.
28. Treviranus and Casasola, "Canada's private sponsorship of refugees program: A practitioners perspective of its past and future," p. 185.
29. Carter et al., "The Resettlement Experiences of Privately Sponsored Refugees: Phase Two Report Preapred for Manitoba Labour and Immigration," p. 18.
30. Research supports this claim, that privately sponsored refugees often are not aware of their right to access settlement services outside of the connections made by their sponsors, or feel uncomfortable at the prospect of bypassing them. See ibid.
31. Patti Tamara Lenard, *Trust, Democracy and Multicultural Challenges* (University Park: Pennsylvania University State Press, 2012).
32. Kumin, *Welcoming Engagement: How Private Sponsorship Can Strengthen Refugee Resettlement in the European Union*.

Disclosure statement

No potential conflict of interest was reported by the author.

The ethics of people smuggling

Javier Hidalgo

ABSTRACT
People smugglers help transport migrants across international borders without authorization and in return for compensation. Many people object to people smuggling and believe that the smuggling of migrants is an evil trade. In this paper, I offer a qualified defense of people smuggling. In particular, I argue that people smuggling that assists refugees in escaping threats to their rights can be morally justified. I then rebut the objections that people smugglers exploit migrants, have defective motivations, and wrongly violate the law. My conclusion is that people smuggling is sometimes a permissible way of helping refugees to evade unjust immigration restrictions and compelling states to bear their fair share of the global refugee population.

1. Introduction

People smugglers assist migrants in crossing international borders without official authorization and in return for compensation. People smugglers are guides who escort migrants to and from specific points, drivers who transport migrants in trucks or boats, staff who operate safe houses for migrants, guards who protect migrants on their journeys, or coordinators who handle the logistics of smuggling operations.[1] Every year millions of migrants hire people smugglers to help them to immigrate (Kyle and Koslowski 2011). In recent years, people smugglers have transported hundreds of thousands of refugees who are fleeing wars and political collapse from the Middle East to Europe.

People smuggling is generally illegal. Over a hundred countries have signed a United Nations protocol that commits signatories to criminalizing people smuggling (United Nations 2011). The European Union has even initiated military operations against smugglers in order to disrupt their activities in the Mediterranean. The illegality of people smuggling reflects widespread moral condemnation of this practice. The Australian Prime Minister Kevin Rudd expressed a common view when he remarked: 'People smugglers are engaged in the world's most evil trade and they should all rot in jail because they represent the absolute scum of the earth. People smugglers are the vilest form of human life' (Missbach and Sinanu 2011, 58). Why do people object to people smuggling? Some critics argue that smugglers take unfair advantage of desperate migrants. On their view, smugglers wrongfully exploit vulnerable migrants. Other critics argue that people smugglers only benefit migrants in order to secure profits and that this is a defective motivation.

We may also have duties to obey the law and people smugglers violate these duties. There are other objections to people smuggling as well.

In this paper, I will argue that people smuggling is sometimes morally justified. Roughly speaking, I will defend the view that people smugglers act permissibly when they help refugees to escape threats to their human rights. I have organized this paper as follows. In Section 2, I will argue that people smuggling can be presumptively permissible. In Section 3, I will respond to the objections that people smuggling is exploitative. In Section 4, I will consider the objection that smugglers have defective motivations. In Section 5, I will rebut the objection that people smuggling is impermissible because smugglers violate the law. In Section 6, I will conclude the paper.[2]

2. Permissible smuggling

In this section, I will argue that people smuggling is *prima facie* permissible in certain cases. By 'prima facie permissible,' I mean that there is a strong reason to believe that people smuggling is *normally* permissible when smugglers satisfy the conditions that I will specify below, but this reason is defeasible. I will examine whether other considerations defeat this reason in later sections of the paper.

To motivate my argument for people smuggling, I want to start with a stylized case. Consider:

> *The Smuggler*. Ibrahim is a smuggler who operates in Libya. Ibrahim rents and staffs cargo ships to transport migrants across the Mediterranean to Europe. One of these migrants is Khaled. Khaled wants to flee the ongoing civil war and political collapse in Libya and claim asylum in Europe. The voyage across the Mediterranean is risky. But Ibrahim is honest with Khaled about the risks and Khaled nonetheless agrees to use Ibrahim's services. Ibrahim's boat transports Khaled and other migrants to the Italian coastline where the smugglers turn off their motors and send out emergency signals. Italian coastguards rescue the passengers and these passengers claim asylum once they reach the mainland. Khaled pays Ibrahim for his services and Ibrahim makes a small profit from this exchange.[3]

It seems to me that Ibrahim acts permissibly in smuggling Khaled to Europe.

Why though? Here is my argument for the claim that Ibrahim acts permissibly:

(1) While Ibrahim has moral reasons to transport Khaled to Europe, it is false that Ibrahim is morally required to transport Khaled to Europe without compensation.
(2) If it is permissible for Ibrahim to refrain from transporting Khaled to Europe without compensation, then it is *prima facie* permissible for Ibrahim to transport Khaled in return to compensation if (i) Khaled consents to use Ibrahim's services, (ii) Khaled benefits from using Ibrahim's services, and (iii) this interaction avoids violating the rights or entitlements of other agents.
(3) Ibrahim secures Khaled's consent, Khaled benefits from the exchange, and Ibrahim avoids violating the rights of third parties.
(4) So, it is *prima facie* permissible for Ibrahim to smuggle Khaled to Europe.

Let me clarify and justify each premise in turn.

The first premise says that Ibrahim can permissibly refrain from smuggling Khaled without compensation. This premise is just the denial of the view that Ibrahim is morally required to unconditionally aid Khaled. To be clear, I believe that Ibrahim has strong moral reasons to aid Ibrahim. Assume that civil war and the breakdown of political order in Libya means that Khaled's rights are insecure and that he is vulnerable to violence from militants. Imagine that Khaled's rights would be better protected if Khaled could reach Italy or another part of Europe. Ibrahim is in a good position to aid Khaled and other refugees by smuggling them to Europe (by 'refugee,' I mean broadly any migrant whose human rights are credibly threatened in his or her country of origin). If you are in a good position to help another person in need, then you have moral reasons to do so irrespective of whether you have any prior relationship or interaction with this person. This explains why Ibrahim has significant moral reasons to smuggle Khaled and other refugees.

But most people think that our duties to aid other people are sensitive to costs. If it is too costly or risky for you to aid other people, then these costs or risks release you from an obligation to aid them.[4] Suppose that you could reduce poverty and suffering by transferring most of your income to the citizens of poor states. This would probably be a good thing to do, but most of us would deny that you are required to give away most of your income because this sacrifice is too costly. Of course, people disagree about what counts as unreasonable or excessive costs. But, while it may be unclear where the threshold lies, there is plausibly some threshold of cost that undercuts duties of assistance. If that is true, then it seems permissible to refrain from helping other people when aiding them generates sufficiently large costs to the duty-bearer.

If duties to aid other people are sensitive to costs, then it is plausible that Ibrahim lacks a duty to assist Khaled and other refugees without compensation. Let's stipulate that, in The Smuggler, it is costly and risky for Ibrahim to smuggle Khaled and other refugees to Europe. For one thing, Ibrahim incurs financial costs in transporting Khaled. Suppose that it is expensive to secure a boat and hire a crew to man it. Ibrahim also confronts risks of punishment from the authorities because people smuggling is illegal. If Libyan or European officials catch Ibrahim, they could imprison him or harm him in other ways. If significant risks and costs undercut duties of assistance, then it seems false that Ibrahim has a duty to unconditionally aid Khaled. Ibrahim could reasonably refuse to bear the costs and risks of aiding Khaled without compensation. This is surely true about people smugglers in general as well. While people may have duties to help refugees in some way, it seems unlikely that bystanders are morally required to smuggle refugees across borders for free in large part because the risks and costs of doing so can be great.

The next step in my argument is that, if it is permissible for Ibrahim to refrain from engaging in smuggling without compensation, then it is *prima facie* permissible for him to participate in smuggling insofar as migrants consent to his assistance, this assistance benefits them, and Ibrahim avoids violating the rights of third parties. Here is the rationale for this premise. If you can permissibly refuse to benefit someone, then it stands to reason that you can permissibly benefit this person in a consensual way. You have moral reasons to benefit other people and, if they consent to these benefits, it is hard to see how you could wrong these people by benefiting them when it was permissible to deny them these benefits altogether. Suppose, as I have argued, that it is generally permissible for Ibrahim to refuse to smuggle refugees to Europe for free. If it is permissible for Ibrahim to refrain from benefiting migrants without compensation, then how could be wrong for Ibrahim to make his assistance conditional on payment for his services if his clients consent to these terms and this interaction does not violate the entitlements of other people?[5] Remember though that premise 2 is a claim about *prima facie* permissibility. I leave open for now whether it is sometimes all-things-considered impermissible in these kinds of cases for you to benefit someone in a consensual manner if, say, these benefits are unfair. But we have reason to believe that it is normally permissible to consensually benefit someone if you can permissibly refuse to benefit this person in the first place.

Let's now turn to the conditions of premise 2 and examine more closely how they apply to The Smuggler. As I noted above, Ibrahim benefits Khaled and other migrants by smuggling him to Europe. If Khaled could reach Europe, his rights would be substantially more secure. While the voyage across the Mediterranean is risky, the expected benefits of migrating to Europe can outweigh the risks of the voyage for Khaled. Thus, the *ex ante* prospects of attempting to migrate to Europe are positive for Khaled and other migrants.[6] Khaled also consents to Ibrahim's services. This fact is important because Ibrahim exposes Khaled to risks by smuggling him to Europe. Normally, it is wrong to expose people to large risks. But we can waive our rights against these risks. If someone imposes risks on you but you consent to these risks, then it may be permissible for this person to expose you to these risks. For this reason, Khaled and other refugees can waive their rights against the risks that Ibrahim imposes on them.

You might worry that the refugees who hire Ibrahim are in a desperate position. Refugees may face the option of contracting with Ibrahim and undergoing a risky ocean voyage or continuing to live in dire conditions in Libya. But a person's consent can be morally transformative even if this person has only bad options. Consider an example. Suppose that a patient, Susan, is suffering from a life-threatening condition. Susan has two options. First, Susan can undergo a risky surgery that might cure her, but it might also kill her. Second, Susan can forgo surgery and face a high probability of death in the next year. If Susan takes the first option and consents to surgery, then it seems permissible for the surgeon to operate on her. Although Susan has terrible options, she remains capable of waiving her right against the risks that the surgeon imposes on her.

The same goes for refugees. Khaled's options are severely constrained. Khaled has the options of continuing to live in Libya under the threat of violence or trying to reach Europe via a dangerous ocean voyage. Yet Khaled retains the normative power to waive his rights against the risks to which Ibrahim exposes him. Perhaps it would still be wrong to expose Khaled to risks if the risks of harm from smuggling substantially outweighed the benefits. Along similar lines, some people think that it is wrong for a surgeon to expose Susan to high risks of harm if the expected benefits of the surgery were low, even if Susan consented to these risks. But I am assuming that the *ex ante* expected benefits of smuggling Khaled outweigh the risks of harm in the case that I am describing. So, Ibrahim avoids wronging Khaled by smuggling him to Italy.

It can still be impermissible to engage in a mutually beneficial and consensual interaction if this interaction violates the rights of third parties. For instance, Ibrahim's actions could impose unfair costs on the citizens of recipient states. When states admit refugees, they must typically spend funds on processing asylum-claims and providing refugees with housing, food, and job training. The migration of refugees can impose other indirect costs on citizens, such as increased competition for jobs, housing, and other scarce goods. However, the citizens of recipient states are often obligated to bear the costs of admitting refugees. Almost every political theorist who writes about the ethics of immigration agrees that states are morally required to admit and resettle *some* refugees. For instance, Michael Walzer, Christopher Wellman, and David Miller argue that states have rights to self-determination that permit them to restrict immigration. But each of these authors accepts that states' immigration policies are constrained by general duties to assist foreigners, and that these duties can require states to admit refugees (Walzer 1984, 48–51; Wellman and Cole 2011, 120–122; Miller 2013).

If states are obligated to admit refugees, then it is generally false that smugglers impose unfair costs on these states by transporting refugees to their borders. Here is an analogy to illustrate why. Imagine that a busing company transports people from a poor inner city to an affluent suburb, and some of these people move to the suburb. The residents of the inner city tend to be much poorer than the residents of the suburb. As a result, they consume more social services and receive more welfare payments than do the average residents of the suburb. Suppose also that these services are financed by local taxes on the suburbanites and the migration of people from the city to the suburb causes taxes to go up. So, by transporting people from the inner city to the suburb, the busing company contributes to imposing costs on people in the suburb. Nonetheless, the busing company does nothing wrong in transporting people from the inner city to the suburb. This is the case because it would be wrong for the suburb to forcibly exclude people from the city and deny them the benefits that other residents receive. If the suburb is obligated to admit them and provide them with benefits, then the busing company avoids violating the entitlements of the suburbanites by contributing to the imposition of these costs.

The underlying principle here is that, if agent A is obligated to bear certain costs, then it is permissible for some agent B to act in a manner that imposes these costs on A. If this principle is correct, then Ibrahim's conduct may refrain from violating the entitlements of recipient states. As I noted above, political theorists generally think that rich democracies have obligations to admit at least some refugees when these refugees face significant threats to their human rights. Khaled faces significant threats to his rights. So, it is plausible that other states, such as affluent democracies, are obligated to admit Khaled. Assume for the moment that European states are obligated to admit the Khaled and other refugees. If European states are required to admit and resettle Khaled, then they are also obligated to bear the costs of his integration. So, the citizens of these states might lack entitlements against the costs that smugglers like Ibrahim help impose on them.

For these reasons, it seems that Ibrahim acts in a permissible manner. To generalize from Ibrahim's case, my argument for the permissibility of people smuggling goes like this:

(1) While people smugglers have moral reasons to transport refugees to states that can adequately protect their human rights, it is false that smugglers are, in general, morally required to transport refugees across borders without compensation.
(2) If it is permissible for potential smugglers to refrain from transporting refugees to other states without compensation, then it is *prima facie* permissible for smugglers to transport refugees in return for compensation if (i) these refugees consent to this interaction, (ii) refugees benefit from interacting with smugglers, and (iii) this interaction avoids violating the rights or entitlements of other agents.

(3) In some cases, refugees consent to interacting with smugglers, refugees benefit from interacting with smugglers, and this interaction avoids violating the rights or entitlements of other agents, such as recipient states.
(4) So, it is *prima facie* permissible to engage in people smuggling in these cases.

Call this: *the presumptive argument* for people smuggling.

The presumptive argument is compatible with the claim that most people smugglers act wrongly in practice. Some smugglers deceive migrants, negligently expose them to risks, kidnap them, and abuse them in other ways. These smugglers are engaged in serious wrongdoing. Furthermore, this misconduct is predictable. People smugglers operate in black markets. Participants in black markets are often unable to appeal to courts or other legal institutions to resolve conflicts or report abuse. Smugglers have incentives to use violence to settle disputes and customers often lack effective recourse if smugglers defraud or exploit them. These incentives explain why many smugglers violate the conditions of permissible smuggling.[7]

But some smugglers avoid wronging their customers. People smugglers usually want to make money. It is a bad business strategy to acquire a reputation for abusing clients and violating their rights. After interviewing smugglers (or 'coyotes') on the Mexico–United States border and the migrants who employ them, the sociologist David Spener reports:

> Migrants typically chose their coyotes based on information they obtained by word of mouth in their social networks …. Thus, to the extent that they need to attract customers, coyotes needed to be concerned with their reputations 'on the migrant street,' since word of failure, imposition of hardships, or malfeasance on their part was likely to travel throughout the region in which they operated.
>
> (2009, 187)

Studies of smugglers operating in Europe and Australia arrive at similar conclusions (Van Liempt 2007; Missbach and Sinanu 2011). In their research on migration to Austria, Veronika Bilger, Martin Hofmann, and Michael Jandl report that 'the commonly held view of smuggled migrants being fully at the mercy of their smugglers in many cases does not correspond to reality' (Bilger, Hofman, and Jandl 2006, 87). Smugglers usually prefer to protect their reputations. To protect their reputations, smugglers generally need to treat their customers well (Palacios 2015; Sanchez 2015). Smugglers often have other incentives to respect the rights of their customers as well. They may want to avoid social stigma and some of them are morally motivated to help migrants. Some smugglers respond to these incentives by protecting the welfare of their customers and securing their voluntary consent.

Smugglers may also avoid violating the entitlements of recipient states in practice. This is the case because many states, particularly affluent democracies, should arguably admit more refuges than they currently do. Why? One reason is that the standard definition of refugees is under-inclusive. According to the definition of refugees embodied in international law, refugees are migrants who are fleeing well-founded fears of persecution on grounds of race, religion, political opinion, nationality, and membership of a particular social group. But people face other urgent threats to their human rights besides persecution. Severe poverty, disease, natural disasters, and war constitute grave threats to human rights as well. Yet migrants are often unable to claim refugee status under international law if they are fleeing these threats, as these migrants are not the victims of political persecution. As a result, states may exclude and deport migrants who face urgent threats in their countries of origin but nonetheless fail to qualify for refugee status.

In addition, rich democracies host a relatively small fraction of the global refugee population. Most refugees in the world live in poor and middle-income states, such as Ethiopia, Pakistan, and Turkey (UNHCR 2015). For example, Lebanon and Jordan currently host more refugees from the Syrian civil war than do all European countries combined (UNHCR 2014). It seems unfair for relatively poor countries to shoulder the burden of hosting and resettling most of the world's refugees, as rich states can more easily bear these costs than can poorer states. But rich democracies have actually implemented immigration policies that make it difficult for refugees and asylum-seekers to immigrate through legal channels. These states have limited offshore applications for asylum, interdicted asylum-seekers in international waters, created international zones in airports and other locations where they can turn back refugees, imposed carrier sanctions that encourage airlines to refuse to transport unauthorized migrants, and enacted other measures to prevent the migration of refugees and asylum-seekers (Gibney 2005). Moreover, the international refugee regime lacks mechanisms to compel rich states to admit more refugees. The international regime is unable to enforce burden-sharing.

People smugglers can help compensate for these defects in the international refugee regime. Smugglers can assist migrants in moving to states where their human rights are adequately protected despite the fact that these migrants would be ineligible for refugee status under international law. For example, suppose that a refugee is escaping war or severe poverty, but she is not a victim of persecution. Under international law, this person lacks a legal claim to asylum. However, the distinction between political persecution and other threats to human rights seems to be morally arbitrary (Gibney 2004; Ferracioli 2014; Betts 2015). If people have moral claims to international protection because their human rights are threatened through persecution, then people also have claims to protection when their rights are threatened in other ways. Imagine that a people smuggler assists a migrant who is fleeing war or destitution to cross borders without official authorization and this migrant's human rights are adequately protected as a result of immigrating. The smuggler in this case helps secure protection for a refugee who merits asylum from a moral perspective, but may not be legally entitled to protected status because it is false that she is escaping persecution.

People smugglers also transport refugees from states that host a disproportionate number of refugees to rich states that host relatively few. In fact, to evade the border restrictions and immigration agents of rich states, refugees often need to rely on the expertise of smugglers. This explains why perhaps a majority of refugees in high-income democracies employed smugglers in order to immigrate. According to some estimates, over 50% of asylum-seekers in European states, such as the Netherlands and Germany, were smuggled there (Koser 2011, 260–262). It seems unlikely that smugglers who transport refugees to rich democracies would be imposing excessive costs on these countries or otherwise violating their rights. Smugglers that transport refugees to rich states may merely be inducing rich states to bear their fair share of the global refugee population. If affluent democracies should accept more refugees than they currently do, then we have reason to conclude that people smugglers who transport refugees to these states avoid violating the rights of recipient states in practice.[8]

3. Exploitation

I will now examine objections to the presumptive argument for people smuggling. One common objection to people smuggling is that smugglers take unfair advantage of vulnerable migrants. Dimitris Avramopoulos, the European Union's Commissioner for Migration, Home Affairs, and Citizenship, contends that the European Union 'cannot allow ruthless smugglers to make a fortune through criminal acts, exploiting migrants looking for a safe passage to Europe' and that 'smugglers are finding new routes to Europe and are employing new methods in order to exploit desperate people who are trying to escape conflict and war' (2015). On this view, people smuggling is objectionable in virtue of the fact that people smuggling is wrongfully exploitative. Call this: *the exploitation objection* to people smuggling.

I agree that people smuggling can be wrongfully exploitative. Consider the following case:

> *Exploitative Smuggling*. Khaled wants to immigrate to Europe and Ibrahim is the only smuggler in the area who can assist Khaled in reaching Europe. If Khaled is unable to immigrate, he will likely suffer serious harm at the hands of militants in Libya. Ibrahim could smuggle Khaled to Europe for the equivalent of $1000 without bearing any large costs or risks. But Ibrahim decides to charge Khaled $5000 instead and Khaled is willing to pay this amount, although Khaled is penniless after paying Ibrahim. Ibrahim makes a significant profit from this exchange.

On a standard definition of exploitation, person A wrongfully exploits person B if A extracts unfair benefits from interacting with B. It seems to me that Ibrahim wrongfully exploits Khaled in this example by extracting excessive benefits from him. As this example illustrates, people smugglers can in fact wrongfully exploit migrants.

But I deny that people smuggling is necessarily or generally exploitative. Consider another case:

> *Fair Smuggling*. Khaled wants to immigrate to Europe. Ibrahim is one of many smugglers in the area who can assist Khaled in reaching Europe, and these smugglers compete against each other for customers. Ibrahim offers to smuggle Khaled to Europe for $1000, which is about the competitive market price for this service. At this price, Ibrahim will make a small profit, although Ibrahim would also incur significant risks and costs by smuggling Khaled. If Khaled declines Ibrahim's offer, he can easily find another smuggler to help him to reach Europe.

It appears that Ibrahim avoids exploiting Khaled in this case. The interaction between Khaled and Ibrahim seems fair. Cases like this one are possible. Therefore, it is false that smugglers *necessarily* exploit migrants.

What is the difference between Exploitative and Fair Smuggling? I lack the space to develop a theory of exploitation here. But we can take some prominent theories of exploitation off the shelf and use them to explain the difference between Exploitative and Fair Smuggling. Here is an illustration. In an influential paper, Valdman (2009) argues that one person A wrongly exploits another person B if and only if A extracts excessive benefits from B when B cannot reasonably refuse A's offer. Valdman says: 'To wrongly exploit someone is to *extract* excessive benefits from him – it is to use the fact that his back is to the wall, so to speak, to get him to accept lopsided and outrageous terms of exchange' (2009, 13). To explain Valdman's account, consider Exploitative Smuggling. In this case, Khaled is unable to reasonably refuse Ibrahim's offer because Khaled confronts a threat of violence if he stays in Libya and Ibrahim is the only person who can help Khaled escape. In other words, Ibrahim has an effective monopoly over a service that is necessary for Khaled to secure his basic rights and Ibrahim uses this monopoly to extract benefits from Khaled.

Moreover, the benefits that Ibrahim gains from interacting with Khaled are excessive. Valdman claims that person A extracts excessive benefits from person B if A charges B more than A would receive in a competitive market. In Exploitative Smuggling, the market for smuggling services is non-competitive because there are few providers in the market. As a result, Ibrahim can charge Khaled more than the competitive market price and thus Ibrahim reaps excessive benefits from the exchange. Valdman's theory of exploitation can explain why Ibrahim avoids exploiting Khaled in Fair Smuggling as well. In this case, Khaled can reasonably refuse Ibrahim's offer because Khaled can easily hire another smuggler to assist him. Ibrahim lacks a monopoly on essential services. Ibrahim also charges the competitive market price for his assistance. So, Ibrahim refrains from extracting excessive benefits from Khaled. Their interaction in this case is non-exploitative on Valdman's theory of exploitation.

It is a difficult empirical question whether actual smuggling markets more closely resemble Exploitative Smuggling or Fair Smuggling. But we have some reason to believe that, in at least *some* cases, the interactions between smugglers and migrants resemble Fair Smuggling. Social scientists who study human smuggling find that smuggling markets are sometimes fairly competitive. There are typically low barriers to entry for engaging in smuggling and the large potential supply of smugglers might make the smuggling market competitive. In his fieldwork on smugglers, Spener observes that no single smuggler or group of smugglers monopolized the market along the United States–Mexico border (2009, 174). Bilger, Hofmann, and Jandl report that the smuggling market in Europe is characterized by 'intense rivalry between smugglers competing for the same pool of clients' (2006, 65). Competition reduces the bargaining power of smugglers. Economists have documented how people can develop mechanisms to mitigate market failures even in the absence of legal regulation (Leeson 2014; Stringham 2015). These mechanisms are present in smuggling markets. For example, while there are information asymmetries between smugglers and migrants, smuggling markets evolve mechanisms that compensate for these asymmetries. Smugglers offer insurance and 'money back' guarantees, and they rely on social ties and reputations to signal information about their trustworthiness (Bilger, Hofman, and Jandl 2006). If smuggling markets are sometimes reasonably competitive, then it is less likely that these markets involve significant exploitation.

So far, I have been relying on Valdman's theory of wrongful exploitation in order to show that it is false that people smuggling is necessarily exploitative. But perhaps his theory of exploitation is incorrect. Even if this theory turns out to be wrong, we still have reason to doubt whether people smuggling is exploitative. To see why, consider legal analogs to people smuggling, such as commercial airlines, busing companies, and shipping companies. It seems that these services are often non-exploitative. Few people argue that commercial airlines are inherently unjust because they exploit their customers. Yet it is hard to see how people smuggling is fundamentally different from these legal services. After all, both people smuggling and commercial airlines or busing companies involve transporting people to new locations in return for compensation, but people smuggling just happens to be illegal. At first glance, if people smuggling is necessarily exploitative, then it seems that we must conclude that airlines or busing companies are necessarily exploitative too. It is unlikely that any theory of wrongful exploitation can show that people smuggling is necessarily or generally exploitative without implying that many ordinary commercial transactions are wrongfully exploitative as well. As it is implausible that airlines and busing companies are necessarily exploitative, we should also reject the view that people smuggling must be exploitative.

4. Defective motives

People often level a related objection against people smuggling. This is the objection that people smugglers are selfish. Commentators in popular discourse frequently criticize people smugglers on the grounds that they are solely motivated by greed. Gerhard Øverland says that smugglers 'help desperate people solely for the money' and that 'smugglers might be liable to condemnation for profit maximization' (2007, 182).[9] In other words, people smugglers have morally defective motivations and this fact explains why people smuggling is impermissible. This objection seems to go:

(1) If person A helps person B for the wrong reasons, then A acts impermissibly.
(2) People smugglers help needy migrants for the wrong reasons, such as profit-seeking rather than other-regarding concern for the welfare of these migrants.
(3) So, people smugglers act impermissibly.

Let's call this *the motivational objection* to people smuggling.

One problem with the motivational objection is that it is unclear why bad motivations would transform actions that would otherwise be permissible into impermissible actions. Many philosophers argue that we should distinguish between the moral status of actions and the status of motives (Mill 1998; Scanlon 2008). Your motives can be defective while your actions are permissible. If you aid people in need solely for selfish reasons, then this impeaches your character and motivations. Your motivations are worse than they ought to be. Yet your actions can still be morally justified. Consider the following variations on The Smuggler. In Variation 1, Ibrahim aids needy refugees in Libya solely in order to make a profit and Ibrahim tries to make as much money as possible. So, Ibrahim only helps refugees to reach Europe for selfish reasons. In Variation 2, Ibrahim wants to make a sufficient income to support himself, but he also assists refugees because he cares about protecting them from harm. Let's stipulate that Ibrahim's activities in Variations 1 and 2 are otherwise identical.

Ibrahim's character and motivations are morally worse in Variation 1 than in Variation 2. Ibrahim's character would be better if he were motivated to assist refugees for other-regarding reasons. But it is difficult to see why this fact would entail that his actions are objectionable. It is more natural to say that Ibrahim's actions are permissible and his motivations are faulty. People can do good things for bad reasons. If we can distinguish between moral evaluations of a person's character and evaluations of their conduct, then my argument in this paper is compatible with the claim that 'smugglers might be liable to condemnation for profit maximization.' This is so because we can condemn the motivations of people smugglers and nevertheless conclude that their actions are permissible. Thus, if a person can perform permissible actions for defective reasons, then premise 1 is false.

We should also reject premise 2. Premise 2 says that people smugglers assist migrants for the wrong reasons, such as the desire to maximize profits. The implication is that smugglers should help migrants for the right reasons, such as a concern for their well-being and a desire to protect their rights. That is, smugglers should act out of other-regarding concern, but smugglers fail to do so. However, while smugglers are generally motivated by the desire to make money, motivations for smuggling can be over-determined. To see how this is possible, consider an analogy. Suppose that someone wants to earn a high income and she trains to become a surgeon in part because surgeons are well paid. But this person also wants to save lives and this fact motivates her to become a surgeon as well. This person's motivations are over-determined. She is motivated both by financial considerations and other-regarding concerns.

The same can hold true for smugglers. The anthropologist Gabriella Sanchez interviewed 'smuggling facilitators' and many of them report that they are motivated by a desire to help migrants. Many smugglers are unauthorized migrants or refugees and they say that they want to assist people like themselves. Sanchez writes:

> Many were adamant that their participation contributes to the wellbeing of others. The recognition of similar experiences to their own among their clients was a constant theme in the interviews .... Among respondents, there was also an ethical element to their participation – namely the assistance provided to people who, as facilitators or clients, would otherwise face high levels of risk and vulnerability.
>
> (2014, 77)

These respondents might be exaggerating their moral motivations. Yet it is surely the case that some smugglers are motivated by ethical considerations. Furthermore, many smugglers report that they engage in smuggling because they have a family to support and they lack alternative employment options. These smugglers are motivated by other-regarding concerns and it is for this reason that they desire a higher income.[10] Thus, a desire to make money and other-regarding concerns are sometimes compatible. Some people smugglers may act for the wrong reasons. But it is false that people smugglers generally act for the wrong reasons.

5. Law-breaking

A final objection to people smuggling is that smugglers violate the law. People smuggling is illegal and states often impose significant criminal punishments on people smuggling. Many people think that it is wrong to break the law. If it is impermissible to break the law, then people smuggling is also wrong. Call this: *the law-breaking objection* to people smuggling.

Philosophers disagree about whether we have content-independent obligations to obey the law (a content-independent duty is a duty to obey laws irrespective of the content of these laws). But let's assume for the sake of argument that we do have content-independent duties to obey the law. Nonetheless, it is doubtful whether law-breaking *per se* involves significant wrongdoing when the law forbids an activity that is not intrinsically impermissible. Consider some examples to illustrate. Suppose that you drive slightly over the speed limit in order to make an appointment in time. Or suppose that you jaywalk in the middle of the night when no one else is around. Or imagine that you drink an alcoholic beverage on the day before your twenty-first birthday and you live in a jurisdiction that prohibits the consumption of alcohol before you are 21. In each of these cases, you have violated the law. Yet it is rather implausible that you have engaged in serious wrongdoing in any of these cases.

Perhaps we do have moral reasons to obey the law as such. But, as the above cases suggest, these reasons must be relatively weak. It is not intrinsically wrong to go slightly over the speed limit or jaywalk when doing so avoids endangering others. In cases where it is not independently morally wrong to engage in the conduct in question, it appears that even minor considerations can override the reasons to comply with the law. For example, I suspect that most people would say that your promise to meet your friend for lunch at a certain time could justify going slightly over the speed limit if you are late and you avoid imposing excessive risks on other people. If my arguments in this paper are correct, we should reject the view that there is anything intrinsically wrong with people smuggling. Furthermore, smugglers have moral reasons to engage in people smuggling and these reasons are often far from minor. The smuggling of refugees is often necessary to protect human rights and there are strong reasons to protect the human rights of vulnerable people. If even weak reasons can defeat content-independent duties to comply with the law, then the reasons to engage in people smuggling can surely defeat the moral reasons to obey the law at least in cases where the people smuggling in question satisfies the conditions of permissible smuggling.

Let's suppose that the foregoing claims are wrong and that we in fact have weighty content-independent duties to obey the law. Even if we have stringent duties to obey the law, most people would still agree that you could permissibly violate the law in exceptional cases. Consider the necessity defense in the common law. A necessity defense holds that a person's illegal conduct is justified if this conduct prevented a greater evil than her conduct caused, there was no legal alternative action that would have averted the harm, and this person was not responsible for creating the threat that she helped avert (Mancilla, forthcoming). When successful, a necessity defense nullifies criminal liability, as this defense establishes that the illegal behavior in question was all-things-considered permissible or required. People who think that we have weighty duties to comply with the law agree that it is in principle permissible to violate the law in cases of necessity.

People smuggling can sometimes satisfy the conditions of a necessity defense because people smuggling may be necessary to rescue people from grave harm. Consider the following case:

> *Rescue Smuggling.* Moutassem is a resident of Damascus, Syria. There is intense fighting between the government and rebel armies near Damascus. This fighting poses a grave threat of injury or death to Moutassem. Even if Moutassem avoids injury, the government will soon conscript him and force him to serve in the army, which will also expose him to high risks of harm. To avoid imminent conscription and collateral harm from the fighting, Moutassem plans to immigrate to Turkey. If Moutassem can reach Turkey, he will be reasonably safe and his human rights will be better protected. But imagine that Turkey has begun closing the border to Syrian refugees. Moutassem locates a smuggler, Anas, who can secretly transport Moutassem across the border to Turkey. Suppose also that it is unlikely that Moutassem can locate another smuggler who can help him escape before he is conscripted. Anas successfully transports Moutassem to Turkey and Moutassem pays Anas for his assistance.

In this example, Anas rescues Moutassem from a threat of harm in Syria by smuggling him to Turkey. Anas' actions are necessary to prevent severe and imminent harm to

Moutassem and Anas refrains from causing equal or greater harm to anyone else in smuggling Moutassem. It is easy to imagine that there are no alternative legal means of preventing harm to Moutassem. As I noted in Section 2, many refugees are unable to immigrate to another state legally and it is implausible that Anas has another way of averting the threat to Moutassem. Anas also lacks any responsibility for the threat of violence against Moutassem. Anas has a strong necessity defense for violating the law. If the necessity defense is valid, then Anas' actions may still be permissible despite the fact that he violates the law.

An objector might argue that Anas is unable to appeal to a necessity defense because Anas receives compensation for his services. This objector could argue that, while smuggling Moutassem out of Syria is necessary to protect Moutassem from harm, it is false that Anas needs to charge for his services in order to aid Moutassem. So, Anas' actions are not in fact necessary to protect Moutassem from the threat of harm. But we can imagine version of the case in which Anas must charge for his services in order to continue to rescue people like Moutassem from harm. Imagine that, unless Anas charges for smuggling, he will be unable to pay for the expenses of smuggling Moutassem and other refugees out of Syria. Smuggling can be expensive. Smugglers may need to pay for transportation, food and shelter for migrants, false documents, and so on. If Anas must receive compensation in order to finance his smuggling operations, then compensation is necessary to avert harm to Moutassem and other refugees that Anas assists.

The law-breaking objection fails to condemn people smuggling in general. On any reasonable view, it is morally permissible or even morally required to violate the law in certain cases. It seems to me that we need only weak moral reasons to justify violating laws that prohibit actions that are not intrinsically wrong. If that's true and the rest of my arguments in this paper are correct, then people smuggling can often be permissible despite its illegality. But, even if we need strong moral reasons to justify illegal behavior, people smuggling can meet this justificatory burden in certain instances, as people smuggling may be necessary to prevent grave harm.

6. Conclusion

According to a common view, people smuggling is an evil trade. But my argument in this paper suggests that an indiscriminate condemnation of people smuggling is mistaken. People smuggling can be a permissible means of assisting migrants. There is also some reason to believe that many smugglers actually act in a permissible way in practice, especially when these smugglers aid refugees in crossing borders. Some smugglers help compel rich states to bear their fair share of the world's refugee population and assist refugees in evading threats to their human rights. People smuggling can be a weapon of the weak against immigration restrictions that prevent refugees and other migrants from escaping threats to their lives and liberties.

Notes

1. For a description of the different activities that people smugglers engage in, see Sanchez (2015, 69).
2. Few philosophers or political theorists have considered the ethics of people smuggling. Gerhard Øverland (2007) and Kukathas (2013) briefly discusses the ethics of people smuggling

in arguing that the smuggling of refugees should be decriminalized. But, apart from these exceptions, I am unaware of a sustained treatment of the ethics of people smuggling.
3. For a description of an actual, similar case, see Yeginsu (2015).
4. For defenses of the claim that general positive duties are sensitive to costs, see Wellman and Simmons (2005), Fabre (2006), and Barry and Øverland (2013).
5. Zwolinski (2008) and Wertheimer (2011, chap. 6) argue in favor of a related principle that they call the 'nonworseness claim.' The nonworseness claim says that it cannot be worse for person A to interact with person B than to refrain from interacting with B if this interaction is mutually beneficial, A and B consent to the interaction, and this interaction has no negative effects on third parties. If the nonworseness claim is true, then it follows that Ibrahim acts permissibly in assisting Khaled in return for payment, as it was permissible for Ibrahim to refrain from aiding Khaled for free. However, I will take no stand here on whether the nonworseness claim is always true. As I will discuss in Section 3, it seems at least possible to me that it can be worse to interact with people than to abstain from interacting with them if these interactions are exploitative.
6. This aspect of the case is realistic. Many migrants incur substantial risks of harm in order to immigrate successfully and believe the benefits are worth the risks (Mbay 2014).
7. For an analysis of how black markets can generate violence, see Miron (1999).
8. I have argued that people smuggling is sometimes permissible. But might people smuggling also be obligatory? The answer to this question seems to be 'yes.' Suppose that a person, A, faces a dire and imminent threat to A's human rights and that another person, B, can only avert this threat by smuggling A to another country. Assume also that B can smuggle A without bearing excessive costs or risks and there is no other viable way of aiding A. It is plausible to me that B is required to smuggle A across borders in this case. But the conditions under which people smuggling is obligatory are probably much rarer and exacting than the conditions under which it is permissible. For this reason, I focus on permissible rather than required people smuggling in this paper.
9. It is unclear whether Øverland actually endorses this objection to smuggling or is merely entertaining it for the sake of argument.
10. In fact, people smuggling is not particularly lucrative. According to Sanchez, most smugglers engage in smuggling on the side in order to supplement their incomes and few of them experience upward economic mobility (2014, 74–75).

Disclosure statement

No potential conflict of interest was reported by the author.

References

Avramopoulos, Dimitris. 2015. "Recent Smuggling Incidents in the Mediterranean." The European Commission Press Release Database. http://europa.eu/rapid/press-release_SPEECH-15-3262_en.htm.

Barry, Christian, and Gerhard Øverland. 2013. "How Much for the Child?" *Ethical Theory and Moral Practice* 16 (1): 189–204.

Betts, Alexander. 2015. "The Normative Terrain of the International Refugee Regime." *Ethics & International Affairs* 29 (4): 363–375.

Bilger, Veronika, Martin Hofman, and Michael Jandl. 2006. "Human Smuggling as a Transnational Service Industry: Evidence from Austria." *International Migration* 44 (4): 59–93.

Fabre, Cecile. 2006. *Whose Body Is It Anyway?* New York: Oxford University Press.

Ferracioli, Luara. 2014. "The Appeal and Danger of a New Refugee Convention." *Social Theory and Practice* 40 (1): 123–44.

Gibney, Matthew. 2004. *The Ethics and Politics of Asylum*. New York: Cambridge University Press.

Gibney, Matthew. 2005. "Beyond the Bounds of Responsibility: Western States and Measures to Prevent the Arrival of Refugees." *Global Migration Perspectives* 22: 1–23.

Koser, Khalid. 2011. "The Smuggling of Refugees." In *Global Human Smuggling: Comparative Perspectives*, edited by David Kyle and Rey Koslowski, 256–272. Baltimore, MD: John Hopkins University Press.

Kukathas, Chandra. 2013. "In Praise of the Strange Virtue of People Smuggling." *Global Policy*. http://www.globalpolicyjournal.com/blog/03/05/2013/praise-strange-virtue-people-smuggling.

Kyle, David, and Rey Koslowski. 2011. "Introduction." In *Global Human Smuggling: Comparative Perspectives*, edited by D. Kyle and R. Koslowski, 1–32. Baltimore, MD: John Hopkins University Press.

Leeson, Peter. 2014. *Anarchy Unbound: Why Self-governance Works Better Than You Think*. New York: Cambridge University Press.

Mancilla, Alexandra. Forthcoming. "What the Old Right of Necessity Can Do for the Contemporary Global Poor." *Journal of Applied Philosophy*. doi:10.1111/japp.12170.

Mbay, Linguère. 2014. "Barcelona or Die: Understanding Illegal Migration from Senegal." *IZA Journal of Migration* 3 (21): 2–19.

Mill, John Stuart. 1998. *Utilitarianism*. Ed. Roger Crisp. New York: Oxford University Press.

Miller, David. 2013. "Border Regimes and Human Rights." *The Law & Ethics of Human Rights* 7 (1): 1–23.

Miron, J. A. 1999. "Violence and the U.S. Prohibition of Drugs and Alcohol." *American Law and Economics Review* 1 (1): 78–114.

Missbach, Antje, and Frieda Sinanu. 2011. "'The Scum of the Earth'? Foreign People Smugglers and Their Local Counterparts in Indonesia." *Journal of Current Southeast Asian Affairs* 30 (4): 57–87.

Øverland, Gerhard. 2007. "The Illegal Way In and the Moral Way Out." *European Journal of Philosophy* 15 (2): 186–203.

Palacios, Simón. 2015. "Coyotaje and Drugs: Two Different Businesses." *Bulletin of Latin American Research* 34 (3): 324–339.

Sanchez, Gabriella. 2014. *Human Smuggling and Border Crossings*. New York: Routledge.

Sanchez, Gabriella. 2015. "Human Smuggling Facilitators in the US Southwest." In *The Routledge Handbook on Crime and International Migration*, edited by Sharon Pickering and Julie Ham, 275–286. New York: Routledge.

Scanlon, Thomas. 2008. *Moral Dimensions*. Cambridge, MA: Harvard University Press.

Spener, David. 2009. *Clandestine Crossings: Migrants and Coyotes on the Texas–Mexico Border*. Ithaca, NY: Cornell University Press.

Stringham, Edward. 2015. *Private Governance: Creating Order in Economic and Social Life*. New York: Oxford University Press.

United Nations. 2011. *Protocol Against the Smuggling of Migrants by Land, Sea and Air, Supplementing the United Nations Convention against Transnational Organized Crime*. https://www.unodc.org/documents/southeastasiaandpacific/2011/04/som-indonesia/convention_smug_eng.pdf.

UNHCR. 2014. *Syrian Refugees in Europe*. Geneva: United Nations.

UNHCR. 2015. *The 2014 Statistical Yearbook*. Geneva: United Nations.

Valdman, Mikhail. 2009. "A Theory of Wrongful Exploitation." *Philosophers' Imprint* 9 (6): 1–14.

Van Liempt, Isle. 2007. *Navigating Borders: Inside Perspectives on the Process of Human Smuggling INTO the Netherlands*. Amsterdam: University of Amsterdam Press.

Walzer, Michael. 1984. *Spheres of Justice: A Defense of Pluralism and Equality*. New York: Basic Books.

Wellman, Christopher Heath, and Phillip Cole. 2011. *Debating the Ethics of Immigration: Is There a Right to Exclude?* New York: Oxford University Press.

Wellman, Christopher, and John Simmons. 2005. *Is There a Duty to Obey the Law?* New York: Cambridge University Press.

Wertheimer, Alan. 2011. *Rethinking the Ethics of Clinical Research*. New York: Oxford University Press.
Yeginsu, Ceylan. 2015. "The Promise of Europe Lures Syrians and Smugglers." *The New York Times*. http://www.nytimes.com/2015/02/06/world/europe/promise-of-europe-lures-syrian-refugees-and-smugglers-to-turkish-coast.html?_r=0.
Zwolinski, Matt. 2008. "The Ethics of Price Gouging." *Business Ethics Quarterly* 18 (3): 347–378.

Who owes what to war refugees

Jennifer Kling

ABSTRACT
The suffering of war refugees is often regarded as a wrong-less harm. Although war refugees have been made worse off in severe ways, they have not been wronged (in some cases), because no one intentionally caused their suffering. In military parlance, war refugees are collateral damage. As such, nothing is owed to them as a matter of justice, because their suffering is not the result of intentional wrongdoing; rather, it is the regrettable and unintended result of necessary and proportionate wartime actions. So, while the warring national or extra-national groups might help war refugees, such aid is regarded as humanitarian, not as justice.

I challenge the view that war refugees are harmed but not wronged when those harms directly result from necessary and proportionate wartime actions. War refugees are innocent bystanders, and so are an exception to the principle that permits defense by any necessary and proportionate means. Just as an individual may not kill or seriously harm an innocent bystander to save herself, so too national or extra-national groups may not create refugees to win a war. If such groups do create war refugees during the legitimate pursuit of military goals, they have wronged those refugees, and so owe them recompense.

War refugees[1] have been harmed in many ways – they have lost their jobs, their homes, much if not all of their physical property, their economic stability, and often many of their loved ones. Furthermore, they have not been harmed by some natural phenomena, such as a tsunami or a tornado. Rather, the harm that they have sustained is the result of war.[2] War is not a natural phenomenon – it is a complex social and political phenomenon that is created and sustained by people who are organized (by other people) into national and extra-national groups of various kinds. However, despite this fact, the suffering of war refugees, in the western just war tradition, is often regarded as a sort of wrong-less harm; that is, although war refugees have been made worse off in many severe ways, they have not been wronged (at least in some cases), because no one intentionally caused or brought about their suffering.[3] As Paul Ramsey writes, 'direct attacks on a civil population can never be justified; but … a good many incidental deaths and extensive collateral damage to civil society *may still be knowingly done*' (2002, 159, emphasis added).

In typical military parlance, war refugees are often regarded as collateral damage. And as the collateral damage of legitimate military actions, nothing is owed to them as a matter of justice, because their suffering is not the result of intentional wrongdoing; rather, it is the regrettable and unintended result of doing what is right.[4] As explicitly stated in the 1907 Hague conventions,

> the attacker may, given the presence of innocents in a combat zone, do anything that it would be permissible to do if there were no innocents there – subject to the restrictions entailed by the principle of proportionality ... This ... allows ... the shelling or bombing of defended areas containing innocents so long as those innocents are not targeted. (as quoted in Zohar 2014, 157)

According to the western just war tradition, then, unintentionally but knowingly harming civilians in war is 'overall permissible as a lesser evil ... [when] the overriding reasons are proportionately weighty' (Lazar 2015, 5). War refugees are sometimes the unintentional byproduct of war, and, at least sometimes, they are created via necessary and proportionate wartime actions (*viz*, by actions that are right, in the parlance of the western just war tradition).[5] It is these cases that I am concerned with – the cases where war refugees are the unintentional byproduct of right (or legitimate) wartime actions. In these cases, while the national or extra-national groups that are at war might – and often do! – help such war refugees as a matter of course, they do not do so because they owe the refugees anything as a matter of justice. After all, they have neither wronged the refugees, nor are they politically responsible for the refugees – they have, all things considered, acted permissibly. Rather, the groups at war provide aid to such war refugees because of humanitarian impulses, feelings of generosity, or, more cynically, because it makes for good press.

In what follows, I challenge the view that war refugees are harmed but not wronged when the harms in question directly result from necessary and proportionate wartime actions. War refugees, I argue, are innocent bystanders, and so are an exception to the principle that permits defense by whatever means are necessary and proportionate. Just as an individual may not kill or seriously harm an innocent bystander in order to save herself, so too national or extra-national groups may not create war refugees in order to win a war. If such groups do create war refugees in the course of the legitimate pursuit of their military goals, they have wronged those refugees, and so owe them recompense. Importantly, this conclusion holds despite the widely accepted – at least in the western just war tradition – doctrine of double effect.[6]

Assuming that my arguments are successful, I close with a, brief discussion of the implications of my view for the ongoing refugee crisis. The current debates about the refugee crisis, especially in the American political arena, are deeply misguided, because they reflect a fundamental refusal to consider and acknowledge the fact that the refugees have been wronged by American military actions and so are owed some degree of recompense by the United States. In addition, the relevant national and extra-national groups that are actually handling the current refugee crisis ought to be sensitive to the justice of refugees' claims: they are not looking for a handout, but for what they are owed. In more concrete terms, this means that many of the contemporary governmental policies surrounding refugee aid, resettlement, and return need to be altered and/or changed in their entirety.

1. The harming and wronging of war refugees

It is uncontroversial that war refugees have been harmed, *viz*, made worse off; my more controversial claim in this section is that they have been wronged, *viz*, their rights have been violated, as well.[7] Now, many war refugees have been both harmed and wronged; refugees that are created via unnecessary and disproportionate wartime actions, for instance, are commonly recognized in the western just war tradition as having been both harmed and wronged (Rodin 2004; Walzer 1977, esp. 144–146; McMahan 2009; Lazar 2015). As I said above, however, I am here concerned with war refugees who are created by necessary and proportionate wartime actions.

For instance, let us consider a defensive military action; the targeted bombing of a city in which a military base is located. Let us assume that the military base needed to be destroyed in order for the defending group to block the annexation of their land and people by an aggressive, illegitimate, extremist religious group. Let us further assume that there was no other less harmful way to take out the military base; sending in combat troops would have resulted in excessive casualties and would have created 'boots-on-the-ground'-type complications, sending in a commando unit to take the base by stealth would not work because of the religious group's close-knit nature, and furthermore would result in reprisals against the local civilian population, etc. Conversely, military estimates claimed that the bombing would create only a few hundred to a thousand refugees at most. Under such circumstances, it seems that the defending group's bombing the base was the right thing to do; it was both necessary and proportionate, and it was a legitimate military target.[8] However, as a byproduct of the bombing, the civilians of that bombed and ruined part of the city are now war refugees. Have they been wronged by the military actions that displaced them?

The western just war tradition would say no. Sheldon M. Cohen writes that, in such cases, 'the rights of innocents are defeasible' and so the harm caused to civilians is 'morally licit' (1989, 3). Put another way, Noam Zohar argues that, in such situations, 'soldiers are allowed to kill [or harm] non-combatants as long as that is not what they intend' (Zohar 2014, 158). Such refugees are collateral damage; although their creation is regrettable and undesirable (in the sense that we wish it had not been necessary), so long as their creation is unintentional, it is permissible, according to the doctrine of double effect (DDE). F.M. Kamm states the traditional view quite simply:

> The DDE has been used to distinguish morally between (1) terror bombing civilians in wartime and (2) bombing military targets, foreseeing with certainty that civilians will be killed [and harmed] as a side effect. The first is said to be impermissible; the second may be permissible [if the conditions set forth by the DDE are met]. (2012, 24)

As Michael Walzer (1977, 152–153) argues, the DDE, at its heart, claims that well-intended actions with bad side effects are permissible, so long as the action itself is good (or at least neutral, if that is possible), the good done by the action outweighs the harm done, the harm is not the means to the good end, and the harm is not intended as an end in itself.[9] By these criteria, the creation of the war refugees that we are considering is permissible: the bombing of the military base is a legitimate act of war, the good of destroying the military base outweighs the harm of creating a few hundred to a thousand war refugees, the creation of the war refugees is not the means to the end of destroying the military base[10], and the creation of the war refugees is not intended by the defensive military force, although it is foreseen. Thus, while the war refugees have been harmed, they have not been wronged, because their creation is 'morally permissible all things considered', according to the standard interpretation (in the just war tradition) of the DDE (Lippert-Rasmussen 2014, 139).[11]

This doctrine has been widely accepted by military forces around the world, in no small part because military forces must fight around civilians, and so it is inevitable that some civilians will be harmed or killed in the fighting. As John Locke (2004, II.176–181) points out, short of the ability to fight battles on the sea, away from all civilians, military forces must either accept the DDE or accept responsibility for all of the wrongs that they do to un-consenting civilians in the course of their wars. (A third option, of course, would be to accept pacifism, but that is not a conclusion that a just war theorist is likely to accept.) Now, wide acceptance is no guarantor of moral correctness; however, there is no doubt that the DDE is widely accepted in warfare, and that its wide acceptance is part of what makes modern warfare morally possible.[12] So, we can view the DDE within the just war tradition as follows: it does not always make harming civilians permissible, because it is possible for the proportionality calculation to come out such that the harm done outweighs the good achieved, but it does sometimes, in many if not in most instances, make it the case that civilians who are harmed by legitimate acts of war are not thereby wronged as well.[13] Noam Zohar agrees that this is the standard view: he writes that 'permission for such unintended killing [of civilians] is commonly asserted by citing the classical doctrine of double effect (DDE)' (2014, 156).

However, this response to the creation of war refugees by necessary and proportionate defensive military actions, while common in the just war tradition, is mistaken. The war refugees in our example have been wronged as well as harmed, and so they are owed recompense of some sort. The reason that the war refugees have been wronged is that they are innocent bystanders, and as such are an exception to the rule – common from discussions of both individual self-defense and the just war tradition – that permits any defensive actions that are both necessary and proportionate. As David Rodin (2002, 81) writes, this rule (on which the DDE is based) has innocent bystanders as its boundary; that we may not kill innocent bystanders, even to defend ourselves from being killed, is a deep and important moral intuition that provides a clear edge to our thinking about self- and other-defense. As Judith Jarvis Thomson puts it plainly, 'it is everywhere impermissible to kill a bystander in defense of one's life' (1991, 298).[14] Further support for this view, which I shall refer to as the innocent bystander exception, comes from Thomas Nagel (1972, 130–132) and, more recently, Jeff McMahan (2009, 110–115), who both argue that, while the defensive killing of those individuals who objectively pose a threat is permissible, the defensive killing of those individuals who are not involved in the altercation at issue, who just happen to be physically nearby when it occurs, is impermissible. Thus the innocent bystander exception maintains that, to the extent that innocent bystanders are harmed by a nearby defensive action, they are the victims of injustice (in the sense that their rights have been violated), even when that defensive action is necessary and proportionate. Innocent bystanders, when they are inadvertently harmed by acts of self- and other-defense, are wronged as well.

To see this, consider a case analogous to the targeted bombing case described above. Here, imagine that Al Capone, the mob boss who ran Chicago during Prohibition, has been targeted by a rival mobster. This rival mobster knows nothing of the ways in which Capone has benefitted Chicago and the men who work for him (Capone was famous for, among other good works, donating to various charities [Bergreen 1994], offering pensions to his employees [Kobler 1992], and opening soup kitchens during the Depression [Murray 1975]); he is simply interested in taking over Capone's lucrative mob businesses. Capone is walking down a sidewalk in Chicago when the rival mobster attacks. Capone ducks behind a nearby car for shelter, which happens to contain a family – two partners and a child. Capone can defend himself against the rival mobster by shooting through the car. He would rather not shoot through the car, because he recognizes that his doing so will result in his severely, if not lethally, wounding the members of the family, but that is the situation in which he finds himself. If Capone defends himself against the rival mobster by shooting through the car, and in the process wounds the family members, has he wronged as well as harmed those family members? I think yes, because Capone's right to defend himself stops where the innocent bystanders (the two partners and their child) begin. Incidentally, Yitzhak Benbaji (2005) and George Fletcher (1973) agree that the innocent bystander exception holds in cases like this one, and that Capone may not kill innocent bystanders to save himself or others, even if doing so is necessary to his or others' defense.

And crucially, this case is closely analogous[15] to the targeted bombing case (especially when we consider that many governments that engage in defensive warfare are not that dissimilar from mob bosses). In the targeted bombing case, the civilians just so happen to be in the way of the enemy military base that the defensive military forces need to destroy in order to defend themselves and their people. The defending group would rather not engage in the targeted bombing of the centrally – located military base, because they recognize that their doing so will destroy civilians' houses and livelihoods, if not civilians' lives and families, but that is the situation in which they find themselves. So, I conclude that like Capone shooting through the car, when the defending group bombs the military base, they have wronged as well as harmed innocent bystanders, civilians whose only connection to the altercation at issue is incidental physical proximity. (Civilians, after all, cannot be expected to control who is in residence in their city, just like the family in Chicago cannot be expected to control who walks near their car.) As Daniel Statman concludes, 'just as individuals are not allowed to kill innocent bystanders in order to save their own lives, collectives [defending groups] are not allowed to do so either' (2006, 63).[16] The defending group's right to defend themselves stops where the innocent bystanders begin. Thus, the war refugees have been wronged as well as harmed by the military actions that displaced them, and so are owed recompense of some sort.

2. Other considerations and various responses

This is a stark conclusion, one that appears to have many serious consequences for both the just war tradition and the ongoing international refugee crisis. As of June 2015, the UNHCR (The United Nations Refugee Agency) estimated that there were roughly 58 million refugees and refugee-like persons[17] worldwide, and estimated that that number would grow to 60 million by 2016.[18] Over half of those refugees are children (UNHCR 2015b). While not all of these persons are refugees due to necessary and proportionate defensive military actions, surely a great number of them are. And if that is correct, then they are owed recompense of some sort for having been wronged by the military actions that displaced them. As the revisionist just war theorist David Rodin argues, 'it may be right to burn a farmer's field to stop a wild fire, but still the farmer's rights have been violated ... for which he deserves some form of compensation or apology' (2002, 52). Furthermore, if we follow the implication of my position above, the group that owes them recompense is the group that is responsible for wronging them.[19] Just as Al Capone, we might think, owes recompense to the family that he wronged, so too does the defending group owe recompense to the war refugees that they wronged. I am happy with this: it is my view that when defending forces wrong innocent bystanders in the course of prosecuting just defensive wars (as surely they must), then those defensive forces owe the innocent bystanders recompense for the wrongs they have suffered at the defensive forces' hands (or bombs or drones, as the case may be). Of course, this is not to say that the aggressive forces involved in the relevant war owe nothing. Insofar as the aggressive forces *also* wronged the innocent bystanders – by starting the war, if nothing else – they also owe them recompense; but it is to say that it is not only the aggressive forces that are at fault for the wrongdoing suffered by the war refugees.

2.1. Transference of responsibility

But perhaps my view is mistaken; surely there is a response to be made that lets the defending group off the hook. After all, they, like Al Capone, were simply defending themselves from aggressors who forced them to choose: either fight back in self-defense, or die. And in fact, this intuitive reaction does contain the seeds of a plausible response. Both the Al Capone case and the targeted bombing case could be what are sometimes referred to as transference of responsibility cases.[20] Let us take the Al Capone case first. We might say that, because the rival mobster started the firefight (in philosophical parlance, he is the aggressor), the responsibility for the harm and wrong done to the family members transfers to him. According to this view, although Al Capone pulled the trigger, he is not morally responsible for the wrong suffered by the family members, because he did not intend to shoot them. Rather, the rival mobster, through his attack on Capone, put the family in harm's way, and so is morally responsible for the subsequent harm and wrong done to them. Analogously, the aggressive extremist religious group started the war, we might say, and so responsibility for the harm and wrong done to the civilians transfers to them. Although the defensive military forces actually engaged in the targeted bombing run, they are not morally responsible for the wrong that was done to the civilians, because they did not want to create war refugees. Rather, the extremist religious group, through their illegitimate, aggressive war, put the civilians in harm's way, and so are morally responsible for the subsequent harm and wrong done to them. Moral responsibility in both cases, according to this response, transfers from the defender to the aggressor, because of the aggressor's initial responsibility for the start of the fight.

While this is a plausible response, it is not ultimately successful. Moral responsibility does not transfer in this way when the agents in question are both (or all) moral agents, and the defending moral agent/s had a choice about how to respond. To say that the defending moral agents literally had no choice in how to respond is to deny the reality of the situation, which is that they faced a difficult, but real, moral choice. As Walzer puts it, when the choice is between defense and capitulation, 'there is no reason to think that the decision was predetermined ... stand in imagination with [the defender], and one can still feel a sense of freedom' (1977, 10). Because there was a choice, moral responsibility in these kinds of cases, rather than transferring, spreads to both the aggressor and the defender who chooses to take up arms in response. The rival mobster certainly aggressed against Capone; perhaps Capone, all things considered, took the correct course of action in defending himself against the rival mobster. However, in the course of doing so, he did wrong the innocent bystanders. The fact that Capone was aggressed against does not erase his moral responsibility for his subsequent choices, although it does allow that he was coerced into a morally difficult choice. Given this, it is more accurate to say that both Capone and the rival mobster, rather than one or the other, are morally responsible for the harm and wrong done to the innocent bystanders.

Analogously, the same goes for the defensive forces and their targeted bombing of the military base in the city. The fact that the defending group was aggressed against does not erase their moral responsibility for their military actions; although they may have taken the correct action, all things considered, in bombing the military base, they still bear moral responsibility for the civilians that they harmed along the way. So, it is more accurate to say that both the aggressive religious extremist group and the defending group, rather than one or the other, are morally responsible for the harm and wrong done to the civilians (now war refugees), and so both owe the war refugees recompense of some sort. Daniel Statman sums up this conclusion nicely in his discussion of transference of responsibility cases:

> What [the argument from transference of responsibility] seeks to achieve is a kind of denial of the defender's part in the killing, by transferring the killing, so to say, in its entirety, to the aggressor. This transference is supposed to show that although the killing carried out by [the defender] is unjustified, it is still somehow morally all right, or at least imposes no blame upon [the defender], because all blame is absorbed, so to say, by [the aggressor]. But this just doesn't work. That [the aggressor] is to blame for creating a situation in which [the defender] can save his life only by killing an innocent person, does not entail that [the defender] cannot also be blamed for actually killing that person. (Statman 2006, 71)

Both Statman and I agree that the argument from transference of responsibility cannot absolve the defending group of moral responsibility for the wrong done to the war refugees. The best it can do is show that aggressors *as well as* defenders are morally responsible for the wrongs done to innocent bystanders by defenders in the course of defending themselves. But this is not enough to get the defenders off the hook; they have still wronged the war refugees, and so still owe them recompense of some sort. So much for transference of responsibility.[21]

2.2. Moral dilemmas

But perhaps there is another, more general, response that will work: perhaps both the Capone case and the targeted bombing case are moral dilemma cases. Moral dilemmas, simply put, are those situations where, no matter what an agent does, she does something wrong (Walzer 1973, 160; Statman 1995, 16; Sayre-McCord 2013, 1–2). If Capone has a strong obligation to himself or others to stay alive, in addition to the equally strong obligation, outlined above, to avoid severely injuring or killing innocent bystanders, then perhaps he is stuck in a moral dilemma. And analogously, if the defending group has a strong obligation to defend themselves and their people, in addition to the equally strong obligation to avoid severely harming or killing innocent bystander civilians, then perhaps they too are stuck in a moral dilemma. However, if these are moral dilemma cases, then it is true that no matter what Capone or the defending group does, they have still failed to meet one of two equally strong obligations (i.e. they have failed to not wrong the innocent bystanders); this is what makes it a dilemma case. But this conclusion is precisely in line with my argument – I am happy to say that the defending group, whatever else they have done, have wronged the war refugees. So, to say that Capone, or, somewhat more plausibly, the defending group, is caught in a moral dilemma does not help matters. If it is a moral dilemma, then my contention that the defending group has wronged the war refugees is fundamentally correct, albeit not the whole ethical story.

Still, understanding the targeted bombing case as a moral dilemma may yet impact my conclusion. If an agent is in a moral dilemma through no fault of her own[22], such that no matter what she does she fails to meet one of two (or more) equally strong obligations, then perhaps it follows that she is not to blame for her wrongdoing. After all, there was nothing less wrong that she could have done, so to blame her for what she did would be to fail to recognize the nature of her dilemmatic situation. This is certainly a plausible response to the presence of a moral dilemma; as Nagel writes, 'the idea of a moral blind alley is a perfectly intelligible one … it is naïve to suppose that there is a solution to every moral problem with which the world can face us' (1972, 143–144). And it is for precisely this kind of reason that I put my argument in terms of recompense, rather than blame. I am not arguing that we should blame the defending group; rather, I am simply arguing that they owe recompense to the war refugees created by their targeted bombing run, because they wronged those refugees. The war refugees have a legitimate claim against the defending group because that group violated, or at least infringed on, their property and security rights, and so the defending group owes them recompense in response to that claim. To say this is entirely different from saying that the defending group ought to be blamed for engaging in the targeted bombing run that created those war refugees. In short, owing recompense and being blameworthy can come apart in some instances, and this is one of those times. So even if we accept that this is a moral dilemma case, and we accept that moral dilemma cases cancel out blameworthiness, it does not follow from those two claims that the defending group does not owe recompense to those innocent bystanders who are wronged by their targeted bombing run.

2.3. Moral remainders

However, the existence of moral dilemmas is subject to much debate in the philosophical literature[23], and so I do not want to rest my argument on either their existence or their applicability to the issue at hand. Instead, I agree with Thomson (1991), Benbaji (2005), Rodin (2002), and Fletcher (1973), among others, that the innocent bystander exception holds in cases of individual self- and other-defense, and also maintain that, by analogy, the exception holds in cases of defensive military action. But perhaps both I and those theorists who argue for the innocent bystander exception are mistaken in thinking that killing or severely wounding innocent bystanders is impermissible. Perhaps what we should say instead is that such actions are permissible, if not required, depending on the circumstances, but that they leave behind a moral remainder.[24] First popularized by Bernard Williams, the notion of a moral remainder is the idea that, in cases where 'something morally disagreeable is clearly required', the 'moral disagreeableness of these acts is not merely cancelled' by the conclusion that they are morally required, but properly produces, in the person/s who does the morally disagreeable act, agent-regret and a recognition that some reparation is owed to the victims of the act (1982, 60). Feeling the weight of such a moral remainder, according to Williams, may well be irrational, but he concludes that it is nevertheless moral: 'we must rather admit that an admirable moral agent is one who on occasion is irrational' (1965, 113).

In line with this view, we might say that the defending group does what needs to be done in bombing the military base – perhaps their actions are not only permissible but morally required, given their obligations to defend themselves and their people – but that they should recognize that their doing so involves committing a morally disagreeable act (turning innocent bystanders into war refugees). The thought is that the justification for bombing the military base – the group's defense of itself and its people – does outweigh the moral reasons for not bombing the military base – that it will violate the rights of hundreds, if not a thousand, innocent bystanders and turn them into war refugees. However, this outweighing does not thereby cancel out the wrong done to the civilians; to see this, consider that

> the victims can justly complain that they have been wronged. It is undeniable ... that the agent [the defending group] has ... let them down, or used them. It may be that when it is all explained, they understand, but it is foolish to say, even then, that they have no right to complain. (Williams 1982, 59–60)

The war refugees have been wronged; that is the moral cost of the targeted bombing run, and it does not get erased by the countervailing reasons to bomb. And that cost comprises a moral remainder that makes it appropriate for the defending group to recognize both that they did the necessary thing and that they owe recompense to the war refugees that they created.

The subject of moral remainders is a complicated one, and there is some question about whether they are best understood in terms of justice, or in some other way. Williams himself certainly thought that moral remainders were most likely to appear in political cases like the one we are considering: as he writes, 'there are features of politics which make it specially liable to produce ... such a remainder' (1982, 60). These features of politics, according to Williams (1982, 60–61), include both the common clashing of rights-based justifications and the common clashing of consequentialist, or maximizing, justifications with rights-based justifications. So whether we understand the targeted bombing case as a clash of rights (the defending group's defensive rights versus the civilians' security and property rights) or as a clash between consequences and rights (what will lead to the best state of affairs overall versus the civilians' security and property rights), it is clearly a political problem, and hence one which is likely to produce a moral remainder. So then, is the proposed moral remainder in the targeted bombing case best understood in terms of justice? Does it make sense to claim, as I have done, that the war refugees are owed recompense by the defending group as a matter of justice? I do think that this would be an appropriate way to understand and make sense of the proposed moral remainder, both because justice is the normative concept most closely linked with politics, and because justice has essentially to do with giving people what they are owed (either because that is what is fair, or because that is what they deserve, or because that is what they are entitled to as rights-holders, etc.). If this is a moral remainder case, then, we should understand that moral remainder in terms of justice; the agents who caused the relevant harmful wrongs to the civilians, despite the fact that they did what was required, owe those civilians recompense, and that 'owing' falls under the domain of justice.[25]

2.4. Moral repair

Much like moral dilemmas, though, the existence of moral remainders is highly contentious in academic philosophy, and so I do not want to rest my argument on their both existing and being as Williams (1965, 1982) describes.[26] Perhaps Williams is mistaken, and there are no moral remainders, and perhaps I am mistaken, and it is sometimes permissible to harm innocent bystanders in the course of conducting defensive military actions, either because some version of the DDE holds, or for more broadly consequentialist reasons. However, even if both of these claims are correct, there is still hope for my argument. This hope takes the form of the idea of moral repair, a concept more familiar in philosophy of race than philosophy of war. Consider the following passage from Beverly Daniel Tatum, wherein she compares racism to pollution: 'To say that it [racism] is not our fault does not relieve us of responsibility, however. We may not have polluted the air, but we need to take responsibility, along with others, for cleaning it up' (1997, 6). Here, Tatum points out that sometimes we are responsible for fixing, or repairing, large-scale wrongs that we did not cause, especially when our inaction makes it worse. Responsibility for the wrong in question and responsibility for its repair do not always go hand-in-hand, especially when the problems (like racism, like pollution, and like, I argue, the ongoing refugee crisis) are almost overwhelmingly large and complex. Of course, the idea that people are sometimes morally obliged to repair wrongs for which they are not at fault does not hold across the board; as Tatum (6–7) suggests, this concept primarily applies to those large-scale, complex wrongs in which everyone, or at least most people, are implicated to a minimal degree. But, to the extent that the ongoing refugee crisis is an issue of this kind, the concept of moral repair can be helpfully applied to it.

So even if we assume, contrary to my own position, that the targeted bombing run is a case where, all things considered, the defending group did what they ought to do, and that the defending group did not wrong the civilians, even though they harmed them, this does not close off the response that the defending group has some responsibility to help repair the problem. Of course, according to this line of argument, the defending group does not have a special or unique responsibility to help repair the problem; nevertheless, it is true that they, like every other group that is able to help, do bear some responsibility for helping to fix the ongoing refugee crisis, because of the general duty of moral repair. This is especially true when we remember the overwhelmingly large and complex nature of the problem. At the time of writing, about 1 in every 122 humans is a refugee (UNHCR 2016, 9). Refugees face serious, life-threatening problems: 61% lack basic shelter, 59% lack sufficient food and clean drinking water, and 50% of children refugees have no education available at all (20). The UNHCR, the main international organization dedicated to protecting refugees and solving refugee problems, is vastly underfunded – humanitarian aid is simply not keeping up with demand. In the first half of 2015, the

UNHCR was able to resettle just 33,400 refugees in foreign countries, and help 63,800 return to their countries of origin (UNHCR 2015a). That is roughly 97 thousand cases solved, out of 58 million refugees and refugee-like persons. Given these numbers and the severity of the problems that refugees face, although no one defending group may have caused the harms and wrongs that the refugees suffer, they nevertheless, along with others, bear the responsibility for alleviating those harms and wrongs. Sometimes, justice demands that you fix things that you yourself did not cause.

Ultimately then, war refugees are owed recompense as a matter of justice, even when they are created by defensive military actions that are necessary and proportionate. This is because such refugees are innocent bystanders, and so have been wronged by the relevant military actions. Alternatively, we could say that the war refugees are the focus of a moral remainder; but if this is the case, then they are still owed recompense as a matter of justice, because recompense to them by the agents that engendered the moral remainder is, as Williams might put it, morally appropriate. Or, we could say that the refugees are the focus of moral repair. In this case, they are still owed help as a matter of justice, because moral repair is a responsibility that falls to everyone who is in a position to help when the undeserved harms in question are human-caused, widespread, complex, and severe.

3. Implications and policy recommendations

Once we recognize that war refugees are owed recompense as a matter of justice, it becomes apparent that current governmental policies surrounding refugee aid, resettlement, and return are woefully inadequate. First, it should be clear that the United States, in particular, as well as other so-called Global North[27] states, have an obligation not to block war refugees from entering their borders.[28] This is partially because the Global North has been deeply involved in the military conflicts that have created the majority of the world's war refugees[29,30], and partially because the Global North is in a position to help. As I argued above, those who are responsible for the wrongs that war refugees have suffered owe those refugees recompense; the Global North is, in many cases, one of the parties responsible, and so owes recompense.[31] Since the wrongs suffered by war refugees include primarily the violation of their security rights, the Global North ought to compensate them in part by providing them with opportunities to regain and enjoy those rights (which allowing war refugees to enter Global North states would presumably do, given the high levels of individual security generally enjoyed by Global North populations). Furthermore, as I discussed in the previous section, the Global North has a moral responsibility to help repair the ongoing refugee crisis, precisely because the problem is so large and complex and because it is in a position to help. As Simon Caney points out, in discussing who is responsible for solving the problem of climate change (another large-scale, complex problem), 'the most advantaged [wealthy individuals and countries] *can* perform the roles attributed to them, and, moreover, it is reasonable to ask them (rather than the needy) to bear this burden since they can bear such burdens more easily' (2005, 769, emphasis added). Global North states could alleviate the worst of the refugee crisis by opening their borders, and they *can* accommodate many, many refugees within their borders[32], and so it is reasonable to ask them to do so, or at the very least it is reasonable to ask them not to block war refugees from entering their borders, given the responsibility of moral repair that everyone shares in cases like these.

This contrasts sharply with the rhetoric in the American political arena after the refugee crisis made national news during the summer of 2015: consider the response by many of the leading presidential candidates at the time that we should suspend entrance for all refugees (Kaplan and Andrews 2015), and the responses of many US state governors that they would attempt to block any and all refugees from resettling in their states (Seipel 2015). Their oft-repeated concern is the worry that it would be possible for a terrorist to enter into the United States under the guise of being a war refugee, and so the US should block all refugees from entrance. Putting aside the factual inaccuracies of this worry (the vetting process for refugees to be resettled in the US is one of the most comprehensive worldwide [Cone 2015; 'Refugee Processing' 2015]), its underlying logic is mistaken. The implied premise of the worry is that any risk is too much to take; but this is simply false, given both the US's obligation to provide war refugees recompense and its ability to do so. As Walzer (1977, 155–156) ably points out, fulfilling our moral obligations to others requires us to take certain risks. The risk that the US, and the Global North in general, is obliged to take in regards to war refugees is, at the very least, not to block them from entrance.

Secondly, there is a clear global obligation to fully fund the UNHCR. Currently, the UNHCR is only able to cover 47% of its comprehensive budget (UNHCR 2016, 19). Functionally, this means that the UNHCR has to prioritize the funds it does have toward emergency situations (e.g. the South Sudan situation, the Iraq situation, and the Syria situation), and must leave underfunded long-term refugee solutions such as support for self-reliance, sustainable development initiatives, educational initiatives, peacemaking initiatives, and political stabilization efforts (19–21). This is problematic because it means that, essentially, the root causes of the refugee crisis are not being addressed; the UNHCR is forced instead to act as little more than a band-aid for the vast majority of refugees and refugee-like persons. However, the UNHCR is in the best position to address the root causes of the refugee crisis; thus, funding it fully would go a long way toward discharging the Global North's obligation to provide recompense to war refugees.

Of course, there is a difference between arguing that the Global North states are obligated to fully fund the UNHCR, and arguing that any individual or national or extranational group has the standing to enforce that obligation. I have not argued for this latter claim, and in the absence of such an argument, the UNHCR should continue to be funded voluntarily. However, just because some action should be voluntary (i.e. not enforced by some outside authority), it does not follow that that action is not obligatory. To borrow an example from Daniel Layman (2012), we might think that parents getting their children vaccinated should be a voluntary choice, *and* that it is obligatory for those parents to do so. Assuming, then, that we can separate obligations from enforcement, I conclude that while no one may have the standing to enforce the Global North states' fully funding the UNHCR, those states are nevertheless obliged to do so. And while this may seem somewhat minimal, it does represent an important moral shift; historically, moving closer to justice begins with a recognition that certain actions are obligatory, rather than optional or supererogatory.[33] Fully funding the UNHCR is one such action.

Thirdly, every war refugee, as a matter of justice, should be provided with a chance for a minimally decent life, that is, a life where they can regain and enjoy their basic security and property rights. Such provision is what recompense for the severe wrongs that they have suffered requires. To see this, consider what recompense means: it means to provide redress or restitution, to replace or re-constitute what was wrongfully destroyed or taken.[34] To re-constitute war refugees' severely violated security and property rights, they must be provided with a chance for a minimally decent life. At a minimum, this will involve securing the human rights of war refugees, as outlined in the Universal Declaration of Human Rights (UDHR). However, while the UDHR (1948) provides the relevant conceptual scheme, it does not – and cannot, given its nature – provide the specific economic, social, and political details desired by those whose job it is to formulate and enact such baselines. But even though the formulation of such worked-out policies is extraordinarily difficult, it is not politically impossible, as evidenced by the implementation of crime victim compensation programs throughout the United States ('Crime Victim Compensation' 2014). Such compensation programs are without a doubt controversial, but, I contend, they are better than no baseline at all. And much like crime victims are owed compensation as a matter of justice, so too are war refugees owed a chance for a minimally decent life as a matter of justice. Thus, in part because we have evidence that we can, we have an obligation to work out the relevant details, within the structure provided by the UDHR, so that refugees receive the recompense that they are owed.

Although I have neither the space nor the expertise to work out the relevant details here, a few recommendations come easily to mind. No war refugee should be in a refugee camp, meant to be a temporary solution before return, resettlement, or local integration (UNHCR 2006, 105–109), for more than two to five years.[35] There are now third-generation refugees living in the camps (UNHCR 2012), and the average stay in a refugee camp is roughly seventeen years (Smith 2004). In addition, when return to their state of origin is not possible, war refugees must be either resettled or locally integrated within two to five years, and such resettlement or integration must include not only physical relocation, but also social, economic, and political support. While it might seem demanding, such support is owed to war refugees not as a matter of optional or supererogatory humanitarian aid, but as a matter of justice; they have been wronged, and so deserve recompense.

Notes

1. I here rely on the UNHCR's definition of a refugee as a person who has been forced to flee their country of nationality or habitual residence because of a well-founded fear of being persecuted because of their race, religion, nationality, membership in a particular social group or political opinion, and who is unable or unwilling to avail themselves of the protection of their country, or to return there, for said fear of persecution (UNHCR 2011, esp. 3–4). This definition coincides nicely with our commonplace, everyday understanding of who counts as a refugee, and it is that group of people with whom I am concerned in this paper. Of course, there are interesting problems with determining who, precisely, should count as a refugee; much of the philosophical literature surrounding refugees focuses on just this question. But while that is an important topic, I leave it aside for the purposes of this paper, which is focused primarily on war refugees' moral status.
2. This contrast is important to note for two reasons. First, although people can be harmed by natural disasters, they cannot be wronged; wrongdoing requires human agency (McMahan 2009). Secondly, it is worth pointing out explicitly that war is not a natural disaster, despite its often being characterized as such (consider talk of being 'swept up in' or 'engulfed by'

war, the metaphor of war as a 'rampaging beast', the idea that war is 'inevitable' and 'unstoppable,' etc). To speak, and think, of war in this way is to let the human agents involved in its creation and perpetuation off the moral hook, so to speak.
3. This is similar to the view that many people have about the harms that black people suffer as the result of institutional racism. Although it is undeniable that black people are made worse off by such racism, and that such racism is a social and political phenomenon, many people argue that no one intentionally caused the harms in question, and so black people have not been wronged, even though they have been harmed (see Boxill [2003] and Coates [2014] for explication and critical discussion of this view). Of course, this is mistaken in a multitude of ways: first, political institutions are often designed with racist agendas, in which case, the harms suffered by black people are intentionally caused, and second, institutional policies can perpetuate racist implicit biases in individuals, which can cause those individuals to non-intentionally infringe on the rights of black people. See Megan Mitchell (2014) for more on this last point.
4. While the First Additional Protocol to the Geneva Conventions (1977) discusses the ways in which parties to armed conflict should minimize incidental harm to civilians, it does not, at any point, straightforwardly outlaw incidentally harming civilians. The implication seems to be that if all of the stated precautions are taken, then the resulting military action, even if it does incidentally harm civilians, is permissible, at least according to the laws of war. See especially Articles 48, 51, and 57.
5. As Michael Walzer (1977, esp. 138–159) argues, necessary and proportionate wartime actions are not merely the least wrong actions that militaries can do under the circumstances. Rather, it is right for militaries to take all necessary and proportionate actions in pursuit of their legitimate war aims. (Of course, what counts as a legitimate war aim is a separate and further question.)
6. For one useful discussion of the doctrine of double effect, see Philippa Foot (1967). The doctrine of double effect has been widely discussed; while I cannot survey the literature here, Foot's article is a useful starting place for those interested in the topic. See also, among others, Kamm (2012).
7. For a useful discussion of the distinction between harming and wronging, see Joel Feinberg (1990). For those readers who do not want to think of wronging in terms of rights, think of it instead in terms of being harmed in such a way that recompense is owed. So long as we can make a distinction between cases where recompense is owed and cases where recompense is not owed, I think that we can keep the distinction between wronging and harming, regardless of whether we cash that distinction out in terms of rights or not.
8. I do not mean this example to be contentious; if you find it unconvincing, feel free to change the example until it becomes, for you, a case of a necessary and proportionate military action that also has the byproduct of creating war refugees. If you think that there is no such case, then I suspect that you already agree with the core claims of my argument.
9. According to philosophical tradition, the doctrine of double effect is first worked out in writing by Thomas Aquinas (1965, II.64.7) in his *Summa Theologica*. There are various understandings and interpretations of the doctrine of double effect throughout the philosophical literature; indeed, the doctrine of double effect has engendered quite a philosophical cottage industry. Walzer's interpretation, and those like it, remain fairly standard in contemporary just war theory; for that reason, I focus primarily on it. (A quick count reveals that over three-fourths of the articles and books cited for this paper reference Walzer's interpretation of the doctrine of double effect.) However, it is worth noting that not all interpretations of the doctrine of double effect are amenable to my argument. In particular, Warren Quinn's formulation regards the doctrine as providing a kind of amplifying effect: as he understands it, the doctrine of double effect holds that 'the pursuit of a good tends to be less [morally] acceptable where a resulting harm is intended as a means than where it is merely foreseen' (1994, 176). Here, actions are not made morally permissible or impermissible in part by the intentions of the relevant actors; rather, morally acceptable acts are made somewhat less (or more) acceptable by the actors' intentions, and (presumably) morally unacceptable acts are made even more (or

less) unacceptable by the actors' intentions. So it is not clear that Quinn's version of the doctrine of double effect would permit the unintended but foreseen creation of war refugees in the first place, insofar as it does not make certain kinds of (unintended but foreseen) harming straightforwardly permissible. In which case, he should agree with me that the war refugees have been wronged, because the violation of their security rights is not made permissible by his version of the doctrine of double effect. Conversely, if he maintains that the creation of war refugees is morally acceptable in such a case, I would refer him to my argument below about the inviolability of the rights of innocent bystanders.

10. To see this, consider that the location of the military base did not play a major role in the defensive military force's decision to bomb the base (except as a deterrent). If the defenders could have bombed the base without harming any civilians, they would have done so, and in fact would have been happy to do so. The creation of the war refugees, in other words, does not serve the defenders' cause; it is no part of their plan, but rather is an undesired and unwished-for side effect. Contrast this with killing the large man in the famous trolley case; there, the death of the large man is part of the pusher's plan, and is in fact necessary to his plan's success, considered as a whole. See Judith Jarvis Thomson (1985, esp. sections VI and VII) for more on this point.
11. As Lippert–Rasmussen rightly points out, the harm done to the civilians is only permissible 'all things considered' so long as proportionality is built into the doctrine of double effect. Walzer (1977) builds proportionality into his understanding of the doctrine; other theorists, such as Jeff McMahan (2009, 18–32), maintain that it is a separate, and further, principle of *jus in bello*.
12. As Keith Pavlischek argues, both international law and the just war tradition put the 'moral and legal obligation to enemy civilians … [precisely] where the traditional doctrine of double effect locates it: Never attack them directly. Never attack them as means to get at the enemy. And limit the unintended harm likely to fall upon them to that which is proportional to the just tactical and strategic objective … within these limits, harms caused to enemy civilians are permissible' (2010, 34).
13. Support for this view in the just war tradition can be found in, among others, Thomas Aquinas (1965, *Summa* II.64.7), Michael Walzer (1977, 152–154), Thomas Hurka (2005), and Brian Orend (2006, 105–140). Of course, there are different interpretations of the doctrine of double effect, and not all readings of it support this conclusion (see especially Note 9). For a good summary of various interpretations of the doctrine of double effect, as well as some good discussion regarding which interpretations are 'standard' and which are 'non-standard,' see Woodward (2001).
14. See also her Section 4, for an interesting and helpful discussion of the different variations of innocent bystander cases.
15. Of course, the two cases are not perfectly analogous. The sheer amount of wronging that occurs in each case is different (a family being severely wronged versus hundreds of people being severely wronged), and the Capone case is a spontaneous act of self-defense, while the defensive military bombing is pre-calculated. However, these differences, in my view, are not enough to make a crucial difference to our overall moral assessment of the cases. They might make a difference to precisely how bad we determine the relevant wronging to be, but I do not think they are sufficient to change the overall view that both cases are instances of wronging innocent bystanders.
16. Statman, in further exploring the framework of self-defense, writes that 'harming an innocent person is morally forbidden whatever the results' (2006, 61). While he does not use the language of wronging and rights here, to say that harming innocent bystanders is 'not allowed', that it is 'morally forbidden whatever the results', is, I take it, to say something quite similar to my own claim, which is that such actions are rights-violations and thus wrong the bystanders.
17. The UNHCR (2015b) distinguishes in this way between those persons who have received official refugee status from the UNHCR, and those who have applied for refugee status but who have not yet been processed, due to both the limited bureaucratic capacities of the UNHCR and the extraordinary strain currently being placed on the organization. For the purposes

of this paper, I will not distinguish between refugees and refugee-like persons; morally, I think, they are all refugees.
18. The number reported in the text does not include stateless persons (persons who have never been citizens of any state), who are also of concern to the UNHCR. All told, the population of concern to the UNHCR, as of June 2015, was 59.5 million (2015b).
19. As Joel Feinberg (1978) points out, in most standard cases of individual rights-violations, we think that it is the wrongdoer who owes recompense to the victim, even when the wrongdoer was coerced into violating the victim's rights. In discussing his famous cabin in the woods case (where a hiker breaks into a cabin to save himself from an approaching killer storm), Feinberg writes that 'almost everyone would agree that you [the hiker] owe *compensation* to the homeowner for the depletion of his larder, the breaking of his window, and the destruction of his furniture. One owes compensation here for the same reason one must repay a debt or return what one has borrowed' (102, emphasis in original). In other words, the rights-violation by the wrongdoer incurs a corresponding obligation of compensation, an obligation that falls to the wrongdoer because his actions are what incurred it. As Feinberg puts it a page later, if I blow up an innocent child in the course of defending myself, my actions might well be justified; however, 'I would have a strong obligation to set things straight somehow with her parents' (103). While there might be some instances where the obligation to compensate does not fall to the wrongdoer – presumably, this is why we purchase certain kinds of insurance – in the ordinary run of things, the obligation to compensate is borne by the person or persons whose action/s incurred that obligation in the first place. And this is true even when the persons in question are coerced into, or are justified in, violating others' rights. I elaborate more on these points below.
20. These types of cases are also sometimes called shifting responsibility cases. For an interesting discussion of this type of argument in the context of human shields, see Michael Moore (1989).
21. Importantly, my argument here does not take into account degrees of responsibility. While you might agree that both the aggressors and the defenders are responsible for the wrongs in question, and so both owe duties of compensation, you might maintain that the aggressors are more responsible, and so their duty of compensation is lexically prior and/or larger than that of the defenders. While I am not sure whether responsibility admits of degrees in this way, I am perfectly happy to admit that if it does, it might well turn out to be the case that the aggressors' obligation to compensate is, at the least, lexically prior to that of the defenders. In which case, the defenders' obligation might only kick in, so to speak, if the aggressors both fail to meet their obligation and it cannot be enforced by an outside party. I elaborate on this point below, as it does have implications for the practical recommendations that I offer at the end of the paper. Thanks to an anonymous reviewer for bringing this point to my attention.
22. Many theorists claim that the 'through no fault of their own' clause is essential, or at least strongly related to, something's being a *true* moral dilemma. See, among others, Walzer (1973, 160–161), David Daiches Raphael (1981, 64–66), Thomas Nagel (1972), and Walter Sinnott-Armstrong (1985, 322). Whether this aspect of theorizing about moral dilemmas is correct or not, though, has no bearing on my argument, because my conclusion holds regardless of whether the defending group is in a moral dilemma or not.
23. For discussion of this debate, see, among others, Sayre-McCord (2013), Conee (1982), Walzer (1973), Ross (1939), Sidgwick (1907), and Kant (1964).
24. Typically, individual self-defense against unjust aggression is viewed as permissible, but not required. However, Williams (1982, 57–62, 1965, 110–114) points out that in many political cases, we view self- and other-defense as required; to fail to defend in such cases would be to fail to do what is right, all things considered. Nevertheless, he maintains that such right actions can still carry with them moral remainders. Additionally, Walzer in places seems to take up the view that political or military defense can sometimes be morally required. See especially his discussion of the Winter War (1977, 70–73).

25. I follow David Sussman (2013) here, who argues that, in cases where there is a moral remainder, recompense of some sort is appropriate, even though the agent who brought about the moral remainder did what she ought to do.
26. For worries about moral remainders, see, among others, Susan Wolf (2004), Jay Wallace (2013), and Joseph Raz (2012).
27. Global North states are sometimes referred to as 'first-world' countries or 'developed' countries. Alison Jaggar (2014) and Thomas Pogge (2008) have successfully argued that these terms are derogatory and oppressive; so, following their lead, I shall refer to them instead as Global North states.
28. My argument as stated extends only to war refugees. While I do believe that the United States and the Global North should also make provision for migrants and climate change refugees, nothing I have said in this paper straightforwardly supports this more sweeping conclusion (although an argument analogous to mine could, it seems to me, be made regarding climate change refugees). Thanks to an anonymous reviewer for bringing this point to my attention.
29. The Global North has been deeply involved in the recent and on-going conflicts in Afghanistan, Iraq, and Syria, which is where roughly one-third of the world's refugees and refugee-like persons are from. See, among others, the U.S. Department of State's report on the Iraq conflict (2006), V. Felbab-Brown (2012), Thomas Pogge (2008), Helen Stacy (2007), and the BBC's (2015) report on worldwide displacement. In addition, the US and other Global North states have also been integral in the conflicts in Colombia, which accounts for 23% of internally displaced persons (Graham 2015; Barry 2002).
30. Importantly, none of this is to say that the Global North's involvement in these conflicts is altogether wrong, all things considered. If the Global North, and in particular the United States, had not gotten involved in these conflicts, the refugee crisis might be much worse than it currently is. (Such a hypothetical is very difficult, if not impossible, to evaluate, but it strikes me as not completely implausible.) However, it is to say that, as things stand, the Global North, because of its involvement, is partially responsible for the wrongs that many currently-existing war refugees have suffered. Not totally responsible – the aggressor groups share in responsibility for those wrongs – but partially responsible, and that responsibility incurs an obligation of recompense. Thanks to an anonymous reviewer for bringing this point to my attention.
31. Of course, the aggressor groups owe recompense as well, and their obligations of compensation might be lexically prior to the obligations of the Global North (see Note 21). However, given the general unlikelihood of aggressor states and/or groups either voluntarily admitting or being forced – either by their own people or an international tribunal – to fulfill their compensatory obligations to war refugees, practically speaking the obligation will fall on the Global North. Thus, I make recommendations regarding what the Global North ought to do, while bearing in mind that these same sorts of recommendations might well (and probably do!) apply to the relevant aggressor groups as well.
32. Joseph Carens (1987, 2015) argues convincingly that many, if not most, Global North states could, functionally speaking, accommodate very large numbers of refugees.
33. For copious examples, consider both the Women's Suffrage movement and the Civil Rights movement in the United States.
34. For an excellent discussion of recompense, see David Rodin (2002, 44–46).
35. This is an arbitrary deadline; any similar deadline would be equally arbitrary. However, the inclusion of some such deadline is important for two reasons. First, both individuals and groups tend to work better when given a public deadline (Burnett 2015). Insofar as the goal of this paper is to push for recompense for war refugees, then, a deadline is helpful. Secondly, the populations of refugee camps do not, for the most part, enjoy basic security and property rights (Dunn 2015); thus, the more time war refugees spend in such camps, the more wronged they become. So, in order to minimize the wrongs done to war refugees, they need to be returned, resettled, or locally integrated as soon as practically possible. And again, having a deadline is pragmatically useful for achieving that goal.

Acknowledgements

Many thanks to Kiran Bhardwaj, the attendees at the 2015 Concerned Philosophers for Peace conference, the attendees at the 2015 Rocky Mountain Ethics Congress, and two anonymous reviewers selected by guest editors of this issue for their insightful and very helpful comments. Any remaining mistakes or errors are my own.

Disclosure statement

No potential conflict of interest was reported by the author(s).

References

Aquinas, Thomas. 1965. *Aquinas: Selected Writings of St. Thomas Aquinas*. Translated and edited by Robert P. Goodwin. Indianapolis, IN: Bobbs-Merrill.
Barry, John. 2002. "From Drug War to Dirty War: "Plan Colombia" and the U.S. Role in Human Rights Violations in Colombia." *Transnational Law & Contemporary Problems* 12 (1): 161–193.
Benbaji, Yitzhak. 2005. "Culpable Bystanders, Innocent Threats and the Ethics of Self-Defense." *Canadian Journal of Philosophy* 35 (4): 585–622.
Bergreen, Laurence. 1994. *Capone: the Man and the Era*. New York: Simon and Schuster.
Boxill, Bernard. 2003. "A Lockean Argument for Black Reparations." *The Journal of Ethics* 7 (1): 63–91.
Burnett, Dean. 2015. "The power of deadlines." *The Guardian*, April 20.
Caney, Simon. 2005. "Cosmopolitan Justice, Responsibility, and Global Climate Change." *Leiden Journal of International Law* 18 (4): 747–775.
Carens, Joseph. 1987. "Aliens and Citizens: The Case for Open Borders." *The Review of Politics* 49 (2): 251–273.
Carens, Joseph. 2015. *The Ethics of Immigration*. Oxford: Oxford University Press.
Coates, Ta-Nehisi. 2014. "The Case for Reparations." *The Atlantic*, June Issue.
Cohen, Sheldon M. 1989. *Arms and Judgment: Law, Morality, and the Conduct of War in the Twentieth Century*. Boulder, CO: Westview Press.
Cone, Devon. 2015. "The Process for Interviewing, Vetting, and Resettling Syrian Refugees in America Is Incredibly Long and Thorough." *Foreign Policy*, November 30.
Conee, Earl. 1982. "Against Moral Dilemmas." *Philosophical Review* 91 (1): 87–97.
Crime Victim Compensation: Resources for Recovery. 2014. Alexandria, VA: NACVCB (National Association of Crime Victim Compensation Boards).
Dunn, Elizabeth Cullen. 2015. "The Failure of Refugee Camps." *Boston Review*, September 28.
Feinberg, Joel. 1978. "Voluntary Euthanasia and the Inalienable Right to Life." *Philosophy & Public Affairs* 7 (2): 93–123.
Feinberg, Joel. 1990. *Harmless Wrongdoing*. Oxford: Oxford University Press.
Felbab-Brown, V. 2012. "Slip-Sliding on a Yellow Brick Road: Stabilization Efforts in Afghanistan." *Stability: International Journal of Security and Development* 1 (1): 4–19.
First Additional Protocol to the Geneva Conventions. 1977. Geneva: United Nations.
Fletcher, George. 1973. "'Proportionality and the Psychotic Aggressor.'" *Israel Law Review* 8 (3): 367–390.
Foot, Philippa. 1967. "The Problem of Abortion and the Doctrine of the Double Effect." *The Oxford Review* 5: 5–15.

Graham, David A. 2015. "Violence Has Forced 60 Million People From Their Homes." In *The Atlantic*, June 17.
Hurka, Thomas. 2005. "Proportionality in the Morality of War." *Philosophy & Public Affairs* 33 (1): 34–66.
Jaggar, Alison M. 2014. "Introduction: Gender and Global Justice: Rethinking Some Basic Assumptions of Western Political Philosophy." In *Gender and Global Justice*, edited by Alison M. Jaggar, 1–17. Cambridge, MA: Polity Press.
Kamm, F. M. 2012. "Justifications for Killing Noncombatants in War." In *The Moral Target: Aiming at Right Conduct in War and Other Conflicts*, edited by F. M. Kamm, 24–35. Oxford: Oxford University Press.
Kant, Immanuel. 1964. *The Metaphysical Principles of Virtue*. Translated and edited by James Ellington. Indianapolis, IN: Bobbs-Merrill.
Kaplan, Thomas, and Wilson Andrews. 2015. "Presidential Candidates on Allowing Syrian Refugees in the United States." *New York Times*, November 17.
Kobler, John. 1992. *Capone: The Life and World of Al Capone*. New York: Da Capo Press.
Layman, Daniel. 2012. "The Compatibility of Locke's Waste Restriction and his Political Voluntarism." *Locke Studies* 12: 183–200.
Lazar, Seth. 2015. *Sparing Civilians*. Oxford: Oxford University Press.
Lippert-Rasmussen, Kasper. 2014. "Just War Theory, Intentions, and the Deliberative Perspective Objection." In *How We Fight*, edited by Helen Frowe, and Gerald Lang, 138–154. Oxford: Oxford University Press.
Locke, John. 2004. *Two Treatises of Government, and ; A Letter Concerning Toleration*. New Haven, CT: Yale University Press.
McMahan, Jeff. 2009. *Killing in War*. Oxford: Oxford University Press.
Mitchell, Megan. 2014. "'Everything's (At Least) a Little Bit Racist:" An Account of Implicit Bias as Institutional Racism." PhD diss., University of North Carolina at Chapel Hill.
Moore, Michael. 1989. "Torture and the Balance of Evils." *Israel Law Review* 23 (2–3): 280–344.
Murray, George. 1975. *The Legacy of Al Capone: Portraits and Annals of Chicago's Public Enemies*. New York: Putnam.
Nagel, Thomas. 1972. "War and Massacre." *Philosophy & Public Affairs* 1 (2): 123–144.
"Number Displaced Worldwide Hits Record High – UN Report." 2015. BBC (British Broadcasting Company), June 18.
Orend, Brian. 2006. *The Morality of War*. New York: Broadview Press.
Pavlischek, Keith. 2010. "Proportionality in Warfare." *The New Atlantis* 27 (Spring Issue): 21–34.
Pogge, Thomas. 2008. "General Introduction." *Introduction in World Poverty and Human Rights*, 1–32. Cambridge: Polity Press.
Quinn, Warren. 1994. *Morality and Action*. Cambridge: Cambridge University Press.
Ramsey, Paul. 2002. *The Just War: Force and Political Responsibility*. New York: Rowman & Littlefield.
Raphael, David Daiches. 1981. *Moral Philosophy*. Oxford: Oxford University Press.
Raz, Joseph. 2012. "Agency and Luck." In *Luck, Value, & Commitment: Themes from the Ethics of Bernard Williams*, edited by Ulrike Heurer, and Gerard Lang, 133–163. Oxford: Oxford University Press.
"Refugee Processing and Security Screening." 2015. *U.S. Citizenship and Immigration Services*, updated 3 December.
Rodin, David. 2002. *War and Self-Defense*. Oxford: Oxford University Press.
Rodin, David. 2004. "Terrorism Without Intention." *Ethics* 114 (4): 752–771.
Ross, W. D. 1939. *Foundations of Ethics*. Oxford: Clarendon Press.
Sayre-McCord, Geoffrey. 2013. "A Moral Argument Against Moral Dilemmas." Unpublished article, University of North Carolina at Chapel Hill.
Seipel, Arnie. 2015. "30 Governors Call For Halt to U.S. Resettlement Of Syrian Refugees," *NPR* (National Public Radio), November 17.
Sidgwick, Henry. 1907. *Methods of Ethics*. London: Macmillan.
Sinnott-Armstrong, Walter. 1985. "Moral Dilemmas and Incomparability." *American Philosophical Quarterly* 22 (4): 321–329.

Smith, M. 2004. "Warehousing Refugees: A Denial of Rights, a Waste of Humanity." *World Refugee Survey 2004*, edited by Merrill Smith, 38–56. Washington, DC: US Committee for Refugees.

Stacy, Helen. 2007. "Humanitarian Intervention and Relational Sovereignty." In *Intervention, Terrorism, and Torture: Contemporary Challenges to Just War Theory*, edited by S. P. Lee, 89–104. New York: Springer Publishing.

Statman, Daniel. 1995. *Moral Dilemmas*. Amsterdam: Rodopi.

Statman, Daniel. 2006. "Supreme Emergencies Revisited." *Ethics* 117 (1): 58–79.

Sussman, David. 2013. "Is Agent-Regret Rational?" Paper presented at the 47th Chapel Hill colloquium in philosophy, Chapel Hill, November 1–3.

Tatum, Beverly Daniel. 1997. "Defining Racism: Can We Talk?" in *Why Are All the Black Kids Sitting Together in the Cafeteria? And Other Conversations about Race*. 3–17. New York: Perseus Books, LLC.

The Universal Declaration of Human Rights. 1948. Geneva: United Nations.

Thomson, Judith Jarvis. 1985. "The Trolley Problem." *The Yale Law Journal* 94 (6): 1395–1415.

Thomson, Judith Jarvis. 1991. "Self-Defense." *Philosophy & Public Affairs* 20 (4): 283–310.

UNHCR. 2006. "Protracted refugee situations: the search for practical solutions." *The State of the World's Refugees 2006*, edited by the United Nations High Commissioner for Refugees, 105–127. Geneva: The UN Refugee Agency.

UNHCR. 2011. *The 1951 Convention Relating to the Status of Refugees and its 1967 Protocol*. Geneva: The UN Refugee Agency.

UNHCR. 2012. *Dadaab – World's Biggest Refugee Camp 20 Years old*. Geneva: The UN Refugee Agency.

UNHCR. 2015a. *UNHCR Global Trends Report: World at War*. Geneva: The UN Refugee Agency.

UNHCR 2015b. *UNHCR Mid-Year Trends 2015*. Geneva: The UN Refugee Agency.

UNHCR 2016. *UNHCR Global Appeal 2016-2017*. Geneva: The UN Refugee Agency.

U.S. Department of State. 2006. "Iraq." *U.S. Department of State Website*, November 17.

Wallace, R. Jay. 2013. *The View from Here*. Oxford: Oxford University Press.

Walzer, Michael. 1973. "Political Action: The Problem of Dirty Hands." *Philosophy & Public Affairs* 2 (2): 160–180.

Walzer, Michael. 1977. *Just and Unjust Wars*. New York: Basic Books.

Williams, Bernard. 1965. "Ethical Consistency." *Proceedings of the Aristotelian Society: Supplementary Volumes* 39: 103–138.

Williams, Bernard. 1982. "Politics and Moral Character." In *Moral Luck: Philosophical Papers 1973-1980*. Chap. 4. Cambridge: Cambridge University Press.

Wolf, Susan. 2004. "The Moral of Moral Luck." In *Setting the Moral Compass: Essays by Women Philosophers*, edited by Cheshire Calhoun, 113–128. Oxford: Oxford University Press.

Woodward, P.A., ed. 2001. *The Doctrine of Double Effect: Philosophers Debate a Controversial Moral Principle*. Notre Dame, IN: University of Notre Dame Press.

Zohar, Noam. 2014. "Risking and Protecting Lives: Soldiers and Opposing Civilians." In *How We Fight*, edited by Helen Frowe and Gerald Lang, 155–171. Oxford: Oxford University Press.

What do we owe refugees: *jus ad bellum*, duties to refugees from armed conflict zones and the right to asylum

Jovana Davidovic

ABSTRACT
In this paper I focus on duties we owe refugees from conflict zones. I argue that it is important to distinguish between two types of duties one might have with respect to refugees from conflict zones. Belligerents from wars that resulted in excess numbers of refugees, I argue, have a stringent *duty to remedy past harms* and provide for resulting refugees. Other states have a *duty to aid* which is context-dependent and can be in some cases as stringent as the duty to remedy past harms. I argue that making a distinction between the grounds and types of duties different actors have with respect to refugees from conflict zones has significant consequences both for just war theory (and in particular proportionality calculations *ad bellum* and *in bello*), but also for practical questions about how best to discharge our duties to refugees from conflict zones.

In this paper, I ask: what do we owe refugees from conflict zones?[1] I argue that both duties to remedy past harms and duties to aid play a significant role in answering this question.

Regarding duties to remedy past harms, I argue that in cases when a war itself or particular strategies in war create an excess number of refugees, belligerents responsible for that war or those strategies have a stringent duty to provide for the resulting refugees. The discussion of duties to remedy past harms grounds one of my central claims: namely, that what we owe refugees from conflict zones should affect our analyses of *jus ad bellum, jus in bello and jus post bellum*. Acknowledging this is particularly relevant for moving just war theory away from proportionality calculations that over-rely on killing and death in war, and that under-focus on other types of significant harm in war, like displacement.

With respect to the duty to aid, I suggest that even though such duty is grounded in a different set of considerations, in most circumstances (albeit not all), it can be as stringent as the duty to remedy past harms. I argue that even though duties we owe refugees are similarly stringent, making the distinction between duties to remedy past harms and duties to aid can help inform a number of interesting practical questions about how we ought to discharge these duties. For example, this distinction can help us say something meaningful about duties to grant asylum, help staff and finance refugee camps, or aid countries which are accepting the largest numbers of refugees.

I start, in the first section, by examining the distinction between the duty to remedy past harms and the duty to aid. I do that by laying out the distinction between negative and positive duties as well as some common problems that this distinction has faced. This distinction (between the duty to remedy past harm and the duty to aid) acts as a foundation for the rest of my argument, which is two-pronged. The focus of the paper is on duties to refugees emerging out of a duty to remedy past harms. However, I also discuss the duty to aid refugees and the relationship between the two types of duties.

In the second section, I discuss the grounds for the duty to remedy past harms and the consequences of acknowledging that duty. I embrace the idea that we have negative duties towards refugees in cases when our war policies have contributed to growing the refugee numbers. For example, I argue that in some cases, like the case of Iraqi refugees (and to some extent Syrian refugees as well), we in the West, and the US in particular, carry a moral responsibility for the excess number of refugees who the wars we fought produced.

In the third section, I argue that this type of analysis, if truly plausible (i.e. if we can actually do careful studies regarding refugee numbers changing as a result of particular military strategies in war) should affect *jus ad bellum, jus in bello* and *jus post bellum* calculations.[2]

In the fourth section, I compare this duty to remedy past harms with a general duty to aid refugees from conflict zones.[3] If we accept that the grounds to duty to remedy past harms and duty to aid are partially different (albeit similarly stringent) this gives rise to two related worries. First, how do we differentiate between those refugees (from same situations) to which we owe negative duties and those we do not? Second, what duties do we owe the other refugees in similar circumstances? I discuss these questions as well as the claim that the stringency of the duty to aid affects the stringency of the duty to remedy past harms and the best way to discharge that duty.

In the final section, I try to show what my argument means for our responsibilities towards Iraqi (and possibly Syrian) refugees. I argue that those states that have contributed to excess numbers of refugees from Iraq (and Syria) have a duty to provide asylum for those refugees and assistance in the form of staffing, infrastructure and monetary assistance to countries and organizations running refugee camps.

A few preliminary remarks are needed before I can move on to the main argument. First, the question of who is a refugee is not only politically controversial, but also philosophically interesting, because such status commonly implies a number of moral and legal obligations (for more see Blake 2016). Here, I focus on refugees from conflict zones, so I accept the rather common definition, which extends the wording of the *1951 Convention Relating to the Status of a Refugee* to include language about refugees from conflict zones. Thus I will use the term 'refugee' as 'referring to a person that has left the country of their nationality and cannot return because of a founded fear of persecution' (UNHCR 1951) and

> every person who, owing to external aggression, occupation, foreign domination or events seriously disturbing public order in either part or the whole of his country of origin or nationality, is compelled to leave his place of habitual residence in order to seek refuge in another place outside his country of nationality. (OAU 1969)

Second, since my focus in this paper is on refugees resulting from armed conflict, the main example I will be using will be that of Iraqi and to some extent Syrian refugees. I take this to be a particularly interesting case, in part, because Iraqi (and Syrian) refugees are primarily fleeing due to armed conflict violence in the region or persecution and economic conditions that are directly precipitated by armed conflict. The Iraqi/Syrian refugee crisis is not the largest recent crisis, but it is one of the most visible crises for the Global North because of its implications for Europe. In fact, a very small percentage, according to some sources as little as 1%, of refugees is being resettled in the West. A vast majority of refugees instead end up either being sent back or living in refugee camps or being resettled in the Global South or neighboring, often developing, countries (UNHCR 2014). All of that being said, I focus in this paper on refugees who result from armed conflict and who jointly with the (probably unjustified) increased visibility of the Syrian and Iraqi refugees' plight make those useful cases to consider. In other words, I do not mean to imply that this recent crisis is in anyway the worst – even if it is the most visible to those in the West.

Positive and negative duties as a tool for distinguishing between a duty to remedy past harms and a duty to aid

Much of the interesting conversation surrounding the recent so-called European refugee crisis has been about what refugees are entitled to and what duties we owe them. I discuss that question in the rest of this paper and I start by differentiating between two types of duties that we might owe refugees.[4] I believe that there are good reasons to consider the two types of duties to refugees, namely duty to remedy past harms and duty to aid, separately. This is because many of the interesting (practical) questions one might ask about discharging our duties to refugees will have differing answers depending on whether the duty is to remedy a past harm or a duty to aid. The sorts of morally salient facts that ground which agents have a duty to aid refugees and what type of a duty they have as well as how it ought to be discharged are going to vary based on whether or not the agent in question has a duty to remedy past harm or duty to aid or both. For example, a duty to aid refugees is much more closely tied to relative ability and geographic location, than is a duty to remedy past harm. The sorts of morally salient facts that will pick out the agents that have a duty to aid refugees are going to be significantly different in other words than the sorts of facts that pick out those that have a duty to remedy past harm. Possibly more important for us at this point in the argument is that the grounds for these duties, that is, what justifies the claim that there is a duty we owe refugees, are significantly different between the duty to aid and the duty to remedy. This is in part, I believe, because the duty to remedy past harms arises out of the same sorts of considerations as negative duties in general, while the duty to aid is a positive duty.

This is why I start here by looking at the distinction between positive and negative duties. While I am skeptical about the robustness and relevance of the distinction between positive and negative duties in general, I do believe that it is a worthwhile tool for differentiating between some aspects of the duty to aid and the duty to remedy past wrongs or injustices. So in discussing the distinction between positive and negative duties I do not mean to assert anything stronger about the nature of rights and duties than what I explicitly state.

To start, we should make a distinction between talk of positive and negative rights and talk of positive and negative duties. The idea of positive and negative rights seems greatly mistaken for a number of reasons – but the most obvious ones were well discussed in Henry Shue's 'Basic Rights' (1980). The argument against making the distinction between negative and positive rights as opposed to negative and positive duties is that the content of rights is filled out by duties and that a same right can pretty straightforwardly give rise to both positive and negative duties. It makes no sense then to ask whether, for example, a right to basic necessities is a positive or a negative right. The right to basic necessities gives rise to negative duties that I do not burn your entire farm or pollute your well, and it also gives rise – probably more controversially – to at least some positive duties of aid in cases when you are starving. The distinction between negative and positive duties is more plausible, albeit still controversial.

Traditionally the distinction between negative and positive duties is a distinction between a duty to refrain from harming and a duty to aid. But the distinction is not as clear cut as one would want it to be, as numerous cases in the literature have pointed out (see Rachels 1975). Nonetheless, the distinction I want to make between duty to aid and duty to remedy a past injustice can benefit from analyzing the distinction between positive and negative duties. In particular, it seems to me that *some of the conceptual tools* that underpin the distinction between positive and negative duties can be useful in explaining the distinction between the duty to remedy past harm and the duty to aid. For example, Pogge's work on severe poverty as a human rights violation can help us in making sense of the difference in the grounds of our duties to refugees in cases when the refugees are displaced because of our past actions and foreseeable consequences of our past actions and in cases when refugees are displaced for some other reasons (2002, 2004). In his 'Severe Poverty as a Human Rights Violation' Pogge (2004) argues that the duty to remedy a past injustice is more akin to a negative duty than a positive duty. He gives a number of examples in an effort to explain this, including one in which a factory starts polluting a river that is the primary source of clean water and food for the communities downstream. Pogge argues that the factory has a negative duty to refrain from polluting and as such commits a human rights violation when they engage in such polluting. He further goes on to argue that the duties that the factory now has with respect to the local communities' lack of access to basic necessities emerge out of a violation of the negative duty not to destroy access to basic necessities. This is just a part of Pogge's argument. His argument is significantly more complicated and is primarily focused on duties that those of us who participate in the imposition of rules and institutions that act like that factory have. His focus is less so on the question of what duties to remedy past harms we have, but there are good reasons to think that his argument can be either understood as or extended to suggest that the duties we have to remedy harms that emerge out of our previous actions are grounded in similar types of considerations as negative duty not to harm. I turn to that argument next.

Negative duty: remedying past harms

There is an interesting question of whether Pogge's examples are actually cases of negative duties at all. After all there is a straightforward way of understanding negative duties as simply duties one has not to act. But his cases do clearly rest on the intuition that the duty not to cause harm and the duties that result from violations of duty not to harm are grounded in the same sort of morally salient considerations. I stress this because it is the only aspect of the controversial positive vs. negative duty distinction that I rely on, namely I am just using the terminology to point to the distinction between the grounds of duties that emerge from past wrongs and harms and those that do not. As we will see shortly I will argue that it is not simply the resulting harm but also the resulting wrong that explains why and when the duty to remedy is stringent. While the duty is to remedy the resulting harm, it is because one committed a wrong and violated a past duty. This plays an important role in thinking about what our duties are in cases when we harm others, but act with an all-things-considered justification and in cases when we act without such justification. In practice this will be relevant when we ask: what do we owe refugees in cases when we start a (justified) war, knowing there would be a large number of displaced persons and refugees? In other words, this will be relevant when we try to distinguish between what we owe refugees who result from wars that are not just and those that are. I will argue that in both cases we have a duty to remedy past harms because we still cause harm (albeit justified), but we are not responsible for fixing it to the same extent as when such harm is unjustified. To illustrate, consider the following set of cases:

> *Murdering Husband*: Jack decides to throw a bomb out his window and into the street in the hopes of killing his wife who he has grown to greatly dislike. There are a number of bystanders in the area and one of them – Larry – requests that X let him into his house to avoid the explosion. Doing so will increase the risk to X's life to some extent.

Whether or not X has a moral duty to let Larry in will depend on a number of considerations. In the case where X is Jack, it seems like Jack has a duty to take the risk of his action upon himself for two reasons: one, because he is threatening unjustified harm to bystanders and, two, because he is threatening harm to bystanders. Now consider a slightly altered case. If X is not Jack, but some other bystander – then whether or not he has a duty to let Larry in and how stringent that duty is will depend on (a) whether Larry has any alternatives, (b) what those alternatives are, (c) what the risk of harm to Larry is (including the extent of the harm and likelihood of that harm) and (d) what the risk of harm to non-Jack X is. The greater the risk of harm to Larry and the lower the risk of harm to non-Jack X, the greater the obligation to let Larry in. Similarly, if Larry has Jack's house as a practical alternative, then lesser the obligation to let him in. But much of this calculus, I believe, is altered if Jack has a justification for throwing the bomb. Consider the following case.

> *Children Rescuer*: Jack is trying to rescue a group of children from a villain. Jack (correctly, given the evidence) decides that the only way to do so is to throw a bomb out his window- killing the villain and possibly endangering some of the children, and certainly endangering Larry. Larry requests that X let him into his house to avoid the explosion. Doing so will increase the risk to X's life to some extent.

It seems like the morally salient considerations here are altered both in the case where X is Jack and when X is a house-owning bystander. In the case X is Jack, I think there are good reasons, or *a* good reason, to think Jack has a duty to take upon himself the risk of letting Larry in, namely the fact that he is threatening harm, albeit justified, to Larry (and other innocent bystanders). The reasoning here is similar to the reasoning scholars like Jeff McMahan (2004, 2015) and others have employed in related cases regarding inescapable harm. So in the case where some amount of inescapable and indivisible harm has to be distributed between two individuals where one of them is (even minimally) morally responsible for that harm it is more just that the harm be distributed to the minimally responsible individual. In our case, the harm is neither inescapable (Jack is rightly *choosing* to impose it) nor, more importantly, indivisible (Jack can take upon himself some (small) risk of harm to eliminate or minimize risk to Larry). In other words, in the case where Jack has a justification for imposing the risk of harm on Larry, if Jack can take some of the risk of harm on himself to minimize the risk of harm to Larry he ought to do so. Note that this argument is not meant to be a result of solely a lesser evil calculation. In other words, the moral work being done in this case is not solely grounded in the distinction between the amount of harm Larry will escape and the amount of harm Jack will risk. While the difference between the risks of harm is playing a more significant role here than it did in the *Murdering Husband* case – the responsibility for imposing harm (albeit justified) also plays a role. In other words, it is not the case that the reason Jack ought to let Larry in rests solely on the fact that Larry has a greater chance of being killed if he is not let in than Jack does if he does let him in. Even if the risks were comparable, that is, in the case that the risk of harm (extent of harm and chance of that extent of harm) is equal between Jack and Larry, Jack still has a duty to let Larry in.[5]

It is also the case that non-Jack X has a moral responsibility to let Larry in, but the above considerations (a)–(d) are greatly affected, I believe, by the fact that the harm Jack is imposing is justified. For example, in the original case whether or not Jack's house was an (practical) alternative played an overriding role in whether non-Jack X had a moral duty to let Larry in. In the case where Jack has an all-things-considered moral justification for throwing the bomb – the relative risk of harm to Larry, to Jack or to alternative non-Jack X are all significant in answering who (if anyone) has a moral duty and how stringent that moral duty to let Larry in is.

Ultimately, it seems like the sorts of factors that are morally salient in deciding whether Jack has a moral duty to let Larry in are affected by his decision to throw the bomb in the first place. This is the case both when such action is morally justified and when it is not morally justified. The duty is *significantly* more stringent in the case when there is no moral justification for the action that threatens to impose harm on the bystanders, but the duty is still present (albeit much more likely to be overridden) when one does have a moral justification for their actions. This is because saying that an act of intervention (in this case throwing a bomb to save children) is morally justified requires that the act be necessary – that is, that there is no other act that causes less harm that can achieve the same morally worthy aim. In this case, assuming that likelihood of success of Jack's intervention does not change – limiting the risk of harm to those that are not liable to be harmed, namely Larry, is required. After all if Jack chooses to engage in an intervention – a fully justified – possibly even required one – and such an intervention foreseeably produces some amount of harm to those not liable to be harmed, then if Jack can take some of that harm on himself without thereby lowering his likelihood of success he ought to do so. The main point here is that the sorts of considerations that play a role in whether or not one has a moral duty to permit another to enter their residence when letting them enter increases some risk of harm to themselves are different in cases when one is responsible for the risk of harm and when one is not. The grounds of such duty and the significance of each morally salient consideration are further affected in branching out between being morally justified and not being morally justified in imposing the harm.

Note also that in the case when Jack has a justification to cause harm it seems like what that justification is can play a role in our intuitions about what is morally required of him. In the case where, for example, Jack is justified, but the children are his own or he is throwing the bomb to protect himself it seems like his duty to let Larry in is greater than in the case when they are children not related to either Jack or Larry and that too seems different than in cases when children Jack is trying to save are Larry's or it is Larry himself. These cases are meant to be parallels to cases of justified national self-defense that causes excess refugees and justified humanitarian intervention, where the first intervention case is meant to parallel cases that produce refugees not benefitting from that intervention and the second case is meant to be a parallel to cases when excess refugees are a result of the intervention (in the first instance) and are the same individuals benefitting from the intervention.

In fact, all of the above is meant to translate with important caveats to the case of refugees in general, but most importantly cases of refugees resulting from conflict, like those resulting from the Iraq war, ISIS and the Syrian crisis. While I do not mean to oversimplify the complex set of circumstances that give rise to refugee crises, I am trying to elucidate one such set of circumstances and ask how does moral responsibility for producing those circumstances affect our duty to provide asylum, assistance to refugee camps or assistance to countries that do provide asylum for refugees.

One significant difference (between my cases and actual refugee crises) lies in the empirical assumption in all of the cases, namely that letting Larry in will increase the risk of harm to Jack. I make that assumption for three reasons, in spite of the fact that significant data sets have shown that in many circumstances refugees actually improve the economy, diversity and overall well-being of the country to which they migrate (in other words they do not harm the country, although the increased risk of harm might be a plausible claim). First, I think that having not committed to the appropriate way to discharge the duty (whether it is in form of asylum or financial and infrastructural assistance) there are cases, especially when only assistance is required where, all-things-considered, the assisting country would be better off if they kept the money for their own economy and their own citizens (for example for their education). Second, there might simply be cases, even in the asylum situations where there is some risk of harm – at least in the short run. Certainly we have evidence that culture clashes and immigrant hatred have given rise to violence that has harmed both the refugee and the domestic population. Thus, assuming a risk of harm is the best way to not be overly optimistic. Third, if there genuinely were no risk of harm, then I would argue there are no philosophically interesting dilemmas (only pragmatically interesting ones) in the question of whether we have a duty to provide (asylum or assistance) for refugees. So having set aside the worry about the empirically problematic assumption about the risk of harm, there are some general claims that one can make regarding our duties to refugees in cases when we are responsible causally (and/or morally) for some excess number of refugees.

The second relevant difference is that rarely (if ever) is a situation such that only one party or one event is responsible for the flow of refugees. This might only be a plausible explanation in cases of natural disasters, but I focus here on refugees escaping political violence and armed conflict. So in most cases a single side in a conflict will not be fully culpable for the harm to civilians as a result of starting the war or fighting in a war.

The third relevant difference is that is most cases of conflict, the decision to enter the war and the individual decisions about strategies in war can all in different ways give rise to refugees (i.e. one might be justified in entering a war, but pursue it in morally unjustified ways).

Both entering a war and making certain strategic decisions regarding the way the war is fought can affect the displacement of civilians. So with respect to entering a war or armed conflict (*jus ad bellum*) which lacks a just cause, war will never be proportionate and the party entering such a war will be morally responsible for the resulting harm – whether in the form of deaths, property loss or displacement. But even in cases of entering a war with just cause (as would be in cases of genuine self-defense or genuine humanitarian military interventions, as opposed to cases of aggression or preventive war) one ought to consider whether such war is proportionate. A war which has a just cause but which is not proportionate is an unjust war and parties entering such a war are responsible for the resulting harm. Recently, conversations in the literature about proportionality (both *jus ad bellum* and *jus in bello* proportionality) have focused on the number of killed and maimed civilians (and sometimes conversations discuss the loss of combatants as well) (McMahan 2004, 2005, 2015; Bazargan 2013, 2014; Lazar 2013). Not much has been said about the relevance of displacement for proportionality calculations, and yet such considerations seem obviously relevant to whether or not entering a war is proportionate. Given that an average refugee spends 17 years in a refugee camp where (currently, as a matter of fact) nearly all of their human rights are left unmet it seems rather obvious that this sort of harm is significant both on the level of the individual and significant on the level of populations and that it ought to be seriously taken into account when one enters a conflict. In cases when one has a just cause, but has failed to take these sorts of harms into account, their war is likely not proportionate and they are morally responsible for the resulting harm to civilians and the excess numbers of refugees (in many cases the 'excess numbers of refugees' will be all of the refugees). In reality most wars fall into one of the above discussed two categories: wars that lack a just cause or those that might have a just cause, but fail *jus ad bellum* proportionality, either because they fail the traditional condition of proportionality or because they have not considered the displacement as a common result of war in their proportionality calculations. So in the vast majority of cases all sides of the conflict have a stringent duty to remedy past harms, in the form of a stringent duty to provide for refugees (whether in the form of asylum or assistance to countries providing asylum).

But this still leaves us with those cases that are similar to the *Child Rescuer* case where a country has a just cause and has (rightly) evaluated the harm they will impose to be proportionate to the harm they are trying to avert, thus making the harm they impose in the form of war and the threat of such harm morally justified. In such cases, I believe the state entering the conflict might still have a moral responsibility for the excess numbers of refugees, but their moral responsibility for those refugees is not grounded in the exact same set of considerations as above. What grounded the moral duty of a state to provide for refugees, in the above cases, was the fact that their refugee status is a direct result of unjustified war of that state. In the case here, what grounds the moral duty of a state to provide for refugees is the fact that the justified harm that such state is imposing (which is leading to displacement) can be divided – that is, it is divisible harm and as such the state and its combatants ought to take some of the harm upon themselves in the form of providing for refugees after war ends or choosing military strategies that minimize displacement in war.

Also, wars are made of a large number of actions and strategies, which may or may not result in displacement. In other words, one might also be morally responsible for the resulting refugees of *ad bellum*-relative just wars in cases when such wars – as almost all do – fail the *in bello* conditions. I will say more about *in bello* conditions of proportionality and necessity and how they relate to the duty to provide for refugees of the conflict shortly.

Duty to remedy past harm and just war theory

A corollary of the above claims is that displacement is a consideration for *ad bellum* proportionality and reasonable chance of success, *in bello* proportionality and necessity and *post bellum* generally. Starting with *ad bellum* proportionality, given the above it seems like foreseeable displacement of civilian populations ought to factor in proportionality calculations – failing to do so could make one's war unjust in the case such calculation would make the act of war disproportionate. Doing so (considering displacement in proportionality calculation), on the other hand, also should affect one's understanding of whether the *jus ad bellum* condition of reasonable chance of success has been met, as well as what is the best way to interpret *jus post bellum* considerations of restitutions and reparations. With respect to the condition of reasonable chance of success, if my argument above is correct, then one is morally responsible for providing for refugees after war ends as well as during the war, which in turn means that what counts as a reasonable chance of success is affected by acknowledging the possible moral responsibility for displacement, even in cases when one is fully justified in engaging in war, especially in cases of national self-defense. With respect to *jus post bellum* considerations, if the above argument is correct, one has a greater moral responsibility to provide for refugees after war ends if they are morally responsible for the excess number of refugees.

The fact that *ad bellum* proportionality calculations are intricately tied with just cause for entering the war, reasonable chance of success and *jus post bellum* considerations is nothing new (see Frowe 2014). But acknowledging the effects that result from taking displacement to be a serious harm (that affects proportionality calculus for *jus ad bellum*) gives new dimension to the claim that *jus ad bellum* proportionality is intricately tied with just cause, reasonable chance of success and *jus post bellum*. Consider, for example, the relationship between *ad bellum* reasonable chance of success and *post bellum* justice. It is a fact that almost all those who enter or start a war assume that theirs is a just war, with a just cause and worth the violent conflict (i.e. proportionate and with a reasonable chance of success). But whether a cause is worth the violent conflict will of course partly depend on acknowledging the responsibility for the resulting displacement. It might very well be the case that one does not have the resources to meet the needs of those displaced by their conflict – if that is the case then the war becomes one without a reasonable chance of success and destined to fail *jus post bellum* – making the war unjust overall.[6]

Parallel considerations regarding the relevance of displacement play a role or should play a role *in bello*. I had noted above that even belligerents who are fighting an *ad bellum*-relative just war (which if we take displacement to be relevant for *ad bellum* proportionality and reasonable chance of success – almost none are) will likely end up with a moral responsibility for displacement and a stringent duty to provide for resulting refugees. This is because considering displacement seriously in analyses of just war requires that we also consider it as relevant for *in bello* proportionality and necessity. The question of *in bello* proportionality traditionally (and in the wide sense) is a question about whether some particular military aim is proportionate to the number of civilians that will foreseeably but unintentionally be killed in the pursuit of that military aim, that is, it is a question of collateral damage. I think there are good reasons to consider displacement as relevant for *in bello* proportionality. After all if proportionality is meant to compare the harm averted and the harm caused, then displacement which leads to years of living in refugee camps (where most of basic human rights are left unmet) and long-term generational harm ought to matter. Similarly, probably more interestingly, the condition of *in bello* necessity is affected by acknowledging the duty to provide for excess refugees caused by our actions. The condition of necessity *in bello* is often understood as a minimal force requirement that says that even if some amount of overall force is proportionate if it is not necessary then it is not justified. No gratuitous harm is allowed. Necessity *in bello* requires that a particular military operation in war, which will destroy property or kill combatants and civilians is necessary for the achievement of the overall military aim. So for example, if our troops need to cross a river and have a number of options to do so with the same likelihood of success, but one requires killing five civilians, while the other requires destroying a small dual-use factory and possibly killing or losing some combatants, even if both options are deemed to be proportionate to the aim of crossing the river (because of its military importance) it would not be permissible that we take the first option – simply because it is not necessary to kill five civilians to achieve that aim. This is why this *in bello* condition is often also understood as a condition that requires that we use the minimum force to achieve our aim. Note what happens then in cases when we have a number of ways to achieve a military aim all of which are proportionate in the traditional sense, but fail to acknowledge displacement seriously. If the above is correct, in such cases, the action is unjustified and one is morally responsible for providing for the resulting refugees. This is because in cases when one could choose a strategy or alternative tactic which results maybe in more harm to combatants but less displacement, that is the strategy/tactic one should employ, if we take displacement to be a significant harm that ought to factor in *jus in bello* analysis. All of this is important since displacement is rarely considered in evaluating necessity or *in bello* proportionality, thus making a vast majority of refugees resulting even from an *ad bellum*-relative just war nonetheless the responsibility of both the just and the unjust side(s).

We are nonetheless (for the sake of completeness of the argument rather than actual practical value) left with cases when we have a significant number of refugees resulting from a conflict for which one has considered displacement and is acting with an all-things-considered (including displacement–considered) justification for a war.

I believe that in those cases it matters what the type of a just war one is engaged in and who is being displaced. If the war is a war of national self-defense, it seems like the state engaged in self-defense is still responsible for providing for refugees, especially if the aggressor becomes unable to do so (e.g. because of the devastation that the just war of self-defense caused). If the war is a war of just humanitarian intervention, things become significantly more complicated. The duty, if it is at all present, seems to depend on whether the refugees caused by the intervention (in the first instance) are the same individuals the intervention is meant to protect or not. It also depends on whether one thinks that humanitarian interventions can be permissible when they are not required, or whether they are only permissible when they are required. Finally, and critically, it also depends on whether other states were able to intervene or were also obligated to intervene and failed to do so. I have elsewhere argued that a humanitarian military intervention is only permissible if it is obligatory (Davidovic 2008). If that is the case, then in most cases of justified humanitarian military intervention, it seems like there will be more than one party that is morally well-situated to intervene and in cases when some state fails to intervene it seems reasonable to conclude that they should share the burden of the consequences of the intervention, which will in most circumstances be a responsibility both for the refugees resulting from the conflict and those resulting from the intervention.

Finally, displacement clearly ought to affect our analysis of *jus post bellum*. *Jus post bellum* conditions (at least on one popular account) include retribution, reparations, restitution, reconciliation, rebuilding and proportionality (see May 2012). How exactly these conditions get affected by excess refugee numbers which are a direct result of the conflict is an important question for further study, which I will not be able to take up here. But, as I have argued above, if one accepts that those fighting the war unjustly or entering an unjust war have a moral responsibility for the resulting refugees which is greater than the duty of other similarly situated states, then *post bellum* justice requires with respect to providing for refugees significantly more of warring states than what is expected or practiced today. If the aim of all wars (or at least all *post bellum* mechanisms) is sustainable peace, we have further albeit instrumental reasons (so different in kind than the primary reasons I have given above) to provide for refugees from conflict zones.

Throughout the paper, I have used a vague term 'provide for refugees', deliberately leaving space for what exactly discharging duty to remedy past harms would mean for refugee populations that emerge out of armed conflict. I turn to that question in the last section. But before I do, I quickly address the question of positive duties to refugees. Much has been said about this in literature, so I give a very cursory coverage to it here, in an effort to complement the above discussion rather than move forward the interesting and complex question regarding the extent to which we are responsible to aid refugees in general (i.e. in cases when we are not responsible for their refugee status) (see Wellman 2008; Wellman and Cole 2011; Blake 2012, 2013).

Positive duty to aid refugees

Nothing that I have said so far is meant to give any substantive answers to the question of what do states, domestic and international institutions, corporations and individuals who did not in a causally proximate way give rise to the excess numbers of refugees owe to those refugees. I do think that whatever duties those are and whatever grounds for such duties they are equally *mutatis mutandis* held by all entities that do also have an additional reasons for action grounded in the negative duty to remedy past harms. Importantly, the grounds of these positive duties to aid are significantly different and to some extent more complicated.

Traditionally, the distinction between positive and negative duties is understood as a distinction between a duty to perform an action and a duty to refrain from performing an action. This in turn often explains, at least in the first instance, why negative duties are commonly thought to be much more stringent (not easily override-able) than positive duties. The distinction helps capture the intuition most people have that the duty to refrain from killing is much more stringent, for example, than a duty to rescue someone from being killed. Of course, this distinction has been problematic in many cases. Consider, for example, the well-known example of a vicious aunt (or cousin) who plans to kill her little nephew hoping to inherit his money. She plans to drown him, but having entered the bathroom realizes he is already drowning and patiently waits to make sure he does in fact drown, so instead of killing him, she 'just' fails to rescue him (Rachels 1975). Most people have the intuition that she is just as blameworthy and culpable in the case when she 'simply fails to rescue her nephew' as she is in the case when she physically holds his head under water. Examples like this and many others give rise (among other things) to worries about the relevance and normative strength we should attribute to the distinction between positive and negative duties. I think it is rather obvious that there are times when the positive duty seems just as stringent as the negative duty, and times when it does not. For example, there seems to be a significant difference between lethally stabbing a surfer because you dislike his board and failing to jump into a riptide to save him from drowning. On the other hand, it seems like there is little difference in the above case of drowning a child or watching him drown and waiting to push him back under water if he resurfaces. The wide range of intuitions about the differences in stringency between negative and positive duties arise, in large part, from the fact that positive duties are significantly *more contextualized and conditional* than negative duties.

When the context is right and some conditions are met a positive duty can be just as stringent as a negative duty. To illustrate this it might be helpful to examine the notion of minimal decency, which, I believe, can act as a bridge between positive and negative duties (see Thompson 1971). Let me shortly explain what I mean by minimal decency. In most cases when we are trying to show that positive and negative duties are not equally stringent what we do is point to a particular value or human interest, like the value of human life, and then ask what sorts of duties does that value and the right emerging from that value (so right to life) give rise to. One's right to life, we might think, gives rise to a strong duty of not unjustifiably killing them and a (overall) much less stringent duty of saving their life in case it is being threatened (by an attacker for example). Commonly scholars sympathetic to the distinction argue that positive duties are by definition not as stringent as negative duties. The reasons given include danger to self, too high a cost, chance of success, etc. However, while this is generally right, in certain circumstances when all of the conditions have been met (so the bystander has reasonable chance of success, is acting proportionately, is acting out of necessity, the danger to self is low, etc.) the underlying value (of life in this case) gives rise to a positive duty that is just as stringent as the similarly grounded negative duty. In other words, it seems like one of the most plausible ways to explain the sliding intuitions regarding the difference in the stringency between negative and positive duties is to assert that in both cases what gives rise to the duty is the same underlying value, but that there are other morally salient and significant considerations quantifying that duty in the case it is a positive duty. So for the concomitant negative and positive duties like a duty not to kill and a duty to rescue one from being killed the same underlying value would be the interest in living. In the case of positive duties a number of other complicating – some morally relevant and some epistemically relevant – factors limits the normative strength of that underlying value. These can include lack of knowledge about how successful your intervention might be, the extent of harm one has to take upon themselves, access to alternative forms of intervention and others. In some subset of cases when all of these conditions have been met (so in cases when we have an epistemically solid set of reasons to think that danger to self and cost to self and others is low, chance of success high and few if any alternatives) the duty to aid becomes minimally decent actions (i.e. just as stringent as the concomitant negative duty with shared underlying interest or grounding value).

The above I think can help us answer or at least start to answer what duties of aid (and how stringent) we have with respect to refugees in cases when we are not responsible for their displacement.

If the above is correct then granting asylum and non-refoulement are minimally decent actions for most Western states with respect to Syrian and Iraqi refugees. This is because it seems that possibly overriding considerations do not seem to be sufficiently significant to override the underlying rights to basic necessities and to life (in cases where refoulement would put them at risk of being killed). The factors that would affect the stringency of such duties are facts about the country where the refugees are seeking asylum, and facts about the numbers and needs of refugees, facts about alternatives and other rather straightforward considerations. I will not get into detail about these facts, since such questions are better left to social scientists- but the key evaluative factors for assessing the duty to provide asylum or assistance will depend on the possible harm to the state or agency providing the assistance or asylum, the chances that the refugees' basic human rights will in fact be provided for (so a country that fails with respect to the human rights of their own citizens has a limited chance of success), the alternative agents that might be able to provide for refugees and the alternative ways that a state can engage with the refugee crisis. The positive duty of states that might for geographic-proximity reasons or affluence-of-state reasons act as places where refugees tend to go can also act as a reason to enforce the negative duty of those states that are morally responsible for excess refugees. Enforcement of that negative duty might be the most cost-effective way for a state to, for example, discharge its positive duty towards the refugees. Furthermore, note that many states that have the negative-like duty to remedy past harms because they engaged in an unjust war or because they fought a war by unjust means also have a positive duty grounded in a completely different set of considerations. This is important because the argument here (about positive duty to aid) that suggests that positive duties can be just as stringent as the negative duties and that at least in some circumstances currently both the states that fought in Iraq and those that did not have duties to provide for Iraqi refugees is not meant to say that the duties to provide are equally demanding between those responsible for the displacement and those that are not. One can think of this in at least two ways. One can think of the duties as strong reasons for action and as such the negative and positive duties could act additively to make the reasons for action preemptory. Or another way to think of the same claim is to suggest that in as much as one has the duty to remedy past harms when they are faced with a positive duty to act, which requires of them the same action as the negative duty to remedy past harms, the harm to self and alternative 'helpers' cannot act as excuses to not discharge that duty. The first of the two elaborations/explanations of the above claim seems, to me, a better way to explain why the overall duty to provide is more demanding in cases when one has a negative duty as well as a positive one. But both of the explanations are meant to be consistent with what was said so far.

Finally, I quickly turn to a brief discussion of alternative ways a state can discharge their duties to refugees. As I have already mentioned at least a part of, if not a large part of, the answer to the question of how one ought to go about discharging their duty to refugees will depend on the case at hand and facts best assessed by social scientists (possible long-term costs and benefits, etc.). In what follows I just give a quick sketch of how the distinction I make above between a duty to remedy past harms and duty to aid affects some of the practical questions regarding what duties we owe to (Iraqi) refugees.

Asylum, assistance and non-refoulement

As Parekh (2016) succinctly explains

> [t]he Refugee Convention contains two sets of normative obligations for states: one set of obligations relates to what states are required to do when asylum seekers arrive on their territory, while the other set has to do with state obligations towards refugees who have fled their own countries and are currently living in refugee camps or informal settlements.

While the relevant laws have consistently been interpreted to prohibit refoulement, namely the return of people to the place from which they escaped, the treaties as well as customary norms provide fewer reasons/examples to act on our obligations to displaced persons in refugee camps, or with respect to those seeking asylum elsewhere. If the above arguments for the varying grounds of obligation (and varying stringency of obligation) with respect to refugees are right, then the states that are responsible for excess numbers of refugees have strong, overriding duties to:

(a) ensure that the refugee camps where refugees resulting from the conflict are situated meet basic human rights needs of those refugees,
(b) provide asylum to a relatively larger number of refugees than they would ordinarily be required to do (given the facts that apply to them and the crisis), and
(c) aid other countries whose duties are solely positive, but for geographic or other reasons end up taking the brunt of the excess refugees and take the brunt of meeting the basic human rights of those refugees.

Because the numbers and distribution of refugees that are a direct result of a conflict one is responsible for vary depending on a great number of factual variables, how one ought to discharge a duty with respect to the above options (a)–(c) will clearly depend to some large extent on other circumstances (other than those that ground their duty to remedy past harms). But what my argument here is meant to show is that, at a minimum, negative duties require significantly more of countries responsible for the displacing conflict than is currently accepted. Consider for example the refugees stemming from the Second Iraq War and ISIS. Given that the war in Iraq seemed to lack a just cause, at least for the vast majority of the conflict and given that some of the tactics the US and allies used were impermissible there are reasons to think that the above argument applies straightforwardly to the refugees from the Iraq conflict. Even prior to the fighting related to the rise of ISIS in Iraq and Syria there were approximately 1.5 million Iraqi refugees from the Iraq war (some displaced internally and others externally). According to at least one source '[t]he 2003 US invasion displaced approximately 1 in 25 Iraqis from their homes, with fighting connected with the Islamic State contributing to additional displacement' (Watson Institute 2015). The number grew to close to 2 million since the conflict with ISIS escalated. Other sources have the numbers even higher. The UN High Commissioner for Refugees suggested in 2007 that there were as many as 2 million Iraqis displaced externally and over 1.7 million internally – 3.5 million in total (Guterres 2007). Many of those who have been displaced have been displaced more than once since the 2003 US-led invasion of Iraq.

With the questions regarding what exactly is the root cause of displacement in Syria, there are good reasons to think that the 2003 invasion of Iraq foreseeably contributed to ISIS and most importantly foreseeably led to weakening Iraq, deepening sectarian divides thus making Iraq less able post US occupation to respond to a threat like ISIS. The main point here is that there are also good reasons to suggest that the refugees from recent violence in Iraq and maybe Syria can to some extent be attributed to the US-led invasion.[7] Nonetheless, I think there are good, pragmatic reasons not to assign a duty to remedy to the US or its allies for refugees currently fleeing Syria and Iraq because of ISIS. One of the main reasons is that we saw that for such a stringent duty – as the duty to remedy past harm – we want to be able to show that a state is responsible morally and in a causally proximate way for displacement. That seems to be the case regarding the refugees from Iraq stemming from the invasion and occupation and its immediate consequences.

Most of the refugees from the 2003 Iraq invasion are still displaced. Many live in refugee camps throughout the Middle East. Others displaced externally moved to Jordan or Syria and live in its main cities. Many have been displaced a number of times. Most of the refugees have no interest in going back to Iraq, even though the host countries have been reluctant to give them residency. This and other reasons in turn have made them unable to meet even their most basic needs. Most cannot find work and their children are almost always unable to get an education. Those displaced internally are by most accounts even worse off than the externally displaced.

My argument is meant to suggest that the US (in the first place and its allies secondarily) has a stringent moral duty to provide for these refugees. The most obvious way to do so would be to increase the number of refugees accepted by the US (and its allies). So far that has not been happening on any meaningful scale. The US has in fact taken only 33,000 refugees from 2003 and 2009 (Schneller 2009). In the years 2010–2015, the US has taken anywhere from 9000 to 18,000 Iraqi refugees a year. European countries have not done much better. Until recently Europe had taken less than 10% of refugees from the Iraqi war. In addition to the fact that resettlement has been slow, many of the Iraqi refugees who are now settled in large cities in the Middle East have little interest in moving to places they see as hostile. This in turn means that the appropriate way to discharge the duty to remedy past harms that the US has towards the refugees from the Iraq war might/should also take the form of helping countries like Jordan, Turkey, Syria once that becomes possible, and others that are overwhelmed by Iraqi refugees both in the cities and in the camps. Regarding the refugee camps the US has a responsibility to ensure that basic human rights of those living in the camps are met. This means providing both personnel and resources. Even though many of the refugees in the camps might not be from the Iraq war, the US has a greater responsibility to provide assistance, because it has both a duty to remedy past harms and an additional duty to aid (given its resources, etc.). While the economic crisis in the US might have for example dampened the general positive duty to aid during the recession, the duty to remedy past harms cannot be overridden by such considerations – unless a country is faced with an economic crisis so severe it would violate the basic human rights of its own citizens in providing such assistance. That has not been the case for the US or most of its allies. Taking this responsibility seriously should actually incentivize the US to act swiftly – limiting the life-long consequences that most refugees and their children suffer. Regarding the refugees living in the cities in places like Jordan, the US ought to ensure access to education, language services (where needed), work permits and civil rights (through, for example, exerting diplomatic pressure to ensure residency status for such refugees).

Finally, regarding non-refoulement, the negative-like duty to remedy requires that states like the US in cases like the Iraq case use their diplomatic resources to advocate against refoulement and to incentivize states considering refoulement against it. This might come in the form of assistance, where such assistance is needed or diplomatic incentives.

Conclusion

My argument is meant to show that contrary to common belief the duty to provide for refugees is in many cases and for many actors a negative-like duty to remedy past harms and a stringent one. I have also argued that for those states that have the duty to remedy past harms the positive duty to aid acts as an added reason for action. I have also suggested that for those states that have only a positive duty towards refugees from an armed conflict zone that duty should act as a motivating reason to enforce the negative-like duty to remedy of the responsible parties. I have argued that the fair distribution of such harm/burden of providing for refugees (if it even is a burden) is partly and relevantly, but not exhaustively, determined by one's moral responsibility for the harm or threat of harm that led to the displacement. This stands in stark contrast to the common view that we owe very little to the refugees in camps, and that majority of our duties ought to be discharged in the form of asylum if and when refugees seek it and meet all other conditions for asylum. Finally, I have taken some beginning steps towards showing what accepting my argument means for just war theory.

Notes

1. I use the Iraq refugee crisis as an example throughout the paper. Also I will use the term 'we' through the paper to refer to the US and those states that participated in the wars that have resulted proximately or indirectly in the Iraqi (and maybe also the Syrian) refugee crisis, unless specifically stated otherwise.
2. In particular, proportionality and reasonable chance of success *jus ad bellum*, proportionality and necessity *jus in bello* and *jus post bellum* generally.
3. While a similar argument can be made for economic harm and economic refugees, for purposes of clarity I will in this paper only focus on excess refugees resulting from wars and the negative duties those engaged in those wars have towards those refugees. If my argument is successful it might very easily be extended to cases of economic harm.
4. This is not meant to be exhaustive – in other words there might be other types of duties with different sorts of grounds.

5. The assumption here is that letting Larry in will not affect the likelihood of Jack's success in stopping the child murderer. If it did then that might make such duty less stringent, or might annul it altogether. I discuss issues related to this shortly – when I discuss whether or not providing for refugees will affect quality of life of those that provide for them.
6. Another way to put this is to suggest that all wars have the aim of sustainable peace as the end goal. *Jus post bellum* considerations signal exactly that claim- not being able to provide for excess refugees is likely (as we are now seeing with the rise of ISIS for example) to add to destabilizing the region and lessening the chance of sustainable peace.
7. For a common argument in support of this thesis see for example, http://www.aljazeera.com/blogs/middleeast/2015/09/iraq-war-root-europe-refugee-crisis-150908151855527.html.

Acknowledgement

I am indebted to a number of people for feedback on earlier drafts of this paper. They include participants at the International Law and Ethics of Armed Conflict Conference, in Belgrade, Serbia, 2016. I am also grateful to exceptionally insightful feedback from referees for this journal.

Disclosure statement

No potential conflict of interest was reported by the author.

References

Bazargan, Saba. 2013. "Complicitous Liability in War." *Philosophical Studies* 165 (1): 177–195.
Bazargan, Saba. 2014. "Killing Minimally Responsible Threats." *Ethics* 125 (1): 114–136.
Blake, Michael. 2012. "Immigration, Association, and Antidiscrimination." *Ethics* 122 (4): 748–762.
Blake, Michael. 2013. "Immigration, Jurisdiction, and Exclusion." *Philosophy and Public Affairs* 41 (2): 103–130.
Blake, Michael. 2016. "Philosophy & The Refugee Crisis: What are the Hard Questions?" *The Critique*. http://www.thecritique.com/articles/philosophy-the-refugee-crisis-what-are-the-hard-questions/.
Davidovic, Jovana. 2008. "Are Humanitarian Military Interventions Obligatory." *Journal of Applied Philosophy* 25 (2): 134–144.
Frowe, Helen. 2014. *Ethics of War and Peace*. London: Routledge Press.
Guterres, Antonio. 2007, February 14. "U.N. High Commissioner for Refugees cited in "More Iraqi refugees are Headed to U.S." by Rachel L. Swarns and Katherine Zoeff." New York Times. http://www.nytimes.com/2007/02/14/washington/14refugees.html?_r=1.
Lazar, Seth. 2013. "Associative Duties and the Ethics of Killing in War." *Journal of Practical Ethics* 1 (1): 3–48.
May, Larry. 2012. *After War Ends*. Cambridge: Cambridge University Press.
McMahan, Jeff. 2004. "The Ethics of Killing in War." *Ethics* 114 (4): 693–733.

McMahan, Jeff. 2005. "The Basis of Moral Liability to defensive Killing." *Philosophical Issues* 15 (1): 386–405.

McMahan, Jeff. 2015. "Proportionality and Time." *Ethics* 125 (3): 1–24.

OAU (Organization for African Unity). 1969. "AU Convention Governing Specific Aspects of refugee Problems in Africa, Art 1.2." http://www.achpr.org/instruments/refugee-convention/#1.

Parekh, Serena. 2016. "Moral Obligations to Refugees: Theory, Practice & Aspiration." *The Critique*. http://www.thecritique.com/articles/moral-obligations-to-refugees-theory-practice-aspiration-2/.

Pogge, Thomas. 2002. *World Poverty and Human Rights*. New York: Polity.

Pogge, Thomas. 2004. "Severe Poverty as a Human Rights Violation." http://portal.unesco.org/shs/en/files/4363/10980840881Pogge_29_August.pdf/Pogge+29+August.pdf.

Rachels, James. 1975. "Active and Passive Euthanasia." *New England Journal of Medicine* 292: 78–80. doi:10.1056/NEJM197501092920206.

Schneller, Rachel. 2009. "No Place Like Home: Iraq's Refugee Crisis Threatens the Future of Iraq." *Terrorism Monitor* 8 (8). https://jamestown.org/program/no-place-like-home-iraqs-refugee-crisis-threatens-the-future-of-iraq/#!.

Shue, Henry. 1980. *Basic Rights*. Princeton, NJ: Princeton University Press.

Thompson, Judith Jarvis. 1971. "A Defense of Abortion." *Philosophy and Public Affairs* 1 (1): 47–66.

UNHCR. 1951. "1951 Convention Relating to the Status of Refugees." http://www.unhcr.org/pages/49da0e466.html.

UNHCR. 2014. "Protecting Refugees." www.unhcr.org/3bb9794e4.pdf.

Watson Institute. 2015. "Iraqi Refugees." Brown University Watson Institute for International and Public Affairs. http://watson.brown.edu/costsofwar/costs/human/refugees/iraqi.

Wellman, Christopher Heath. 2008. "Immigration and Freedom of Association." *Ethics* 119 (1): 109–141.

Wellman, Christopher Heath, and Phillip Cole. 2011. *Debating the Ethics of Immigration: Is There a Right to Exclude?* Oxford: Oxford University Press.

Human security and the international refugee crisis

Aramide Odutayo

ABSTRACT
Despite offering some protection for refugees, realpolitik in international affairs ensures that the paradigm of human security remains aspirational rather than practical. This paper begins by providing a brief snapshot of the current global refugee crisis, encompassing multiple local crises in the Middle East, Europe, Africa, and Latin America. It next details the international community's response to these crises, highlighting the punitive policies used by the Australian government and the European Union (EU) to impede the asylum process. Lastly, the paper will assess whether the framework of human security can support the right to asylum, a right that is enshrined in international law. Following a brief introduction to the concept of human security, the paper will explore its strengths and limitations, examining whether it offers a complementary source of protection to the right to asylum in the face of eroding refugee rights. I argue that human security is a useful but imperfect framework for protecting refugee rights.

Introduction

The world is currently experiencing the greatest refugee crisis since World War II. The most recent report from the United Nations High Commission for Refugees (UNHCR) estimates the total number of refugees and displaced persons at approximately 55 million people (UNHCR 2016). This figure includes over 14 million refugees, 1.8 million asylum seekers, and 32 million internally displaced persons (UNHCR 2016). The single largest cause of displacement is the ongoing Syrian Civil War, a conflict that has killed between 250,000 and 470,000 people, and forcibly displaced approximately 11.3 million people (Crompton 2016). The scope of the Syrian crisis is immense, with the country now comprising the world's largest source of refugees, while Turkey, which shares the longest common border with Syria, is now home to the world's largest refugee population. The civil war has also put significant strain on other surrounding countries, specifically Lebanon, Jordan, Iraq, and Egypt (Amnesty International 2016). Iraq, which currently hosts approximately 300,000 refugees (Amnesty International 2016), is experiencing its own internal refugee crisis as a result of the 2003 US invasion (Giacaman 2015, 2406). The ensuing war and occupation, which also gave rise to the Islamic State, has displaced over 3.3

million Iraqis ("Isis: Worst Refugee Crisis in a Generation as Millions flee Islamic State in Iraq and Syria" 2015).

Elsewhere, renewed fighting in South Sudan has internally displaced over 1.4 million people since December 2013 (UNHCR Country Operations Profile South Sudan 2015b). The UNHCR estimates that the total number of refugees and asylum seekers from South Sudan is approximately 680,000, compared to approximately 123,000 prior to the renewal of conflict in 2013 (South Sudan Situation 2015c). With the re-election of Colombian President Juan Manuel Santos in June 2014, peace dialogues between the Revolutionary Armed Forces of Colombia and the Army of National Liberation continued (UNHCR Country Operations Profile Colombia 2015a). While these peace talks were occurring, however, another 137,000 Colombians were displaced, for a total of 6 million internally displaced persons, with another 350,000 refugees living in the neighboring countries of Venezuela, Ecuador, and Peru (Groll 2015).

To sum up, the UNHCR's most recent report estimates that there are approximately 60 million forcibly displaced people, and 20 million refugees worldwide (Reuters 2015). Between June 2014 and June 2015, conflict and persecution drove an average of 42,500 people each day to flee their homes and seek asylum, either within the borders of their own country or internationally. Since the top three sources of refugees – Syria, Afghanistan, and Somalia – make up 53% of refugees worldwide, addressing the root causes of displacement in the Middle East and North Africa would have the biggest impact in reducing the global refugee crisis (Groll 2015). Unfortunately, the international community has instead imposed a series of punitive policies intended to stem the flow of refugees.

The global response to the refugee crisis: Europe and Australia

> Although forced migration can have serious security implications, it has become over-securitised to the point where it is in danger of creating threats where before there were none, while at the same time undermining the international refugee protection regime in the name of an increasingly amorphous claim to 'security needs (Hammerstad 2008, 2–3).

Over the past few decades, public discourse has increasingly framed the asylum process in negative terms. Asylum seekers in Europe, Canada, the United States, and Australia have been cast as a threat to national security. The imaginary scenario of a state rendered powerless by 'waves' of migrants 'invading' the country has contributed to fears about the porousness of international borders, the integrity of domestic refugee programs, and the vulnerability of the nation-state more broadly. Mobilizing fear to securitize the asylum process has become an effective means for states to justify violations of both domestic and international law by excluding refugees from their sovereign territory (Mountz 2004, 325).

Australia and the European Union both serve as striking examples of this process in action. Specifically, their readmission agreements and safe third-country agreements, made with origin countries, as well as their detention and interdiction practices, all make access to asylum impossible. Taken together, this bundle of policies and spatial practices constitute neo-refoulement – a geographically based strategy intended to prevent asylum by restricting access to territories that ostensibly provide protection to refugees. Such actions are in direct contravention of the principle of non-refoulement (Mountz 2004, 325). Grounded in international human rights and refugee law, in treaty, in doctrine, and in customary international law, non-refoulement holds that states cannot forcibly repatriate individuals to territories in which they may be persecuted, tortured, or otherwise be at risk of serious harm. The principle of non-refoulement follows directly from the right 'to seek and to enjoy' asylum from persecution in other countries, as spelled out in Article 14 of the Universal Declaration of Human Rights (Hyndman and Mountz 2008, 249). While non-refoulement may not immediately correlate with the right to seek asylum, it clearly limits lawful government actions with respect to refugees. Returning asylum seekers to territories where they are at risk of serious harm thus represents an infringement not only of Article 14, but also of connected rights, such as the right to life, the right to freedom from torture or cruel, inhuman or degrading treatment, and the right to liberty and security of the person (UNHCR Note on the Principle of Non-Refoulement 1997).

Australia

Beginning in the 1990s, the Australian government began constructing a more punitive asylum regime, involving detention, interdiction, and deportation, designed to prevent asylum seekers from landing on its mainland territory (Hyndman and Mountz 2008, 249). Between 1993 and 1994, Australia implemented a policy of detaining anyone who arrives in the country without a visa (Hugo 2002, 32). Asylum seekers were subject to imprisonment, and in many cases expulsion, until their cases were resolved (Hugo 2002, 32). This was a response to increasing numbers of illegal migrants being smuggled by sea through South East Asia, many of whom came from Afghanistan, Iraq, and Iran, with smaller numbers from Sri Lanka, Palestine, Syria, China, and Vietnam. Media and government officials used Australia's relative isolation, as well as racialized and xenophobic images of migrants, to create a public perception that the country was under 'invasion'. Fear and moral panic about the 'other', coupled with the emerging consensus that the country must control its borders and protect its territory, resulted in the further entrenchment of an aggressive detention regime (Hyndman and Mountz 2008, 257).

In 2001 Australia inaugurated the Pacific Solution, in which the government began preventing sea-borne migrants from entering its territorial waters (Magner 2004, 56). The detention and processing process was subcontracted out to small, impoverished island nations neighboring Australia, specifically Papua New Guinea and Nauru. The Australian parliament also decided to tighten its borders by retroactively declaring several hundred small islands off the coast of Australia no longer part of its territory (Hyndman and Mountz 2008, 249). This removed the government's obligation to grant asylum to those who reached these islands. The government also established a naval barrier to prevent vessels carrying asylum seekers from entering its territorial waters (Magner 2004. 56). Boats intercepted off the coast of Australia were taken to Papua New Guinea or Nauru, where those on board would be unable to make an Australian asylum claim ("Nauru to Accept Asylum Seekers" 2001).

As part of their agreement with the Australian government, Papua New Guinea and Nauru were given millions of dollars in aid to construct detention centers. The Australian government also paid the entire cost of housing the refugees and reviewing their asylum claims. Because Papua New Guinea has yet to enact any domestic laws governing the admission and processing of refugee claims, while Nauru is not a party to the international refugee convention, these nations were the ideal partners for Australia's offshore processing program, outsourcing the asylum function while absolving Australia from its international obligations to asylum seekers (Magner 2004, 56).

This strategy is complimented by aggressive interdiction policies, whereby the Australian navy patrols, intercepts, and tows boats to Indonesia, another country that is not a signatory to the international refugee convention. As a result, migrants are unable to make an asylum claim after their transportation to Indonesia. Australian officials actually boast of having some 20 bilateral agreements with transit countries such as Indonesia and Malaysia, who either help suppress human smuggling or accept returnees. Their assistance was assured in exchange for informal aid projects (Hyndman and Mountz 2008, 249). Australia's refugee policies have been publically condemned by the United Nations High Commission on Human Rights, Human Rights Watch, and Amnesty International, as contravening the Convention on the Rights of the Child, the Universal Declaration of Human Rights, and the 1951 Refugee Convention.

The European Union

Australia's refugee policy of interdiction and outsourcing asylum seekers is similar to the EU's effort to construct an invisible, yet aggressive policy wall against migration flows, masked under the moniker of 'preventive protection'. Introduced in 1983 by Sadako Ogata, the former head of the UNHCR, preventative protection seeks to diminish the causes of displacement, allowing potential asylum seekers to remain in the safety and dignity of their own homes. For those fleeing violence, the policy advocates concerted efforts to restore peace, ensure respect for human rights, and provide humanitarian assistance, allowing displaced persons to stay in safe areas nearest to their home. But rather than take serious measures to enact preventive protection, European countries have instead sought to manage 'illegal' migration to Europe by preventing potential migrants from entering European territory. More specifically, European nations have closed their borders to would-be refugees, and legitimized their actions by interpreting the concept of 'preventative protection' in self-serving terms, as protection from the flow of asylum seekers (Frelick 1992, 439–440).

This deliberate misinterpretation has been entrenched using a comprehensive set of policies to externalize asylum, in a manner similar to that of Australia. In 1998, the EU released a strategy paper on immigration that signaled a shift away from legal and normative approaches toward more politicized responses that ensured state autonomy, arguing that the Refugee Convention was no longer applicable in the face of increased migration during the 1990s (Samers 2004, 27). During this time period, the removal of restrictions on movement from the former communist bloc generated exaggerated fears about a mass influx of Central and Eastern European immigrants. The expected flows of new migrants only ever materialized in Germany, where a substantial number of ethnic German immigrants from Central and Eastern Europe relocated to Germany, where they were entitled to citizenship. However, there was also a significant rise in the number of asylum seekers as a result of regional civil conflict, particularly from the former Yugoslavia. Increasing refugee flows fostered the belief that traditional domestic instruments were inadequate in managing new flows of unwanted migration (Boswell 2003, 621).

In response to these fears, the EU established the High Level Working Group on Migration and Asylum. The group's recommendations emphasized the importance of increased cooperation between the EU, countries of origin, and transit countries. To that end, the working group suggested the following policies: (a) support for migration management and asylum systems; (b) voluntary return to countries of origin; (c) financial assistance to origin countries that are unable to cope with their readmission obligations; and (d) increased efforts to prevent human trafficking and illegal immigration. The proposed policies were a response to the EU's obligations under international and regional human rights laws, particularly Article 3 of the European Convention of Human Rights, as well as judicial oversight and public scrutiny through parliaments and civil society of immigration policies (Boswell 2003, 621). Consequently, European governments sought to pass on their responsibilities to other states and avoid criticism for essentially punitive immigration policies.

On 21 June 2002, EU heads of state met in Seville, Spain to discuss readmission agreements with transit countries. EU readmission agreements are based on reciprocal obligations, concluded between EU and non-EU countries, to facilitate the return of illegal migrants to either their country of origin, or to a transit country, when it can be shown that an individual passed through the country in question. Illustrating their commitment to readmission and the fight against illegal migration, EU countries promised to provide all necessary technical and financial assistance to receiving countries, and to include clauses on the joint management of migration flows and on compulsory readmission in the event of illegal immigration. The final text of the Seville Conclusions also introduced the policy of negative conditionality in EU relations with third countries, such that countries that do not cooperate with the EU on readmission were to be penalized through cuts to development aid and technical assistance (European Parliament Think Thank 2015).

In yet another example of Europe's support for extraterritorial approaches to asylum processing, Britain also considered implementing offshore transit processing centers in Albania, Croatia, and Ukraine in 2003 (Schuster 2005). Extraterritorial responses effectively de-territorialized the requirement of protecting refugees, so that the temporary protection and processing of asylum claims now take place outside the borders of the given country (Betts 2004, 49). Such policies typically take two forms: first, opening processing centers in third countries; and second, establishing regional protection zones close to refugees' countries of origin. In either case, asylum seekers are effectively excluded from EU members' sovereign territory (Schuster 2005).

An imperfect marriage: human security and the right to asylum

In response to these increasing barriers to refugees, which represent declining respect for the principles of international human rights, refugee advocates have gravitated toward the concept of human security, arguing that this concept offers a complementary source of protection to the right to asylum. The extent to which human security can effectively protect refugee rights in the face of state hostility is a matter of debate, however.

The human security paradigm: an introduction

The United Nations Development Program (UNDP) (1994) annual report argued that the concept of security has traditionally been narrowly construed 'as security of territory from external aggression, as protection of national interest in foreign policy, or as global security from the threat of a nuclear holocaust'. The UNDP called on international actors to move beyond such conceptions toward 'an all-encompassing [trans-boundary] concept of human security' (Human Development Report 1994, 3). The UNDP report offered an extensive definition of human security as: (a) safety from such chronic threats as hunger, diseases, and repression; and (b) protection from sudden and hurtful disruptions in the patterns of daily life (Human Development Report 1994, 3). The report also outlined four essential characteristics of human security: (i) it is a universal concern relevant to people everywhere; (ii) the components of security are interdependent; (iii) human security is easier to ensure through early prevention; and (iv) human security is people-centered (Human Development Report 1994, 3).

The new human security paradigm quickly gained global traction, and a UN Commission on Human Security was established in 2000. Their highly anticipated report was released three years later. It defined human security as:

> Protecting the vital core of all human lives in ways that enhance human freedoms and human fulfillment. Human security means protecting fundamental freedoms – freedom from want, freedom from fear, and freedom to take action on one's own behalf – that are the essence of life. It means protecting people from both critical (severe) and pervasive (widespread) threats and situations. It means using processes that build on people's strengths and aspirations. It means creating political, social, environmental, economic, military and cultural systems that together give people the necessary building blocks for survival, livelihood and dignity. (The United Nations Trust Fund for Human Security 2003)

The commission suggested two general strategies to achieve human security: protection and empowerment (The United Nations Trust Fund for Human Security 2003).

As the language of human rights increasingly failed to protect asylum seekers, refugee advocates turned instead toward the concept of human security, believing that such an approach, which shifts the object of security discourse from states to people, could lead to a resurgence of international support for refugee protection (Edwards 2009, 778). The interests of asylum seekers have typically been seen as separate from national interests, except insofar as migrants were seen as threats to national security. Supporters of this new discourse expressed hope that human security would introduce an important conceptual and policy shift within the international discourse on refugees. Since refugee claimants are non-citizens, they are forced to rely for their protection on international and domestic legal regimes that are only enforced due to humanitarian goodwill (Edwards 2009, 764). These legal regimes have been undermined over time by state noncompliance and the exploitation of legal and policy loopholes. The human security framework seemed to offer a complementary source of protection for asylum rights in the face of declining international support.

The rest of this paper will assess whether the framework of human security can mitigate the current erosion of refugee rights. Through my discussion of the strengths and limitations of the human security paradigm, I will ultimately argue that human security is a useful but imperfect framework for the protection of refugee rights. First, as a result of its broad and all-encompassing framework, it encourages multilateral action. Second, human security offers new ways to conceptualize not only the protection of refugees, but how they are perceived as well. It encourages a shift away from traditional notions of security that privilege the state, toward placing all people, regardless of their legal status, as the primary object of security (Edwards and Ferstman 2010, 5). Third, it has the capacity to reinforce and elevate human rights, offering a new language to promote respect for refugee rights in situations that fall outside existing legal parameters (Edwards and Ferstman 2010, 46).

Despite offering such promise, the concept of human security is limited, in practice, in its ability to protect the right to asylum. The concept has ultimately failed to displace traditional notions of security, which often trump the distinct goals of human security. The human security of refugees too often falls to the wayside in situations where it conflicts with national security (Abass 2010, 172). Third, by defining new duty-bearers tasked with the responsibility of safeguarding human security, the paradigm was understood as a form of 'forward defense' against common threats to humanity (Heinbecker 2000, 13). As evidenced by the Syrian refugee crisis, however, state interests tend to prevent any assertive action. Finally, human security remains rooted in the lexicon of securitization, a vocabulary that undermines the rights of individuals, including migrants (Noll 2003, 279). Although human security offers some protections for asylum seekers and refugees, the continuing centrality of realpolitik in international affairs ensures that the paradigm remains no more than aspirational.

Human security and refugee rights: strengths and limitations

In many ways, the human security agenda inaugurated a new approach to international relations. It has proven an effective tool for mobilizing support due to its expansive and vague scope, encompassing everything from physical security to psychological well-being. The paradigm of human security connects a disparate coalition of middle-power states, development agencies, and NGOs – all of which strive to shift the international community's attention and resources away from conventional security issues to issues of international development. The power of human security is in its lack of precision, enabling it to generate support from diverse players, perspectives, and interests in the international security network (Paris 2001, 88). The intentional ambiguity of the concept has been an effective campaign slogan for causes such as banning the use of anti-personnel land mines (Epps 2008, 1) or the creation of the International Criminal Court (ICC) (Balasco 2013, 47). These are significant accomplishments, and they challenge the claim that human security is merely empty rhetoric. In fact, the alliance of states and advocacy groups who relied on the human security agenda to advance their aims fundamentally altered the post-Cold War landscape of international politics (Paris 2001, 88).

Despite these successes, the overly broad definition of human security has prevented this network from having a sustained impact on the international community's treatment of human rights. The network has been described as lacking focus (Howard-Hassmann 2012, 99), stemming in particular from the concept's lack of any clear definition. Reviewing the varying definitions proves that it is impossible to clearly and consensually define human security. For example, the government of Japan adheres to a holistic definition of human security, which 'comprehensively covers all the measures that threaten human survival, daily life, and dignity – for example, environmental degradation, violations of human rights, transnational organized crime … and strengthens efforts to confront these threats' (Ministry of Foreign Affairs Japan 2000). The Canadian government, on the other hand, has promoted a seemingly more restrictive definition, seeing human security as 'freedom from pervasive threats to people's rights, safety, or lives'. However, even this definition ranges from safety from physical threats, to the right to an acceptable quality of life, rule of law, good governance, and sustainable development. Meanwhile, the Human Security Network – which includes Canada, Norway, and Japan, as well as several other states and an assortment of international NGOs – promises to create a 'more humane world where people can live in security and dignity, free from want and fear, and with equal opportunities to develop their human potential' (Paris 2001, 90–91).

At first glance, the lack of a clear definition is disappointing. Leaving the concept undefined raises serious concerns about its utility for promoting human welfare (Edwards and Ferstman 2010, 90), while the inability to clarify the boundaries of the paradigm provides little guidance in the prioritization of competing values (Paris 2001, 90). However, this should not lead one to prematurely dismiss the concept (Edwards and Ferstman 2010, 30). Human security has enough parameters to give it adequate meaning, and its ability to produce meaningful action can be seen in its impact on the landmine convention and the ICC (Hubert 2004, 351). Even critics must admit that its broadness is preferable to being reduced to a more precise, comprised concept that would undermine its inclusiveness, an inclusiveness that is an asset to the highly diverse, complex issue of asylum (Edwards and Ferstman 2010, 30). Ultimately, the concept's proven ability to affect international policy change makes the best case for its usefulness in protecting refugee rights.

Human security is useful for asylum seekers because it remains fundamentally people-centered, irrespective of one's citizenship status. Under the current regime, asylum seekers take recourse in international human rights law, which for all its lofty intentions still distinguishes between nationals and non-nationals, with less human rights protection for the former. Even the 1951 Refugee Convention grants rights to asylum seekers and refugees incrementally on the basis of one's status with the state. Conversely, human security draws no distinctions between citizens, non-citizens, refugees, and asylum seekers. The security of all people is seen as equally valid and mutually dependent, unlike under the current state-centric international system, which sees refugees as non-persons or outsiders. Instead, they are treated as equal citizens in a global community facing interdependent and universally relevant threats.

Human security has also been criticized because it lacks the binding force of international human rights and international humanitarian law. In 1998 the UNHCR's Division of International Protection echoed criticisms that the concept was, 'vague and undefined in international law' and that 'references to UNHCR's role in safeguarding or reinforcing human security' represented a 'distraction from and dilution of UNHCR's statutory function of providing international protection to and solutions for refugees'. They described the concept as a 'misguided attempt to use the language of security in UNCHR's dialogue with states, at a time when the organization should be speaking unequivocally in terms of refugee protection and the defense of human rights'. The UNHCR concluded that because 'the concept had its origins in the field of development' its use by the UNHCR would be interpreted as an attempt to 'extend its mandate into that domain' (Edwards and Ferstman 2010, 116).

The UNHCR's critique reiterates an important misconception of human security in the context of eroding refugee rights. Many supporters of the right to asylum are suspicious of a non-legal, non-binding framework for refugee protection. This critique is premised on the belief that the current system of refugee protection is near perfect, without acknowledging its myriad weaknesses that allow states to impede the asylum process and avoid their legal obligations to refugees. Additionally, it should be noted that the human security framework was never intended to replace existing legal frameworks, but rather to compliment them. Human security is a useful tool to re-conceptualize both the protection of asylum seekers as well as security issues in general (Edwards and Ferstman 2010, 45).

Human security also offers a new way to deal with those issues that fall outside the purview of existing legal parameters, encompassing the goal of moving the human security discourse toward accepted standards and best practices. The UNHCR's argument that human security undermines hard-won legal gains is misguided, given that human security works with, not against, international human rights law. Agreements such as the Universal Declaration of Human Rights provide a benchmark against which state policies can be judged, as well as a legal framework to which asylum seekers and their advocates can appeal. The limited reach of such agreements, particularly in the face of wider political trends against refugees, has nevertheless contributed to the current retrenchment of asylum rights. Human security offers a new vocabulary with which to appeal to states for protection of refugees, complementing the global human rights regime. Moreover, it also plugs some of the gaps in that framework, including the problem of enforcing human rights guarantees (Edwards and Ferstman 2010, 45–46). By broadening the state's responsibilities to include non-citizens, human security serves as an important complementary player to the state citizen focus of the international human rights regime (Howard-Hassmann 2012, 96).

However, the concept of human security is also no panacea for the weaknesses of the international refugee protection system. At a practical level, the paradigm is ultimately limited in its ability to strengthen the right to asylum. With its focus on individual security, rather than state sovereignty, human security was seen as complimenting the rights of asylum seekers and refugees. Unfortunately, the concept has failed to displace realist national security objectives, which too often undermine the goals of human security.

Human security was originally conceptualized as a challenge to the hegemonic belief that the only form of security that mattered was state security. Whereas state security privileges state actors and interests, human security makes people the focal point of security considerations (Paris 2001, 91). By expanding our understanding of security beyond the nation-state, proponents of human security endeavor to force states to attend to the needs of their citizens. The co-optation of the term security is an intentional effort to persuade governments that people's security *is* state security, thus producing a greater attentiveness to issues of human rights and development. Human security also stresses that national security is threatened by the insecurity of citizens outside the nation's borders. As such, governments should strive to protect the security of both their own citizens as well as those of other states, as a matter of national self-interest. This enlarged responsibility for the security of both citizens and non-citizens is not only exercised through international law, but also through a state's domestic and foreign policies (Howard-Hassmann 2012, 90).

Unfortunately, human security's efforts to serve as a counterweight to state-centric understandings of security pose problems in the refugee context, particularly in situations where national security considerations conflict with those of human security. As evidenced by Australia and the EU's response to asylum seekers, the paradigm of human security too often becomes subordinated to national security concerns, which are often the impetus behind restrictive refugee policies. Such policies throw into doubt the effectiveness of the concept in protecting asylum rights. The danger that the human security approach poses in this regard is readily apparent when both states and international agencies seek to prevent the outbreak of conflict in a region. Because conflict prevention is one of the UNHCR's stated 'durable solutions', it is useful to consider what happens when the desire to avoid conflict from breaking out in a region clashes with the obligation to protect refugees pursuant to international refugee law (Abass 2010, 172–173)?

The answer to this question is perhaps best illustrated by the repatriation of Rwandan refugees from Zaire and Tanzania in 1996, despite concerns that Rwanda remained unsafe. The UNHCR, who assisted in the repatriation efforts, explained that their support was heavily influenced by the threat posed by Rwandan refugees to the security of the Great Lakes Region (Whitaker 2002, 1–2). Sadako Ogata, High Commissioner of Refugees at the time, stated: 'when refugee outflows and prolonged stay in asylum countries risk spreading conflict to neighboring states, policies aimed at early repatriation can be considered as serving [conflict] prevention …' (Whitaker 2002, 13). But while repatriation may help prevent wider regional conflicts, it is clear that it also undermines refugee rights, reducing individual refugees to pawns in regional and global security considerations (Abass 2010, 173).

The Rwandan example demonstrates the second limitation of the human security framework, specifically its failure to address the conflict between the security of state citizens and the security of non-citizen refugees. Human security discourse leaves it unclear which group would take precedence – the citizen or the refugee. This tension bears directly on the usefulness of the human security framework to the issue of asylum, with some scholars interpreting human security as encompassing only the basic security needs of the legal citizens of a state (Upadhyaya 2004, 74), creating obvious problems for asylum seekers who are not citizens of the host state. Scholars have asked:

> whose security counts, that of the refugee fleeing from violence or repression, or that of the host community concerned over job competition, welfare, cultural cohesion, and international crime in the face of large refugee influxes or steady streams of asylum seekers? (Hammerstad 2000, 399)

History has repeatedly proven that states are primarily concerned with asserting their sovereignty and protecting their citizens; rarely do they extend their attention to those perceived as outsiders. Human security is often not strong enough to overcome states' bias toward their own citizens and as such cannot always protect the rights of refugees (Abass 2010, 173).

As previously mentioned, one of the more important innovations offered by the concept of human security is its suggestion that the international community has a responsibility to protect citizens of other states (Brown et al. 2007, xiii). Proponents of human security understand the framework as a form of 'forward defense' against common threats to humanity (Heinbecker 2000, 13). Human security defines new duty-bearers tasked with the responsibility of safeguarding human security, and suggests new mechanisms that they can use to do this (Howard-Hassmann 2012, 90). Thus, the original 1994 human security agenda intersected and complimented the doctrine of Responsibility to Protect (R2P), in an on-going attempt to legitimize and normalize international intervention (Brown et al. 2007, xiii). The R2P report, commissioned by the Canadian government as part of its human security initiatives, clarifies this duty, maintaining that the international community is justified in undertaking military intervention when states fail to protect their citizens from large-scale loss of life that is a product of deliberate state action, state neglect, or inability to act; when there is a failed state situation or when there is large-scale ethnic cleansing (The International Commission on Intervention and State Sovereignty 2001, xi–xii). In 2005 the UN General Assembly agreed in principle with these recommendations, indicating a broad global acceptance of human security and its expanded concept of state responsibility (Howard-Hassmann 2012, 91).

Unfortunately, recent global events undermine human security's claim that 'there shall be no more Rwanda and Srebrenica, or indeed Darfur' (Brown et al. 2007, xiii). The ongoing Syrian Civil War and the resulting refugee crisis show that despite a clear rationale for intervening to remove President Assad, state interests and realpolitik continue to prevent assertive action. The human security implications of the Syrian refugee crisis are indisputable and far-reaching. First, the dire conditions of the Syrian refugee population directly undermine all dimensions of their human security, including their personal, economic, environmental, health, and food security. Second, the hardships of the refugee population affect their host country's human security, undermining their resilience and economic performance, while also heightening social tensions.

For example, a 2013 World Bank Assessment of Lebanon found that the Syrian Civil War had strained the country's already fragile public finances and widened the fiscal deficit. The government of Lebanon spent an additional $2.5 billion to restore social services to pre-Syrian civil war levels. Due to rising prices and increasing unemployment, ordinary Lebanese families are directly financing efforts to manage increased flows of Syrian refugees, pushing an estimated 170,000 Lebanese into poverty in 2014 (The World Bank 2013). Further worsening the situation is the fact that large numbers of refugees have settled in the Bekaa Valley and Northern Lebanon, an area that has historically been underserved in terms of social services and infrastructure.

Economic and political pressures in host countries have exacerbated social tensions between refugees and local residents, and, in the case of Lebanon, between different politico-sectarian sectors of society that support opposing factions in the Syrian civil war, further deteriorating social cohesion. The severe economic and social burden of the refugee crisis, and the growing awareness that refugee flows will not subside in the near future, has led host countries to both restrict the number of asylum seekers and to limit their rights, illustrating the self-reinforcing nature of the human security crisis in the region (Berti 2015, 47). The Syrian crisis provides ample warning that realpolitik will continue to undermine the ability of the human security paradigm to offer a complimentary source of protection to eroding refugee rights.

Human security's ability to protect the right to asylum is further limited by its roots in the lexicon of securitization. The post-911 landscape has proven that the security concept is far from neutral, nor does it apply to states, citizens, and migrants equally. In reality, states have used the language of securitization to justify a range of measures that infringe on the rights of citizens and migrants alike. In this context, the human security framework disingenuously tries to equate the security of the individual with the security of the state, and artificially inflates the importance of individuals in international affairs. In discourses on persecution, flight, and protection, the security concept is employed in an asymmetrical and ultimately paternalistic manner, since it is left to international agencies and organizations to assess whether refugees' security is threatened, while it is left to the humanitarian goodwill of state actors to accept asylum seekers. It is understandable that the UNDP sought to group together the concerns of both individuals and states under the same concept. Unfortunately, the assumptions that underlay the framework of human security obscure the power differences between these very different actors. States not only define and defend their own security interests, they can also usurp the power to define the security interests of individuals, and in certain cases, take measures to defend them. The individual's voice is marginalized in security discourse, and the power to protect individually defined security interests is extremely limited (Noll 2003, 279–280).

Because security is inextricably linked to notions of 'emergency', 'the exceptional', and the legitimacy of force (Noll 2003, 280), invoking the language of human security will not result in the humanization of security discourse, nor will it provide entry points for human rights advocates to enter security debates as originally intended (Edwards 2009, 803). Instead, the security concept trumps any consideration of individual rights, diminishing the legal constraints put on state actors, giving them greater discretion under the guise of emergency measures or exceptional circumstances. As such, applying the discourse of human security to the rights of refugees and asylum seekers only introduces a bias that ultimately works against the rights of individuals, including migrants (Noll 2003, 280).

Affixing the 'security' label to asylum seekers and refugees may prove counterproductive to the interests of refugee advocates, as it perpetuates the view of refugees or other 'outsiders' as security risks (Noll 2003, 280). 'Applying a "security" perspective to examine the needs of "outsiders" and their relationship with the community typically involves assumptions of antagonistic relations and non-tradable interests.' Applying a human security approach nationally may diminish what little public support exists for asylum seekers, and other 'outsider' populations (Newman 2003, 106).

Ultimately, the usefulness of human security to counter the trend of eroding asylum rights is highly suspect. Although well-intentioned, efforts to harmonize state interests with those of asylum seekers are grossly misguided, fated to be imprecise at best and collusive at worst (Noll 2003, 282). The human security of refugees and asylum seekers in the wider security discourse is clearly subordinated to national security interests. Although the paradigm of human security is distinctly aspirational, it obscures the centrality and durability of realpolitik in international affairs.

Conclusion

In his famous poem 'Refugees Born of A Land Unknown', Orcadian poet Edwin Muir described the perilous journey of refugees who once they arrived at their destination were halted in a 'room in a place where no doors open' leading them to conclude that 'the world died many years ago' (Muir 1960). Muir's critique of the international communities dealing with refugees is clear, and many scholars have used Muir's work to emphasize the need for a new philosophy. Is the paradigm of human security the philosophy that Muir envisioned? As this paper has shown, human security cannot be viewed as an effective source of protection for the right to asylum. This is not to say that the paradigm does not have its strengths. Its broad and all-encompassing framework serves as a powerful rhetorical impetus to joint action between diverse actors. Second, human security offers new ways to conceptualize asylum seekers and refugees. It inaugurated a shift away from traditional notions of security that privilege the state towards placing all people, regardless of their status, as the primary referent objects of security. Finally, human security has the capacity to reinforce and elevate human rights, offering a new language to appeal to states to safeguard the rights of refugees in situations that fall outside the purview of existing legal parameters.

Despite this, the paradigm is ultimately limited in its ability to protect the right to asylum, failing to displace traditional notions of security, which often trump the goals of human security. The human security of refugees often falls to the wayside in situations where they conflict with national or citizen security. Although it sought to instill state actors with the responsibility of safeguarding human security, the ongoing Syrian crisis demonstrates that traditional state interests tend to prevent assertive action. Human security is further limited due to its roots in the broader lexicon of securitization, a vocabulary that undermines the rights of individuals, including migrants. Although human security offers some protections for asylum seekers and refugees, the ongoing durability of realpolitik in international affairs ensures that the paradigm remains distinctly aspirational.

Disclosure statement

No potential conflict of interest was reported by the author.

References

Abass, Ademola. 2010. *Protecting Human Security in Africa*. Oxford: Oxford University Press.
Amnesty International. 2016. "Syria's Refugee Crisis in Numbers." Accessed March 23, 2016. https://www.amnesty.org/en/latest/news/2015/09/syrias-refugee-crisis-in-numbers/.
Balasco, Lauren Marie. 2013. "The International Criminal Court as a Human Security Agent." *The Flethcer Journal of Human Security* XXVIII: 46–67.
Betts, Alexander. 2004. "The International Relations of the "New" Extraterritorial Approaches to Refugee Protection: Explaining the Policy Initiatives of the UK Government and UNHCR." *Refugee* 22 (1): 58–70.
Berti, Benedetta. 2015. "The Syrian Refugee Crisis: Regional and Human Security Implications." *The Institute for National Security Studies* 17 (4): 41–53.
Boswell, Christina. 2003. "The 'External Dimension' of EU Immigration and Asylum Policy." *International Affairs* 79 (3): 619–638.
Brown, Oli, Mark Halle, Sonia Peña Moreno, and Sebastian Winkler. 2007. *Trade, Aid, and Security: An Agenda for Peace and Development*. London: Earthscan.

Crompton, Paul. 2016. "Could there be No One Left in Syria by 2031?" *Al Arabiya English*. Accessed October 14, 2016. http://english.alarabiya.net/en/special-reports/syrian-crisis/2016/03/23/Could-there-be-no-one-left-in-Syria-by-2031-.html.

Edwards, Alice. 2009. "Human Security and the Rights of Refugees: Transcending Territorial and Disciplinary Borders." *Michigan Journal of International Law* 30 (3): 763–807.

Edwards, Alice, and Carla Ferstman. 2010. *Human Security and Non-Citizens: Law, Policy and International Affairs*. New York: Cambridge University Press.

Epps, Kenneth. 2008. "The Ottawa Landmines Treaty: A Major Step Toward Human Security." *The Ploughshares Monitor* 29 (1): 1.

European Parliament Think Thank. 2015. "EU Readmission Agreements: Facilitating the Return of Irregular Migrants." Accessed March 29, 2016. http://www.europarl.europa.eu/thinktank/en/document.html?reference = EPRS_BRI(2015)554212.

Frelick, Bill. 1992. "'Preventive protection' and the Right to Seek Asylum: A Preliminary Look at Bosnia and Croatia." *International Journal of Refugee Law* 4 (4): 439–454.

Giacaman, Rita. 2015. "Syrian and Iraqi refugees: A Palestinian Perspective." *American Journal of Public Health* 105 (12): 2406–2407.

Groll, E. 2015. "A Record Year in Misery: the World Has Never Seen a Refugee Crisis This Bad." *Foreign Policy*. Accessed March 23, 2014. http://www.unhcr.org/pages/49e492ad6.html.

Hammerstad, Anne. 2000. "Whose Security?: UNHCR, Refugee Protection and State Security After the Cold War." *Security Dialogue* 31 (4): 391–403.

Hammerstad, Anne. 2008. "Securitization as a Self-fulfilling Prophecy: Refugee Movements and the North-South Security Divide." Accessed August 17, 2016. https://www.researchgate.net/publication/239928108_Securitisation_as_a_self-fulfilling_prophecy_Refugee_movements_and_the_North-South_security_divide, 1–21.

Heinbecker, Paul. 2000. "Human Security: The Hard Edge." *Canadian Military Journal (Spring)*: 11–16.

Howard-Hassmann, Rhoda. 2012. "Human Security: Undermining Human Rights?" *Human Rights Quarterly* 34 (1): 88–112.

Hubert, Don. 2004. "An Idea that Works in Practice." *Security Dialogue* 35 (3): 351–352.

Hugo, Graeme. 2002. "From Compassion to Compliance? Trends in Refugee and Humanitarian Migration in Australia." *Geojournal* 56 (1): 27–37.

Hyndman, Jennifer and Mountz, Alison. 2008. "Another Brick in the Wall? Neo-refoulement and the Externalization of Asylum by Australia and Europe." *Government and Opposition* 43 (2): 249–269.

"Isis: Worst Refugee Crisis in a Generation as Millions Flee Islamic State in Iraq and Syria." 2015. *International Business Times*. Accessed March 24, 2016. http://www.ibtimes.co.uk/isis-worst-refugee-crisis-generation-millions-flee-islamic-state-iraq-syria-1506613.

Magner, Tara. 2004. "A Less than 'Pacific' Solution for Asylum Seekers in Australia. *International Journal of Refugee Law* 16 (1): 53–90.

Ministry of Foreign Affairs Japan. 2000. "Statement by Director-General Yukio Takasu at the International Conference on Human Security, in a Globalized World." Accessed August 6, 2016. http://www.mofa.go.jp/policy/human_secu/speech0005.html.

Mountz, Alison. 2004. "Embodying the Nation-State: Canada's Response to Human Smuggling." *Political Geography* 23 (3): 323–345.

Muir, Edwin. 1960. "The Refugees Born for a Land Unknown." Accessed March 31, 2016. http://thebaffler.com/poems/refugees-born-land-unknown-muir.

"Nauru to Accept Asylum Seekers." 2001. *The Globe and Mail*. Accessed October 14, 2016. http://www.theglobeandmail.com/news/world/nauru-to-accept-asylum-seekers/article22401058/.

Newman, Edward. 2003. *Refugees and Forced Displacement International Security, Human Vulnerability, and the State*. New York: United Nations University Press.

Noll, Gregor. 2003. "Securitizing Sovereignty? States, Refugees, and the Regionalization of International Law." Accessed April 5, 2016. https://works.bepress.com/gregor_noll/46/, 277–305.

Paris, Roland. 2001. "Human Security Paradigm Shift or Hot Air?" *International Security* 26 (2): 87–102.

Reuters. 2015. "World's Refugees and Displaced Exceed Record 60 million: U.N." Accessed April 5, 2016. http://www.reuters.com/article/us-un-refugees-idUSKBN0U10CV20151218.

Samers, Michael. 2004. "An Emerging Geopolitics of Illegal Immigration in the European Union." *European Journal of Migration and Law* 6 (1): 27–45.

Schuster, Liza. 2005. "The Realities of a New Asylum Paradigm." Accessed March 19, 2016. https://www.compas.ox.ac.uk/2005/wp-2005-020-schuster_new_asylum_paradigm/.

The International Commission on Intervention and State Sovereignty. 2001. "The Responsibility to Protect." Accessed April 15, 2016. http://responsibilitytoprotect.org/ICISS%20Report.pdf, 1–91.

The United Nations Development Program. 1994. "Human Development Report 1994." Accessed April 4, 2016. http://hdr.undp.org/sites/default/files/reports/255/hdr_1994_en_complete_nostats.pdf, 3.

The United Nations High Commissioner for Refugees. 1997. "UNHCR Note on the Principle of Non-Refoulement." Accessed March 25, 2015. http://www.refworld.org/docid/438c6d972.html.

The United Nations High Commissioner for Refugees. 2015a. "2015 UNHCR Country Operations Profile – Colombia." Accessed March 23, 2014. http://www.unhcr.org/pages/49e492ad6.html.

The United Nations High Commissioner for Refugees. 2015b. "2015 UNHCR Country Operations Profile – South Sudan." Accessed March 24, 2016. http://www.unhcr.org/pages/4e43cb466.html.

The United Nations High Commissioner for Refugees. 2015c. "South Sudan Situation." Accessed March 24, 2016. http://data.unhcr.org/SouthSudan/regional.php.

The United Nations High Commissioner for Refugees. 2016. "UNHCR Global Appeal Report: 2016-2017." Accessed March 23, 2016. http://www.unhcr.org/564da0e3b.html.

The United Nations Trust Fund for Human Security. 2003. "Human Security Now." Accessed April 5, 2016. http://www.un.org/humansecurity/content/human-security-now.

The World Bank. 2013. "Lebanon: Economic and Social Impact of the Syrian Refugee Crisis." Accessed April 15, 2016. http://www.arabstates.undp.org/content/dam/rbas/doc/SyriaResponse/Lebanon20Economic%20and%20Social%20Impact%20Assessment%20of%20the%20Syrian20Conflict.pdf, 1–180.

Upadhyaya, Priyankar. 2004. "Human Security, Humanitarian Intervention, and Third World Concerns." *Denver Journal of International Law and Policy* 33 (1): 71–91.

Whitaker, Beth Elise. 2002. "Changing Priorities in Refugee Protection: The Rwandan Repatriation from Tanzania." Accessed April 15, 2016. http://www.unhcr.org/3c7528ea4.html, 1–16.

⁸ OPEN ACCESS

The duty to bring children living in conflict zones to a safe haven

Gottfried Schweiger

ABSTRACT
In this paper, I will discuss a children's rights-based argument for the duty of states, as a joint effort, to establish an effective program to help bring children out of conflict zones, such as parts of Syria, and to a safe haven. Children are among the most vulnerable subjects in violent conflicts who suffer greatly and have their human rights brutally violated as a consequence. Furthermore, children are also a group whose capacities to protect themselves are very limited, while their chance to flee is most often only slim. I will then discuss three counterarguments: the first counterargument would be that, instead of getting the children out of a particular country, it would be better to improve their situation in their home countries. A second counterargument could be that those states, which have such a duty to bring children to a safe haven, would be overburdened by it. Finally, the third counterargument I want to discuss states that such a duty would also demand a military intervention, which could worsen the situation even further.

In this paper, I will discuss a children's rights-based argument for the duty of states, as a joint effort, to establish an effective program to help bring children out of conflict zones, as is the case in Syria at present. My argument will be presented in three steps: firstly, children are among the most vulnerable subjects in violent conflicts and that they suffer greatly as a consequence. I will employ a children's rights framework to support this claim. Furthermore, children are also the group whose capacities to protect themselves are very limited, while their chance to flee is most often only slim (and requires others helping them). As such, children are a group that, on the one hand, deserve special attention, and, on the other hand, are not able to move out of danger on their own. This seems to provide a sufficient basis to establish a duty to be proactive and bring children to safe countries. Children also have a right to a family and it is proven that staying with their caregivers, to whom they have close attachment, is critical; as such, this duty should also include caregivers and other close family members. I will then, thirdly, discuss three counterarguments: the first counterargument would be that, instead of getting the children out of the country in conflict, it would be better to improve their situation in their home countries. While I agree that this would indeed be a better outcome, I will argue that this is not very realistic,

---

This is an open-access article distributed under the terms of the Creative Commons Attribution License http://creativecommons.org/licenses/by/4.0/, which permits unrestricted use, distribution, and reproduction in any medium, provided the original work is properly cited.

and in the meantime, we should bring children out of conflict zones, possibly with the option to return them as soon as the situation sufficiently improves. A second counterargument could be that those states, which have such a duty to bring children to a safe haven, would be overburdened by it. I will contend that the duty I propose is limited by external factors but that there are good reasons to believe that the highly developed countries are able to fulfill it without being overburdened. Finally, the third counterargument I want to discuss states that such a duty would also demand a military intervention, which could worsen the situation. I will conclude that this danger exists, but that it can be limited. While bringing children out of conflict zones does not necessarily involve a high level of military engagement in these countries, it does not mean that sides need to be taken.

1. Children in conflict zones

For the purpose of this paper, I will assume that children do have rights and that the UN Convention of the Rights of the Child (CRC) is an adequate expression of these rights within the context of all human rights, but specified according to children's particular needs and competences.[1] I view these human rights of children as both moral and legal rights,[2] while assuming that their reach overlaps in this regard. As moral rights, they are binding even if states choose to ignore them; meanwhile, as legal rights, they are established by international treaties. I am agnostic towards the question about whether children have such rights and how they can be justified philosophically (see, e.g. Archard 2004; Dixon and Nussbaum 2012). The CRC sets out a number of rights derived from the overarching concept of children's dignity, with what is in the best interests of children being of particular interest. For my purpose, it is not necessary to examine each and every right that children have under the CRC, nor how it is violated by living in conflict zones and the hardships that come with it. It is sufficient to point out that the situation is so bad that it clearly constitutes a human rights violation according to the CRC. The CRC states that each and every child has a right, for example, to health, decent living conditions, education, and protection from violence, abuse and neglect.

What is also important is that children's rights under the CRC are universal, with each and every child entitled to the protection of their rights. This means that children's human rights claims do not stop at national borders.[3] This lies within the nature of human rights themselves and has moral and legal importance: from a moral point of view, we need to clarify what constitutes reasonable moral obligations, while, from a legal point of view, we need to ask what kinds of obligation can or do follow on from international human rights treaties, such as the CRC or other relevant laws. Although it has not been proposed as yet that the CRC provides the legal framework for a duty to bring children to a safe haven, I believe that both the moral and legal aspects of children's human rights point in that direction. States and the UN, as well as other international organizations, already impose sanctions in response to human rights violations with a wide range of measures, including interventions and UN-led military operations. I am not concerned with the question about whom is responsible for a violent conflict and who should be punished for it. I am also highly skeptical that sanctions can actually improve the situation for children in conflict zones. It is rather the case that, in countries such as Syria or Iraq at this present time, those kinds of sanctions that are normally used to improve the situation regarding children's rights have no conviction, It is pointless reminding the government of Syria that it is obliged to protect children's rights because they do not have the means to do so effectively. Thus, the intervention from foreign states is permissible, and as I will argue later also obligatory, but in such a way that it maximizes the outcome for children with minimal risks and those who carry out the duty to bring them to a safe haven.

Unfortunately, we do not exactly how many children are currently living in conflict zones such as Syria and Iraq.[4] There are estimations about how many children have arrived in the European Union (EU), while it can be reasonably expected that hundreds of thousands of children are currently living in the aforementioned conflict zones; meanwhile, globally, there are possibly millions of children affected. UNICEF estimated in February 2016 that about six million children are affected by the ongoing war in Syria and that nearly 2.5 million children are awaiting registration as refugees. UNICEF and other humanitarian organizations have reported gross violations of these children's rights. Most of them – one report of the UN counts about two million for whom this is the situation right now – are out of school, and that this particular situation is a persistent issue, which might lead to a 'lost generation'.[5] In October 2015, UNICEF reported that they reached out to more than 430,000 children under five years of age, while pregnant and lactating women received multi-micronutrient supplementation, over 500,000 children aged between 6 and 59 months received nutrient supplements and more than 8000 children aged between 6 and 59 months were treated for global acute malnutrition.[6] The toll on children's minds and souls is maybe even harder to estimate, while it is without doubt that most will be traumatized and experience anxiety and fear in later life (one early study: Quosh, Eloul, and Ajlani 2013). Access to healthcare is also declining and the healthcare system is on the brink of collapse (in many areas, it already has collapsed due to a lack of drugs, electricity, etc.), which leaves millions of children without vaccinations or treatment in cases of illness or injury. Children suffer increasingly from diarrheal diseases, such as cholera, due to a lack of access to clean water, while the risk of pneumonia and other respiratory infections increases due to low temperatures during the winter, together with inadequate shelter, housing or heating. UNICEF reports that it has given winter kits to 152,000 children in the first three months of 2016 alone; 44,000 of those children are living in hard to reach areas. The long-term health effects of the conflict on children can, and unfortunately will, for many, be severe and irreversible (Devakumar et al. 2015). The rate of disabilities, mental and physical impairments, and chronic diseases will be especially high. The situation for all these children is bad, but for those trapped in conflict zones it is even worse:

> The humanitarian consequences of the conflict in Syria has taken the toughest toll on communities, with children trapped in besieged locations where the most basic lifelines to the outside world have been cut off as a deliberate tactic of war. There are an estimated 486,000 people living in 18 locations designated as besieged with limited or no access to food, water, healthcare, electricity and fuel. UNICEF estimates half are children.[7]

Children in conflict zones are difficult to reach for humanitarian organizations; they are in acute danger of being injured or killed as well as often trapped in their situation. World Vision reported in March 2016 that about 12,000 children have been killed in Syria,[8] while many more have been wounded. Since the outbreak of the conflict, over 250,000 people in total have been killed and over one million injured. It can only be estimated how many children have lost one or both of their parents, which leaves them even more vulnerable and in need of assistance and care.

The evidence I have presented in this section only gives a glimpse into the reality of these children's lives in conflict zones. As the aid for them is severely underfunded and the conflict is ongoing, it cannot be expected that their plight will improve anytime soon. It is essential that children experience healthy development, care and protection, with their basic needs fulfilled; otherwise, they will suffer from long-lasting negative consequences. Violent conflicts, such as the war in Syria, undermine such needs beyond the direct and indirect consequences mentioned here, which makes these children more vulnerable to exploitation. There are some troublesome reports about children forced to work in Syria, being sexually abused – especially girls and young women – after they flee[9] or even made to participate in the violent conflicts as child soldiers or human shields.

2. Children's capacities to protect themselves and to flee

So far, I have shown that children are among the most vulnerable in conflict zones and that they suffer greatly under such circumstances. The hundreds of thousands of children actually living in places of civil war, such as Syria, are denied essential human rights, which they are granted under the CRC: namely, the right to life, health, education, safety, a decent living standard and so on. Although children represent a heterogeneous group, involving those who are completely dependent on others, as well as those who are on the border of adulthood, this claim about children's vulnerability holds for them as a group.[10] What is important now is that children are not only among the most vulnerable and the most affected by violent conflicts; they also only have a slim chance to escape and change their situation. This supports the second step in my argument concerning a duty to bring them out of conflict zones.

Children, then, obviously make up a very heterogeneous group, ranging from newborns to near adults until the age of 18 years. This makes it is somewhat more complicated to draw conclusions about children as a group, while it would go beyond the scope of this paper to discuss the concept of childhood in detail (in that respect, see, e.g. Schapiro 1999). Despite that, I want to claim that for all children, when we look at them as a group and not as individuals with differentiating features based on age or maturity, certain characteristics are crucial in terms of the proposed duty to bring them to a safe haven, which are also acknowledged in the CRC. Firstly, they are not fully developed physically and psychologically, which makes it harder, perhaps even impossible, for them to protect themselves from the dangers of violent conflicts and to uphold their human rights. For young children, this claim is uncontroversial since very young children cannot sustain themselves at all and may die without care and protection from others, while younger, preadolescent children are still at risk of being harmed and exploited by adults. Children cannot run a school on their own, nor can they provide themselves with medical care or rebuild their homes. In particular, if their parents are wounded, dead or captured, they are highly vulnerable. The case for older teenagers is certainly weaker in that regard, while some of them will even actively engage in violent behaviors and become combatants themselves, or otherwise take advantage of those who are younger and weaker.[11] That said, those teenagers are not fully matured and still deserve protection. Joel Anderson and Rutger Claassen refer to a 'regime of childhood'

(2012) without implying that children should not be held responsible for their actions.[12] Such a regime does not focus on competences alone, but also on the wider implications of treating teenagers who are not fully mature as adults, even if, as I want to formulate it, this is in their best interest regarding the rights they have under the CRC. It is not, however, because it would certainly benefit the development of these children if they fell under the protection of the CRC, even if their vulnerability is not that different than that of adults. Furthermore, it is certainly the case that not all children are equally mature, while differential treatment would require a thorough analysis, which is not feasible under the circumstances of a conflict zone.[13]

Secondly, children's limited capacities to flee and move to a safe haven themselves are equally limited. The pictures of a dead body lying on a Turkish beach were all over the news a few months ago and can serve as an example of the dangers of fleeing. Those dangers certainly exist for adults as well; but, for children, the dangers are simply higher because they are less prepared for the hardship that comes with fleeing, given that being alone on the run makes them more vulnerable to exploitation or being otherwise harmed by adults and because protection systems are weak, if they exist at all, under such circumstances (for more details, see Kanics et al. 2010). While younger children cannot flee alone, taking them along makes the journey more difficult for the family. It is also important to note that girls are more prone to certain forms of violence and abuse because of their gender. Fleeing alone is a traumatic experience in itself because children suffer from separation from their parents and are constantly facing experiences of loneliness and insecurity (Berman 2001). All these things considered, it is understandable why children are often trapped in conflict zones and only have very limited or no options to get to a safe haven on their own. At the same time, they cannot rely on the protection systems of the state because they are failing under such circumstances or because a law-free space has developed in the absence of authority.

3. The duty to bring children to a safe haven

I have shown that children's rights are grossly violated in conflict zones, such as Syria, and that they are not safe there. I have further indicated that children lack the competences to protect themselves, while their opportunities to get to a safe haven on their own are very limited. Based on these two arguments, I will now flesh out a duty to bring children to safety and argue that this duty falls to those states which are able to fulfill it, not primarily as individual states but as a group under the heading of the UN. Furthermore, this duty also covers the concerned children's families.

Let me begin by stating that the duty to protect children's rights falls first and foremost to the state in which the children reside. This is a moral and a legal claim regarding the CRC, under which all states that signed it pledged to protect and promote children's rights. The moral obligation is similar and I will not explore its basis here. Under some circumstances, states fail to do so, while, in cases of violent conflict and the collapse of state order, at least in some parts of a country, the protection of children's rights becomes even more necessary, but at the same time more difficult, maybe even impossible, because the state in question no longer has the means to do so or simply lacks control over the space where children live. In such cases, a clear-cut attribution of the responsibility to protect children's rights is impossible, although all individuals involved are required to respect those rights just as they have to respect human rights in general. Still, it is unclear who is responsible for providing children with adequate healthcare, education or shelter in cases where they are separated from their families. The reality of (civil) war and conflict often makes upholding such rights impossible. Even if little disagreement exists over the claim that violent conflicts actually violate children's rights in several dimensions, it is less clear why other states may have a duty to protect these children and their rights, even under the scenario that the state, in which those children live, is unable (or unwilling) to do so or that the state no longer exists in a particular region, for example, where control has been relinquished to the Islamic State. In the following section, I aim to clarify why such a duty exists, the extent of this duty, the attribution of responsibility to certain parties and whether they are overburdened by it and why it is the best solution for the problem at hand.

It is widely accepted and recognized that children who are able to flee and come to the borders of safe countries, such as those in the EU, deserve protection and that they should certainly not be returned to the conflict zones from which they fled. These legitimate claims of children are not only moral rights, but also stated in various international laws and treaties, such as the Geneva Convention Relating to the Status of Refugees, the European Charter of Fundamental Rights or case law of the European Court of Human Rights.[14] For my case, it is not important whether this ultimately leads to granting these children refugee status or subsidiary protection. What is important is that, as soon as children arrive at a safe haven, such as within the EU, they have legitimate claims of protection from that state. One can debate how such protection has to be provided. Even such nationalists as David Miller, who denies a human right to cross borders, agree that states cannot send children, or any other person, back to a conflict zone but have to establish protection even if that is not in the country which the migrants want to enter, but in a third state (Miller 2013). So, my argument is also not concerned with the issue of prioritizing asylum seekers over other migrants[15] but simply asserts, and this seems highly plausible, that states have a duty to ensure that they do not send children, or any other person, back to a conflict zone, where their human rights are severely endangered. Now, if we accept that those children who come to our borders are entitled to support and protection (whether or not that translates into granting asylum or transferring them to a different safe country is not of importance here), then we need to ask whether or not it would be unfair to disadvantage those children who were unable to flee and who are stuck in conflict zones. As I have shown, we cannot expect children to flee by themselves. But, if they do flee alone or even with their families, this journey is highly dangerous; it seems that it is too dangerous for this to be the basis for granting them protection. Let me use a strong analogy here: if a police officer witnesses a child being punched, held down and in immediate danger of being abused, he has the duty to intervene, not wait for that child to free himself or herself from the abuser and run towards the officer, if they are lucky enough, in order to expect any kind of child protection.

This brings me to the crucial question. So, then, even if most would agree that children's human rights are violated in conflict zones and that states would have a duty to protect them as soon as they are at their borders, it is not so straightforward as to whether states have an obligation or duty to intervene, and even if they have an obligation to intervene, it is not clear whether this means that this intervention constitutes bringing those children to a safe haven. I will address the first issue concerning whether or not there is a duty to intervene if children's human rights are violated. I will draw on two different sources to make my argument. The first one is Kok-Chor Tan's argument for a duty to protect and the second is Pablo Gilabert's argument for a positive duty to eliminate global poverty. Both are not particularly concerned with children's human rights or the situation of children in conflict zones but, as I will show, both are applicable.

Let me begin with Tan's argument (2006). Tan assumes rightly that an intervention is permissible in cases of severe human rights violations.[16] The main argument against permissibility is that of state sovereignty, which is not strong enough in cases of human rights violations. The intervention I propose, as well as any intervention, would certainly be unproblematic from the perspective of state sovereignty, were the state in question to allow it and agree to allow children living in its territory to be brought to safety. Unfortunately, and for different reasons, a state like Syria may be reluctant to comply in this way, for example, because it fears that this might open up its state borders to a much more far-reaching military intervention or because it does not want to look weak in the eyes of the public or other states. Therefore, if a state refuses to let its children be brought to a safe haven, other normative arguments must be brought forward in order to legitimize such an intervention by foreign states. Firstly, as the value of state sovereignty is not universal, I would argue in particular that the respect of state sovereignty is dependent, partly at least, on the state concerned fulfilling its obligations towards its citizens by protecting their human rights. If a state fails to do that, the demand to have its sovereignty respected is weakened; in cases of gross, enduring and widespread violations, which we now witness in Syria, this argument becomes stronger. It is based both on moral and legal grounds, since the human rights of children are equally morally binding, even if they are not signed by the state in question and because most states, and Syria being one of them , have signed human rights treaties, including the CRC. So Syria has actually agreed to protect children's rights and acknowledged that children have those rights unconditionally. Peters (2009) has argued in a similar vein that state sovereignty is not limited by human rights, but that the normative value of sovereignty is itself derived from, and oriented towards the protection of human rights. Secondly, in the case of a violent conflict, which leads to a situation where a state actually loses control over parts of its territory and therefore cannot protect its citizens living there at all, I see it as even more legitimate for other states to intervene in the way I have proposed. Thirdly, the justification of an intervention can be strengthened if it is carried out as a joint effort by the UN, rather than by one or more foreign states. The UN does not have unlimited legitimacy to overrule state sovereignty, but it has some which is widely acknowledged and has been used in the past. Unfortunately, as the UN is dominated by interests and power games, it can lead to a situation where it cannot agree to undertake such an intervention. In this case, the duty certainly falls back on the states as a joint effort, which could lead to a situation where a coalition of states carries out its duty to bring children out of conflict zones without the backing of the UN. I would also view such an undertaking as legitimate.

So, if there are good reasons to render an intervention to protect the human rights of children as permissible, we can draw on Tan, whose aim is to show that from the permissibility that states have a duty to intervene, or to put it differently in the case of human rights violations, at least severe ones, permissibility and obligation are tied together. He argues that if human rights violations are strong enough to overrule the sovereignty of the state that is intervened with, it is also strong enough to overrule the sovereignty of the state that is obliged to intervene. Human rights violations deny neutrality and, as Tan writes in reference to Henry Shue, generate duties for all states.[17]

A second argument concerning the duty to intervene can be derived from the discussion about positive action towards the global poor based on the violations of their human rights. Gilabert (2005) has argued in opposition to Thomas Pogge, who claims that our duty towards such human rights violations are only negative ones, in favor of a positive duty to assist.[18] Gilabert's argument involves four steps: firstly, he wants to show that positive duties as duties of justice exist in general, such as if a person witnesses an accident and can help or that a state is obliged to tax the rich to help the poor. Secondly, he argues that we need positive duties in order to effectively eliminate poverty because it can have various causes and even if the rich (countries) stop harming the poor (countries), thus realizing their negative duties, poverty can develop and also these people have claims which can be supported. Thirdly, Gilabert distinguishes three types of robust global solidarity: (a) charity, (b) reasonable assistance to secure the conditions of autonomy and (c) harm avoidance. He holds the view that Kants's formula of treating all persons as ends involves not only (c) but also a positive duty of (b). Fourthly, he assumes that the positive duty to assist those in poverty and to secure their human rights is not overly demanding, although some people might feel that way. He criticizes such dominant intuitions as too narrow and that they should not be taken as a benchmark for moral and political reasoning, but rather that we should criticize them.[19] I do not see how such an argument for a positive duty to assist the poor and to protect their human rights would not be applicable to other human rights violations, such as the ones of children in conflict zones. In particular, Gilabert's second step is interesting here. Also, in the case of the violation of human rights in conflict zones, it is unreasonable to expect that following only negative duties would be sufficient to restore the protection of human rights. As I will explore later, there is a difference in how we can and probably should assist the global poor and those in conflict zones, but in both cases positive duties to support them exist and they demand intervention.

The next crucial question is, who would be responsible for protecting the human rights of children in conflict zones, or if the best solution is to bring them to a safe haven, who is responsible for such an intervention? Tan (2006) calls this the agency question. This also implies the need to clarify the moral question about whether such a duty is a reasonable burden on those who should be held accountable. I want to propose that this duty falls to any states that are able to carry it out; not as individual states, but in terms of a joint effort, which is best assigned to the UN. This is also consistent with the pledge of the state in other human rights treaties, such as the Universal Declaration: '[…] Member States have pledged themselves to achieve, in co-operation with the United Nations, the promotion of universal respect for and observance of human rights and fundamental freedoms'. Let me consider some aspects of that pledge. Firstly, I am agnostic in response to questions about whether or not a global state would be the best solution to protect children's rights, since I do not view that as a feasible or realistic option right now. Secondly, the discussion about open borders is only of limited interest to me, since I am focusing on children who have no or only very limited options to flee anyway; therefore, a regime of open borders would not benefit them very much (see, e.g. Higgins 2008). They are trapped and in need of assistance in order to get to a safe haven, where their rights can be protected effectively. Thirdly, my claim rests mainly on the assumed power of other states, and in particular their joint efforts under the heading of the UN, to effectively help those children without being overburdened by this duty. That claim certainly has two sides: the first is whether such a duty can be carried out, which I assume is possible given the significant resources that developed states have at their disposal (one argument that power provides the basis for attributing responsibility was presented in Young 2011). They have military forces, but also technical assistance and know-how in cases of natural disasters, which make it highly likely that they can effectively plan and carry out a humanitarian intervention in a foreign conflict zone. This is certainly not without its risks; but – and this is the second aspect of my claim – these risks can be limited and the protection of these children's human rights is worth the effort. I do acknowledge that there are certain limitations to the duty I propose, which are based on what a state, or a coalition of states, can achieve, but the costs for carrying out such an intervention, as well as the subsequent protection and provision of these children, even if we must assume that this concerns hundreds of thousands of them, are most likely bearable, particularly if the burden does not fall upon one single state. Fourthly, a UN-led intervention, with the explicit goal of bringing children out of conflict zones, will limit the risk that foreign armed forces will become involved in fights within these zones. At best, a temporary ceasefire can be negotiated beforehand and the conflict parties can be involved as little or as much as is deemed necessary. The duty I propose has a clear and limited scope, which is certainly not to solve the conflict or help one side win it.

A final reason that may apply to certain states is based on the causes behind a violent conflict. Several conflicts are initiated and sustained, at least partly, by states such as the USA, Russia or Saudi Arabia because they have their own interests in a particular region. Such involvement can take many forms, ranging from supplying weapons to carrying out so-called 'black' operations. Based on this kind of involvement, states become liable for the consequences of their actions and making sure that children do not suffer from these consequences, or at least ensuring that their suffering is kept to a minimum (this is referred to as the liability model of responsibility in Young 2011). Since almost all states have signed and ratified the CRC or other human rights treaties, they have therefore pledged and accepted the obligation to protect children's rights.

If we accept that children in conflict zones have a right to be protected and brought to a safe haven, this ought to also include their parents. It is already widely accepted that children have a human right to a family and identity, which covers the claim of any children to family reunification (Rohan 2015). Such a right is based on several grounds, including overcoming the trauma of separation and protecting the best interests of children. This complicates the duty I propose because it significantly enlarges the volume of those who can claim to be brought to a safe haven, as well as also involve those who are actively engaged in conflict zones and maybe do not want to leave. My answer to that problem involves two considerations: firstly, children's rights trump parental rights (for such a child-centered view, see Archard 2004). A parent cannot decide whether a child should stay in a conflict zone; if he or she does, then he or she forfeits his or her parental rights, in which case, the state (or, in my case, foreign states and the UN) has an obligation to protect that child. Secondly, under certain circumstances, where parents would not be allowed to join their children in a safe haven, it would be justified to leave them behind. I am concerned about children's rights in this regard and, although the right to a family is one such fundamental right, the right to be protected from getting killed or wounded, or being exploited, hungry or without shelter is more basic and should take priority.

Finally, the proposed duty to bring children to a safe haven is different from other obligations that foreign states and the UN have concerning the protection of children's rights in general, such as violations that result from severe poverty, which is widespread in developing countries (for a detailed account on poverty and human rights, see Pogge 2011). It is certainly possible to alleviate such poverty without endangering those who are engaged in that help. Child poverty can often be effectively alleviated without bringing children to another country, although sometimes such relocation is necessary. In conflict zones, on the other hand, children need to be moved in order to escape danger and for their rights to be protected. It is possible to secure food, build sanitation and run a school in a deprived local context, but in a conflict zone, such an undertaking is almost impossible. That does not imply that I am against the far-reaching duties of rich countries to protect the rights of poor children, some of which have safely evacuated and welcomed children out of conflict zones, but this is simply beyond the scope of my paper.

4. Prioritizing children's human rights

So far I have argued that an intervention to protect the human rights of children in conflict zones is permissible and obligatory and that it can attributed to the community of states and that it is an institutionalized duty, although some states may have duties based on their involvement in the conflict. But why, one can certainly ask, prioritize children's human rights over those of others? Is it not the case that the human rights of other groups are also equally violated? What about the elderly or disabled, who are also stuck, or what about the men in torture prisons? I want to respond to these questions while drawing on two normative sources, but before that let me be clear that there exists a duty to bring children to a safe haven and this does not rule out that there is also a duty to bring other groups of people to a safe haven as well. If possible, the human rights violations need to be stopped altogether. Under non-ideal circumstances though, decisions about priorities have to be made, although I do not find it reasonable to believe that the duty I propose will use up all or even most of the resources of the rich countries. It is certainly possible to invest sufficient resources in alleviating global poverty and to bring all children out of conflict zones and protect their human rights effectively.

The first strand of arguments I want to refer to were developed by Dixon and Nussbaum (2012). They claim that children's physical vulnerability is not sufficient basis to prioritize them, since they share this feature with other groups such as people with disability or the elderly. Instead, they say that prioritizing children's human rights can be based on the particular vulnerability of children as socially dependent beings. They claim that the lack of control, which characterizes the children's social position (which is both based on natural features of children and social, including legal norm), gives them a stronger claim to have their human rights protected. Dixon and Nussbaum, as I understand, argue that since being a child is a position of higher risk they deserve special protection. The second argument of Nussbaum and Dixon states that the prioritization of children's human rights is based on a cost-effectiveness principle. They use the examples of vaccination to make their point. It is cheaper to vaccine a child then to cure her as an adult in case she gets sick. Similar reasoning, they claim, can be applied to many if not most children's human rights.

What does that tell us about children in conflict zones? The cost-effectiveness argument has some merit and force. In Syria, hundreds of thousands of children cannot go to school and to educate them at an older age is much more costly and ineffective since children learn faster (and better under circumstances without deprivation or war). To put it in the language of the capability approach: some capabilities and functionings need to be developed early because they are the basis for others. The vulnerability principle is harder to apply to my case. In conflict zones, everyone is vulnerable and in immediate danger of getting hurt or killed or suffering other deprivations. Still I suppose this argument has some force. It seems as if the inability to protect themselves together with the knowledge that their development is easily – and often irreversibly – distorted speaks for their special treatment.[20]

A second strand of arguments that prioritize children's human rights are widely accepted in health care policy and ethics. One is the fair innings argument (Nord 2005), which states that children's health needs should be prioritized because they have not had their fair innings, while older people have had theirs. The fair innings argument can take two forms: either it defines a threshold, say 70 years, and discriminates everyone above that threshold because they had their fair innings, or it can be used to discriminate in cases where the age difference is substantial, say a 10-year-old and a 40-year-old. Proponents of the fair innings argument would not imply that the 40-year-old has already had her fair innings, but they would claim that she had enjoyed her life for a longer period of time than the 10-year-old meaning that the 10-year-old should be prioritized to give her the chance to also live for another 30 years. Others have advocated for a life-cycle argument, which claims that each person should have an opportunity to live through all the stages of life, because each life stage is valuable and each person should have the opportunity to experience it (Emanuel and Wertheimer 2006). While the fair innings argument looks only at the length of life, it has been argued that this is not a good measure and that we should instead look at quality adjusted life years (Ottersen 2013). If it was established that the 40-year-old can be expected to live a quality life for another 10 years, while the 10-year-old will live a quality life for only three years, we should prioritize the 40-year-old. If one also looks at the population level though, this favors children, because in general children have a greater expectancy of quality life years remaining compared to adults. As my argument covers the population of children, I suppose that the both fair innings and also the quality life years argument support my claims. It is also worth noting that the prioritization of children in healthcare has been supported from the perspective of the capability approach (Anand 2005), so it seems that Nussbaum's and Dixon's arguments and the fair innings and the quality of life years argument could be combined under one normative approach.

Such arguments for the prioritization of children in healthcare can be applied to the case in question, which is the violation of children's human rights in conflict zones. Firstly, many of these violations affect children's health directly (getting wounded, killed, or suffering from poor health due to of lack of food, medical care or sanitation). In this respect, a violent conflict is similar to the outbreak of an epidemic. Secondly, the life-cycle approach also reflects on the particularity of life stages and their value. A child that is deprived of education – which is a violation of that child's human rights – is deprived of an important aspect of that life stage and also of a precondition to enjoy the later stages of life in a decent way. That makes the child different from the adult, who has been educated but is now not able to utilize that education. She has experienced the life stage of childhood, while the child living in the conflict zone right now has not. This argument could be expanded to say that young adults should be prioritized over older adults, but I am not exploring that further here, because my argument is focused around children.

5. Possible counter arguments

The first counterargument I want to discuss states that, instead of bringing children out of their home countries and into safe havens, actions ought to be concerned with improving the situation on the ground in the home countries. I do agree that this argument has some force, but I want to point out two flaws to it. Firstly, to improve the situation for children in conflict zones, such as Syria or Iraq, is a long-term project with an unclear chance of success. Children need help as soon as possible and cannot wait a few years until the situation is stabilized and healthcare and schools are back on track. Putting an end to the immediate violence is certainly a first and necessary step, but children's rights involve more than just not getting killed by a grenade. Children, as rapidly developing beings, do not have the time to wait that long because everything they lack and miss during their childhood (e.g. nutrition, education and care) can lead to long-term effects, which are often impossible to be dealt with later. Furthermore, it is not foreseeable whether such peace-building will work altogether or whether it will fail, thereby making the situation even worse for children. As long as it remains plausible that children's rights will actually be reinstated and protected in the process of bringing children out of conflict zone, we should not gamble with children's lives in that way. Secondly, the improvement of children's rights in their home country will certainly be more demanding than the duty to bring them to a safe haven. History tells us that such peace-building, followed by nation-building, is a high-cost, high-risk adventure with uncertain results. It would probably involve much more engagement in those states than the humanitarian missions that are linked to my proposal. Bringing children out of conflict zones is also dangerous and will also probably involve on-the-ground operations, but they will be on a much smaller scale than those required for deciding the conflict and rebuilding a functioning state, both of which can guarantee children's rights. Furthermore, as I have said, evacuating children does not interfere with the conflict itself, so those engaged in the conflict have fewer reasons to oppose it or even fight those who are getting the children out. The situation is completely different when it comes to peace- and nation-building, which almost certainly implies that there will be one side that has to lose who will fight those who help the winning side. Such a duty is, therefore, linked to a much higher risk and would demand much more involvement on the side of duty-bearing states. Instead of saying that such a duty may be justified, it seems obvious to me that, from a children's rights perspective, the solution that is more effective and has a better chance of successfully protecting children's rights should be prioritized, which is the duty to bring children to safety first and foremost. That said, my argument does not necessarily imply that all children from conflict zones need to be brought to the EU or the USA. The duty I am arguing for demands to bring them to a safe haven, where their rights are sufficiently protected. That can be in a safe zone within the country or in a neighboring country. Only if there are good reasons to believe and sufficient evidence that their rights can only be protected by bringing them to the EU or to any other highly developed country should this be the solution.

A second counterargument could be that those states, which have such a duty to bring children to a safe haven, would be overburdened by it. Is it feasible to assume that states can take in millions of children (and their families)? Without hoping to do justice to the extensive literature on the issue of overdemandingness (see e.g., Sonderholm 2013) I only want to make one point in that respect. Firstly, it seems plausible to assume that, as a collective, the highly developed states which share this duty that I propose would be able to take in and to take care of millions of children (and their families). The crucial question here is how much can we demand from them. Following a Singerian account (Singer 2010), for example, one could assert that as long as the loss in welfare in those countries, which take in these children, does not push them below a sufficient limit of basic welfare, they have an obligation to do so. A more convincing account, in my opinion, would assert that highly developed countries have a duty to sufficiently protect the rights of children (and their families) as well as other people with equal claims as long as it does not endanger the protection of the rights of their citizens, which includes a certain level of welfare and also demands that the state does not deplete all or most of its resources to protect children in conflict zones. The question of when this threshold is reached, so if it is possible to bring 2 million or 20 million children to a safe haven, or if the EU can take in 5 or 25 million refugees before being overburdened, is an empirical one that I cannot answer here.[21] For example, the German Government calculated it will spend about 100 Billion Euros in total for the two million refugees they expect until 2020.[22] A large sum but still only a small fraction of its annual GDP of 3.3 trillion. Certainly the costs associated with the duty to bring children to a safe haven would be lower if these children would be able to live in safe zones in the region and could be provided with everything they need there.[23] The solution I propose is certainly limited by such external factors, as I also acknowledged throughout this paper, but this does not mean that no such solution exists in the first place, and that the highly developed countries are not able to fulfill it properly. At least from an economic point of view, they have more than enough resources to take care of millions of children.

The third, and final, counterargument I want to discuss is whether such a duty would also demand a military intervention, which could worsen the situation even further (for a detailed discussion of potential dangers, see Kydd and Straus 2013). I concede that this danger exists, but it may be limited. The first limiting factor depends upon whom is carrying out the intervention. If it is done by the UN, as I suggest, it is clear that a neutral force would be intervening with a limited agenda. That makes it more likely that these forces, which are necessary to carry out the intervention, will not be targeted or become involved in the conflict. Even if the intervention is carried out by a coalition of foreign states, however, the risks of being dragged into the conflict may be limited, even to a great extent. It needs to be made clear that such an intervention is not being used as a pretense to support one side over the other or to achieve other goals, such as securing access to natural resources. Secondly, the intervention needs to be well-coordinated and carried out without delaying the process. If hundreds of thousands or even millions of children are affected, it will certainly take some time to reach those trapped in conflict zones, where actual war is going on, which comes with certain risks and will certainly not be easy. In such cases, negotiating with the parties in conflict will most likely be the best approach, for example, in order to reach a temporary ceasefire during which those children can be evacuated. It might even be the case that risks to the well-being of those who have sent in to carry out the intervention are too high compared to the possible gains. Such decisions can only be made on a case-by-case basis and, although I wish I were able to make a strong argument for the solution I propose, I am aware that other arguments may outweigh it under certain circumstances. States certainly also have a duty to work towards peace, in particular those which are actively involved in the ongoing war, and to resolve the situation for the better. In the meantime, though, those children who are suffering from the conflict should be brought to a safe haven, where they have their rights sufficiently protected and can wait in peace for the end of the conflict, which made it impossible for them to live there without harm or danger to their life and well-being.

6. Conclusions

I want to conclude my paper with some thoughts on borderline cases, which are actually very important in relation to what is actually happening today. Many children have already left the conflict zones in Syria and moved to safer places there or in neighboring countries, such as Turkey, Lebanon or Jordan. What about these hundreds of thousands of children? Does my duty to bring children to safety also cover them? I would like to say that an expansion of my argument also seems plausible in order to include those children because it is very likely that some of their rights are also being grossly violated. Living in a refugee camp comes with many hardships and restrictions, for example, the lack of adequate nutrition or access to healthcare, education and shelter. Children under such circumstances are often not in immediate danger of dying, but there are convincing arguments that they have justified claims to a better quality of life under the framework of the CRC. These children are also more or less stuck where they are and have little or no chance to improve their situation, at least not on their own, while attempting to move to a European country, such as Austria or Germany, is highly dangerous. It should also not be forgotten that being in a safer zone in Syria or Iraq right now does not necessarily mean that the conflict stays where it is. Even if I am convinced, however, that children in such refugee camps in neighboring countries or living in safer locations in Syria have claims to be brought to safety, I still think that we should prioritize those children who are stuck in conflict zones. The immediate danger for children is greater there.

Notes

1. See the text of the CRC: http://www.ohchr.org/en/professionalinterest/pages/crc.aspx.
2. I am assuming children's rights here as both legal and moral rights for two reasons: firstly, the CRC is a legal document but one which also articulates moral rights and is based, so I assume, also on moral grounds. Secondly, I propose a solution that is primarily a political one – a duty of states and the international community of states – and for that legal considerations on the human rights level are of utmost importance. That said, I am well aware that I am arguing mostly from a moral point of view, but one that hopefully can be connected to the legal dimension of children's rights.

3. Also this claim seem uncontroversial, although there is considerable controversy what follows from the universality of human rights. An argument for the universality of human rights as the necessary content of global justice has been brought forward by David Miller, who is skeptical of the far-reaching claims of cosmpolitanism (Miller 2008).
4. UNICEF has set up and a webpage about the situation of children in Syria, where the newest information can be found: http://childrenofsyria.info.
5. http://www.un.org/apps/news/story.asp?NewsID=53145.
6. http://reliefweb.int/report/syrian-arab-republic/unicef-syria-country-office-nutrition-facts-figures-september-2015.
7. http://childrenofsyria.info/2016/03/31/syria-all-children-everywhere-now-urgent-funding-needs/.
8. https://www.worldvision.org/wv/news/Syria-war-refugee-crisis-FAQ.
9. http://www.aljazeera.com/news/2015/07/syrian-children-increasingly-exploited-labour-150702061339627.html.
10. This reflects the problem that not all children are more vulnerable than all adults, for example chronically sick or disabled adults, but that taken as a group children are more vulnerable than the group of adults. More about the complexity of children's vulnerability can be read here Macleod (2015).
11. The CRC is very clear that, for younger children, this is also a clear violation of children's rights: 'States Parties shall take all feasible measures to ensure that persons who have not attained the age of fifteen years do not take a direct part in hostilities' (§38). I would assume that the CRC is not strict enough in this regard and that children should not be recruited until the age of 18 years, but this lies beyond the scope of my argument here.
12. The case of child soldiers shows how complicated things can get here. Children who are recruited to fight are certainly victims, but they are also not free of all responsibility for their actions. For some child soldiers, returning to a normal childhood is also difficult, maybe even impossible, because they do not want to be treated as children anymore, as they feel and behave adult-like. See, for example, Özerdem and Podder (2011).
13. Such an analysis of the competences of a child, for example, to decide where to live and with whom, is common in custody cases in some countries. To this extent, I would also assume that children should not be allowed to decide whether to stay in a conflict zone. Their view on this matter is not authoritative. For more discussion on this topic, see Archard and Skivenes (2009).
14. See the legal report, 'European Union: Status of Unaccompanied Children Arriving at the EU Borders': https://www.loc.gov/law/help/unaccompanied-children/eu.php.
15. There are good reasons – political ones mainly – to treat migrants differently according to whether they are asylum seekers or not but that does not affect my argument. See: Carens (1992).
16. The literature on these issues is vast, and it is not the aim of this article to add something new to the general debate about humanitarian interventions to protect human rights but to propose and discuss a specific duty that rests on the permissibility of humanitarian interventions, or at least some of them. For an overview see (Hehir 2013).
17. According to Shue (1996) human rights involve three types of duties: the duty to avoid human rights violations, the duty to protect people from human rights violations and the duty to assist people, whose human rights have been violated. In the case of a conflict zone, the respective state fails to do all three, and thus an external agent needs to step in.
18. Gilabert is certainly not the first to argue for such a positive duty. Another theorist would be David Miller, who is in general, as said, skeptical toward duties of global justice, but also he states that remedial duties exist in cases of human rights violations, for example a dictator that deprives his people (Miller 2007, 231–259). But, again, I do not aim to add much to the basics of the debate about positive or negative duties but want to show that if a positive duty to protect the human rights of children exists that this should take the form of such a duty to bring them to a safe haven in cases that they are trapped in conflict zones.
19. A more detailed criticism of the 'overdemandingness' objection against positive duties has been elaborated by Sonderholm (2013).

20. Colin Macleod has made a similar argument, some while ago. He writes (Macleod 2002, 224):

> First, meeting children's claims to just treatment seems to enjoy a general priority over meeting the comparable claims of adults. Let me try to motivate this claim through an example. There is a sense in which children and adults have a similar interest in avoiding suffering severe pain that can give rise to a comparably strong entitlement to access to pain medication. Yet where circumstances force a choice between providing pain-relieving medication to a child and providing medication to adult suffering the same pain, we seem to have reason to give priority to recognition of the child's claim. I suspect that this general priority is grounded in various related factors. Children are vulnerable and dependent in many ways on adults for protection of their most basic interests. Because they cannot effectively represent and secure their own interests we naturally attach moral urgency to ensuring they receive fair treatment. The fact that children are developmentally fragile also seems significant. Children often seem to suffer more and are less able to recover from the ill effects of unjust treatment. So even when their moral claims seem comparable, caution suggests favouring the claims of children. More generally, children's status as innocents who can be assigned no responsibility for their plight or for ameliorating unjust treatment they face supports a general priority of children's claims. There seems to be an important difference in the relative urgency of the particular competing entitlements in this case. In sum, moral ties go to children.

21. Research suggests, contrary to the public opinion and some voices in politics, that the economic burden of the migration movement to the EU in 2015 is in fact low. The situation for children is certainly a bit different but in the long-run similar positive effects can be expected. One recent economic simulation by the Economics and Econometrics Research Institute concludes:

> Our simulation results suggest that, although the refugee integration (e.g. by providing welfare benefits, language and professional training) is costly for public finances, in the medium – to long – run the socio-economic and fiscal benefits significantly outweigh the associated refugee integration costs. (Kancs and Lecca 2016, 26)

22. http://www.reuters.com/article/us-europe-migrants-germany-costs-idUSKCN0Y50DY.
23. A newspaper article in the *The Independent* calculates the costs for one refugee to be 10 times lower in a camp in Jordan. http://www.independent.co.uk/voices/syrian-refugees-will-cost-ten-times-more-to-care-for-in-europe-than-in-neighboring-countries-a6928676.html.

Acknowledgements

I want to thank Norbert Paulo, the participants of the ifz research seminar in Salzburg, the participants of the Bochum/Dortmund research colloquium at the University of Bochum, and two anonymous reviewers for their valuable remarks and feedback.

Disclosure statement

No potential conflict of interest was reported by the author.

Funding

This work was supported by the Austrian Science Fund (FWF) under [grant number P26480].

ORCID

Gottfried Schweiger ⓘ http://orcid.org/0000-0001-5456-6358

References

Anand, Paul. 2005. "Capabilities and Health." *Journal of Medical Ethics* 31 (5): 299–303. doi:10.1136/jme.2004.008706.
Anderson, Joel, and Rutger Claassen. 2012. "Sailing Alone: Teenage Autonomy and Regimes of Childhood." *Law and Philosophy* 31 (5): 495–522. doi:10.1007/s10982-012-9130-9.
Archard, David. 2004. *Children: Rights and Childhood*. 2nd ed. London: Routledge.
Archard, David, and Marit Skivenes. 2009. "Balancing a Child's Best Interests and a Child's Views." *The International Journal of Children's Rights* 17 (1): 1–21. doi:10.1163/157181808X358276.
Berman, Helene. 2001. "Children and War: Current Understandings and Future Directions." *Public Health Nursing* 18 (4): 243–252. doi:10.1046/j.1525-1446.2001.00243.x.
Carens, Joseph H. 1992. "Refugees and the Limits of Obligation." *Public Affairs Quarterly* 6 (1): 31–44.
Devakumar, Delan, Marion Birch, Leonard S. Rubenstein, David Osrin, Egbert Sondorp, and Jonathan C. K. Wells. 2015. "Child Health in Syria: Recognising the Lasting Effects of Warfare on Health." *Conflict and Health* 9 (1). doi:10.1186/s13031-015-0061-6.
Dixon, Rosalind, and Martha Nussbaum. 2012. "Children's Rights and a Capabilities Approach: The Question of Special Priority." *Cornell Law Review* 97: 549–593.
Emanuel, Ezekiel J., and Alan Wertheimer. 2006. "Who Should Get Influenza Vaccine When Not All Can?" *Science* 312 (5775): 854–855. doi:10.1126/science.1125347.
Gilabert, Pablo. 2005. "The Duty to Eradicate Global Poverty: Positive or Negative?" *Ethical Theory and Moral Practice* 7 (5): 537–550. doi:10.1007/s10677-005-6489-9.
Hehir, Aidan. 2013. *Humanitarian Intervention: An Introduction*. 2nd ed. Basingstoke: Palgrave Macmillan.
Higgins, Peter. 2008. "Open Borders and the Right to Immigration." *Human Rights Review* 9 (4): 525–535. doi:10.1007/s12142-008-0068-0.
Kancs, d'Artis, and Patrizio Lecca. 2016. *Long-Term Social, Economic and Fiscal Effects of Immigration into the EU: The Role of the Integration Policy*. No EERI RP 2016/08. EERI Research Paper Series. Brussels: Economics and Econometrics Research Institute (EERI). http://www.eeri.eu/documents/wp/EERI_RP_2016_08.pdf.
Kanics, Jyothi, Daniel Senovilla Hernández, Kristina Touzenis, and Unesco, eds. 2010. *Migrating Alone: Unaccompanied and Separated Children's Migration to Europe*. 1st ed. Paris: UNESCO.
Kydd, Andrew H., and Scott Straus. 2013. "The Road to Hell? Third-Party Intervention to Prevent Atrocities: THE ROAD TO HELL?" *American Journal of Political Science* 57 (3): 673–684. doi:10.1111/ajps.12009.
Macleod, Colin. 2002. "Liberal Equality and the Affective Family." In *The Moral and Political Status of Children*, edited by David Archard and Colin Macleod, 212–230. Oxford: Oxford University Press. http://www.oxfordscholarship.com/view/10.1093/0199242682.001.0001/acprof-9780199242689-chapter-12.
Macleod, Colin. 2015. "Agency, Authority and the Vulnerability of Children." In *The Nature of Children's Well-Being*, edited by Alexander Bagattini and Colin Macleod, 1st ed., vol. 9, 53–64. Dordrecht: Springer. http://link.springer.com/10.1007/978-94-017-9252-3_4.
Miller, David. 2007. *National Responsibility and Global Justice*. 1st ed. Oxford: Oxford University Press.

Miller, David. 2008. "National Responsibility and Global Justice." *Critical Review of International Social and Political Philosophy* 11 (4): 383–399. doi:10.1080/13698230802415862.

Miller, David. 2013. "Border Regimes and Human Rights." *The Law & Ethics of Human Rights* 7 (1): 1–23. doi:10.1515/lehr-2013-0001.

Nord, Erik. 2005. "Concerns for the Worse off: Fair Innings Versus Severity." *Social Science & Medicine* 60 (2): 257–263. doi:10.1016/j.socscimed.2004.05.003.

Ottersen, Trygve. 2013. "Lifetime QALY Prioritarianism in Priority Setting." *Journal of Medical Ethics* 39 (3): 175–180. doi:10.1136/medethics-2012-100740.

Özerdem, Alpaslan, and Sukanya Podder, eds. 2011. *Child Soldiers: From Recruitment to Reintegration*. 1st ed. Basingstoke: Palgrave Macmillan.

Peters, Anne. 2009. "Humanity as the A and Ω of Sovereignty." *European Journal of International Law* 20 (3): 513–544. doi:10.1093/ejil/chp026.

Pogge, Thomas. 2011. "Allowing the Poor to Share the Earth." *Journal of Moral Philosophy* 8 (3): 335–352. doi:10.1163/174552411X588982.

Quosh, Constanze, Liyam Eloul, and Rawan Ajlani. 2013. "Mental Health of Refugees and Displaced Persons in Syria and Surrounding Countries: A Systematic Review." *Intervention* 11 (3): 276–294. doi:10.1097/WTF.0000000000000013.

Rohan, Mark. 2015. "Refugee Family Reunification Rights: A Basis in the European Court of Human Rights' Family Reunification Jurisprudence." *Chicago Journal of International Law* 15 (1): 347–375.

Schapiro, Tamar. 1999. "What Is a Child?" *Ethics* 109 (4): 715–738. doi:10.1086/233943.

Shue, Henry. 1996. *Basic Rights. Subsistence, Affluence, and U.S. Foreign Policy*. 2nd ed. Princeton, NJ: Princeton University Press.

Singer, Peter. 2010. *The Life You Can Save: How to Play Your Part in Ending World Poverty*. 1st ed. London: Picador.

Sonderholm, Jorn. 2013. "World Poverty, Positive Duties, and the Overdemandingness Objection." *Politics, Philosophy & Economics* 12 (3): 308–327. doi:10.1177/1470594X12447779.

Tan, Kok-Chor. 2006. "The Duty to Protect." *Nomos* 47: 84–116.

Young, Iris Marion. 2011. *Responsibility for Justice*. 1st ed. Oxford Political Philosophy. Oxford: Oxford University Press.

Index

Note: Page numbers with 'n' refer to notes

abuse, sexual 36
additionality, principle of 58, 59, 61
Afghanistan 34, 40, 120
aggressor groups 97n30–1
Alternative for Deutschland (AfD) party 47
Amnesty International 1, 3
Anderson, Joel 137
anti-refugee violence 49
Aquinas, Thomas 94n9, 95n13
Army of National Liberation 120
assistance, reasonable 141
Asylum Law 45
asylum seekers 34–5, 114; distribution in EU 38; in Germany 45; human security for 125–30; threat to national security 120, 124
Australia: private sponsorship programme in 57; response to refugee crisis 120, 121–2
Avramopoulos, Dimitris 72

Basic Rights 104
Benbaji, Yitzhak 85, 88
Benhabib, Seyla 21–2
Betts, Alexander 31, 32
Bilger, Veronika 73
'black' operations 142
Blake, Michael 37
Blended-Visa Office Referred (BVOR) programme 56, 58
borders: burnt 13–14; and citizens 13–14; controls 2, 121; of human mobility 1–6
Brezger, Jan 48, 49–50
Britain 123

Canada: Blended-Visa Office Referred programme 56, 58; private refugee sponsorship 56–8; public–private partnerships to sponsor refugees 58–60; refugees resettling to 56
Caney, Simon 91
Capone, Al 84–8, 95n15
Carens, Joseph 17, 37, 97n32
charity 141

children: and capacities approach 137–8; in conflict zones 135–7; duty, to bring into safe countries 134–49; improving situation in home countries 135–6, 145; poverty 143; prioritization of human rights 143–5; rescuer 105; rights of (legal/moral) 135, 138–9; vulnerability of 137, 143
citizens 20–1; benefits to 59–60; and borders 13–14; contributing resources to resettlement project 56; costs concerns 49; duty to accept burdens 51; indirect costs on 68; private 59; protection of 128–9; and refugees 50; and rights 21; state protection of basic needs, absence of 26, 27, 140
civilians, as collateral damage 82
civil society 44, 47–8
civil war 119, 139
Claassen, Rutger 137
Cohen, Sheldon M. 83
Cole, Phillip 4, 15
Collier, Paul 31, 32
compensation 86
conflict zones: bringing children out of 134–49; duties towards refugees from 101–17
conflicts 34, 91, 97n29–30, 107–8, 119–20, 142
content-independent obligations 75
contextualism 29
costs, of admitting refugees 38–9, 51, 59
coyotes 70
crime victim compensation programs 93
Czech Republic 39

Davidovic, Jovana 5, 101
defective motivations, of people smugglers 74–5
detention centers 121
displacement 15–22, 109–10, 115, 119
Dixon, Rosalind 143–4
doctrine of double effect (DDE) 82, 83–4, 94n6, 94–5n9
Duarte, Melina 1
Dublin III Agreement 45, 52

INDEX

duty to remedy past harms 101, 104–9; duty to aid refugees 101, 103–4; and just war theory 109–11

economic migrants 2, 13
egalitarianism 40, 42n2
emotional support 59
equality 22, 35
ethics: of conviction 48; of people smuggling 65–78
European Charter of Fundamental Rights 139
European Convention of Human Rights, Article 3 123
European Court of Human Rights 139
European Union: fair distribution of refugees 34–42; obligation to admit refugees 35–7, 40–1, 49; against people smuggling 65, 72; readmission agreements 123; response to refugee crisis 120, 122–3
exploitation, smuggling as 72–4

fair distributive scheme in EU: implementation of 38–40; restrictions on 40–2
Feinberg, Joel 94n7, 96n19
Fletcher, George 85, 88
Foot, Philippa 94n6
freedom of movement 35, 42n1
Funk, Nanette 4, 44

Geneva Conventions 94n4, 139
Germany, and refugees 39, 44–5; asylum seekers in 45; civil society 47–8; integration policy 46, 51; language and job training courses 46–7; need for holistic view 52; policy 45–8; public sphere 48–52; state 45–7
Gesang, Bernard 49, 50, 51
Gibney, Matthew 37, 38, 41, 63n2
Gilabert, Pablo 140, 141, 148n18
global displacement, in liberal political theory 15–22
Global North states 91–2, 97n27
global poverty 17
Gosepath, Stephan 49, 50, 51
Greece 45, 52

Hague conventions (1907) 82
harm avoidance 141
healthcare: access to 136; prioritization of children in 144
Hidalgo, Javier 5, 65
High Level Working Group on Migration and Asylum 122–3
Hoesch, Matthias 49–50
Hofman, Martin 73
Holtug, Nils 4, 34, 42n1–3
human mobility 1–6
human rights: of children 135, 143–5; duty types 148n17; protection of 35, 76; violations 29, 34, 37, 41, 57, 104, 140–1

human security 124; and international refugee crisis 119–31; paradigm 123–5; and refugee rights 125–30; and right to asylum 123–30
Human Security Network 126
human smuggling *see* people smuggling
Hurka, Thomas 95n13

Imhoff, Simeon 49, 50
immediate vicinity argument 30–1
immigrants, illegal 2, 3, 121, 123
immigration: liberal political theory and 19–20; and welfare states 39
Immigration Act (1976, Canada) 57
Integration Law 45, 46
International Criminal Court (ICC) 125
International Monetary Fund (IMF) 51
Iraq 119; as conflict zone 136; invasion of 115, 119; refugees from 5, 34, 40, 102–3, 113, 119; war in 107, 114–15
ISIS 114–15

Jaggar, Alison 97n27
Jandl, Michael 73
Jordan 36, 71
just war theory 94n9, 109–11

Kamm, F.M. 83
Khalili, Bouchra 8–14, 14n3
Kling, Jennifer 5, 81
Krivenko, Ekaterina Yahyaoui 63n8
Kukathas, Chandra 77–8n2
Kurdi, Alan 15, 60

labour market 39, 46, 57
Lægaard, Sune 4, 24
Layman, Daniel 92
Lebanon 36, 71, 129
Lenard, Patti 4, 55
liberal political theory, global displacement in 15–22
Lippert-Rasmussen, Kasper 1
Lister, Matt 26
Locke, John 84
Lohr, Nikki 13

Macleod, Colin 149n20
Marxism 17
McMahan, Jeff 84, 95n11, 105
Mediterranean Sea: smuggling incidents in 66, 68
membership: and displacement 20; and mobility 21
Merkel, Angela 44, 47
Meyers, Diana 3, 8
migrants: economic 2; smugglers and 73
migration: and liberal political theory 19; and membership 17, 20; and security implications 120
Miller, David 25, 37, 139, 148n3, 148n18; refugee definition 26–30

INDEX

Muir, Edwin 130
museumgoers 11
Muslim refugees, acceptance of 49

Nagel, Thomas 84, 88
nation states 10, 17–18
Nauru 121
Nawi, Diana 9
negative duties 103–4; to remedy past harms 104–9
New Zealand, private sponsorship programme in 57
non-citizens 124
nonrefoulement 2, 3, 24, 26, 113–16, 120–1
'nonworseness claim' 78n5
Nussbaum, Martha 143–4

Odutayo, Aramide 5, 119
Ogata, Sadako 122, 128
Orend, Brian 95n13
Ott, Konrad 48, 49, 51
overdemandingness 146
Øverland, Gerhard 74, 77–8n2

Pacific Solution (2001) 121
Papua New Guinea 121
Parekh, Serena 1, 114
partial compliance theory 26
Pavlischek, Keith 95n12
people smuggling: ethics of 65–78; as exploitation 72–4; fair 72; global 65–78; illegality of 65; incidents in Mediterranean Sea 66, 68; law-breaking objection to 75–7; motivational objection to 74–5; permissible of 66–71; presumptive argument for 70; rescue 76; state punishments for 75
people smugglers, defective motivations of 74–5
persecution 27, 34, 70, 120
Peters, Anne 140
Philosophie Magazin 48
Philosophies of Exclusion (Cole) 20
physical disabilities 18, 19
Pogge, Thomas 97n27, 104
political theory: refugees displaced in 15–22
positive duties 103¬–4; to aid 111–14
poverty 17, 104, 141, 143
prioritarianism 40
private citizens 59
Private Sponsorship of Refugees Program (PSRP), in Canada 56–8
proportionality 95n11, 108–10
public–private partnerships, to sponsor refugees 58–62

Quinn, Warren 94n9

racism 41, 94n3, 121; and pollution 90
Ramsey, Paul 81

Rawls, John 18, 20, 32
readmission agreements, EU 123
realism 29
recompense, for war refugees 88–92, 93
Refugee Convention (1951) 2, 25, 27, 114, 126
refugee crisis 1–6, 8; in American political arena 82; global response to 120–3; human security and 119–31; Iraqi/Syrian 103; as nonideal 25–6; philosophical discussion of 24–32; protections for asylum seekers 123–30; root causes of 92
refugee policies: Australia 121–2; Germany 45–8
refugees, 2–3, 16, 18, 26–30, 35, 119: from armed conflict zones, duties towards 101–17; burden-sharing 36, 41, 71; camps 5, 93, 97n35, 110, 114–15; costs of admitting 38–9, 51, 59; dealing with crisis 35–7; definition of 26–30, 70, 93n1, 102; displaced 15–22; and EU 34–42, 49–50; hostility toward 15, 50; in immediate vicinity argument 30–1; Iraqi 5, 34, 40, 102–3, 113, 119; language and job training courses for 46–7, 59; Muslim, acceptance of 49; positive duty to aid 111–14; resettling 36, 55–64; rights and human security 125–30; Rwandan, repatriation of 128; smuggling of 65–78; sponsorship, private 56–8; sponsorship, public–private cooperation in 58–62; status, in Germany 44–52; stories of 8–14; Syrian 1, 34, 40; *see also* asylum seekers; refugee crisis; war refugees
relocation scheme, EU 35, 37, 38
reparations 89
repatriation 128
rescue smuggling 76
resettlement, of refugees 55–64
residual view, of global poverty 17
resistance, geography of 13
Responsibility to Protect (R2P), doctrine of 128–9
Revolutionary Armed Forces of Colombia 120
rights, of refugees: and human security 125–30; *see also* human rights
Rodin, David 84, 86, 88
Rudd, Kevin 65
Rwanda: repatriation of refugees 128

Sanchez, Gabriella 75
Santos, Juan Manuel 120
Schweiger, Gottfried 5–6, 134
sectarian violence 36
securitization paradigm *see* human security
self-defense 84, 88, 110
Seville Conclusions 123
sexual abuse 36
Shacknove, Andrew 27
Shue, Henry 104, 141, 148n17
Sloterdijk, Peter 49
smuggling, of people *see* people smuggling

INDEX

social cohesion, effect of diversity 39–40, 42n3, 129
social justice 39, 42n2; versus global justice 60
solidarity taxes 51
Somalia 120
Spener, David 70, 73
sponsorship: agreement holders 57; public–private partnerships to refugees 58–62
states: duty to bring children to safe haven 139; immigration policies 45–7, 69; integrative ability of 38; obligations towards refugees 114; protecting citizens from loss of life 128–9; punishments for people smuggling 75; sovereignty 140
Statman, Daniel 85, 87, 95n16
Sussman, David 97n25
Sweden 39
Syria 36, 114, 120; bringing children out of conflict zones 134; and children's rights protection 140; Civil War 119, 129; crisis in 57, 60, 107, 119, 129; refugees from 1, 34, 40; situation of children in 136, 148n4
Syrian Observatory for human rights 3

Tan, Kok-Chor 140–1
targeted bombing 83–9
Tatum, Beverly Daniel 90
taxes 51–2
A Theory of Justice (Rawls) 18
Thomson, Judith Jarvis 84, 88
transference of responsibility 86–7
Turkey 1–3, 36, 37, 52
Twele, Marcel 49, 50, 51

UN Commission on Human Security (2000) 124
UN Convention of the Rights of the Child (CRC) 135, 137
UN Development Program (UNDP) 123–4
UN General Assembly 129
UN High Commissioner for Refugees (UNHCR) 16, 34, 36, 55, 58–9, 85, 90–2, 119, 126–8
Universal Declaration of Human Rights (UDHR) 93, 121, 127, 141; Article 14 121
US-led invasion of Iraq 115, 119

Valdman, Mikhail 72–3
violations: of human rights 29, 34, 37, 41, 57, 104, 140–1; of law 75–7
violence 137, 140: anti-refugee 49; sectarian 36
Vitikainen, Annamari 1
volunteers, civil society 47
vulnerability, of children 137, 143

Walzer, Michael 83, 92, 94n5, 94n9, 95n11, 95n13
war refugees 81–97; harming and wronging of 83–5; implications and policy recommendations 91–3; moral dilemmas 87–8; moral remainders 88–90; moral repair 90–1; recompense for 88–92, 93; transference of responsibility 86–7
wars 29, 108; civil 119, 139
Watson, Lori 22
welfare states 39
Wendt, Fabian 49, 50
Wertheimer, Alan 78n5
Williams, Bernard 89, 96n24
Wilson-Goldie, Kaelen 14n2
women: threats to safety and freedom 49
World Bank 129

xenophobia 41, 121

Zohar, Noam 83, 84
zones, economic 31
Zwolinski, Matt 78n5